Dinner at
Mr. Jefferson's

Previous works by Charles A. Cerami

*Jefferson's Great Gamble: The Remarkable Story
of Jefferson, Napoleon and the Men
behind the Louisiana Purchase*

*Young Patriots: The Remarkable Story of Two Men,
Their Impossible Plan and the Revolution
That Created the Constitution*

*Benjamin Banneker: Surveyor,
Astronomer, Publisher, Patriot*

Crisis: The Loss of Europe

*Alliance Born of Danger: America, the Common
Market, and the Atlantic Partnership*

Dinner at
Mr. Jefferson's

Three Men, Five Great Wines, and the Evening That Changed America

Charles A. Cerami

WILEY

John Wiley & Sons, Inc.

Remembering the incomparable Jean Keats

A reproduction of Charles Wilson Peale's portrait of Secretary of State Jefferson, painted the year after Jefferson's return from France.

Contents

Acknowledgments

My first thought is always to recognize my agent and friend, Bob Silverstein, as a major contributor, for this book would not have come to life without his active role. Bob's uncanny sense of what turns an attractive project into a realistic book played its usual part in guiding my steps, and in making the whole process enjoyable.

Hana Umlauf Lane was clearly born to be a superb editor. I could cite obvious merits, such as a remarkable memory for spotting points that seem repetitious, and an unerring feel for the *mot propre*. But much more significant is her ability to suggest improvements without distorting the original thought. This skill gives a writer the pleasant reassurance that he is flying with just the right pilot.

I am also grateful to Rachel Meyers for doggedly continuing with pinpoint reading until the last possible moments—and coming up with suggestions that were put to good use.

David Robinson helped me to profit from the splendid Rare Books section of the Library of Congress. Dr. Gerard W. Gawalt, a historian at that same great library did me a huge favor by suggesting that there was more to be learned from Professor Kenneth R. Bowling, who was on a special assignment at George Washington University. Professor Bowling is, to my mind, the unquestioned authority on the Dinner-Table Compromise. By opening his extensive library and collection of facts to me, this leading authority on my book subject provided advantages that I could not have found in any other way. I deeply appreciate his openhanded friendliness.

The Lauinger Library at Georgetown University, my own alma mater, was, as usual, a primary resource, with several city blocks' worth of perfectly indexed resources on just the subjects I needed. But I admit to also having been impressed by the fine Eisenhower Library at Baltimore's Johns Hopkins University and overwhelmed by the masses of material at the New York Public Library.

But back in Washington, a quieter and simpler resource, the well-hidden Senate Library, located under one of the Senate Office Buildings, is even more special to me because—not for the first time—an expert lady named Zoe Davis went to considerable trouble on my behalf, this time coming up with many pages of voting records that showed exactly how the hotly disputed Assumption Bill swung in Hamilton's favor some 217 years ago.

And the astonishing letter proving how carefully Alexander Hamilton arranged the steps leading to the U.S. Coast Guard—and how pertinent he is still considered there—was found for me by the guard's historian, Robert M. Browning, bringing to life the fact that Hamilton was indeed the genius who seemed to learn and to dominate every challenging subject that he encountered. The letter, which is reproduced in appendix B, almost makes us hear Hamilton's voice as he conveys his own principles to his new recruits.

Finally, it is a duty and pleasure to thank my daughter and son-in-law, Victoria and James Huckenpahler, and my dearest friend, Mary Ann Gale, for their patient understanding during those exacting hours that somehow resulted in this book.

Introduction

JUST BACK FROM FIVE IDYLLIC YEARS in France, eager for a quiet period at his Monticello home, Thomas Jefferson was jarred by the news that George Washington wanted him to be his secretary of state. When he took a risk by accepting the post without being sure of Washington's political views, he soon found that it had been a mistake.

On reaching the temporary capital, New York City, Jefferson was stunned to find that a majority of the state's people were probably already tired of democracy. The tone of their conversation sounded a distinct preference for the comfort of royal rule. And after he reported for work, he realized that Alexander Hamilton, whom he saw as a monarchist at heart, was on his way to becoming a one-man government, usually able to get his way with Washington and ready with a new plan for every conceivable need. We find these well-known people to be totally different from the way they are usually portrayed, behaving oddly, often close to desperation.

Jefferson was a genius who could spread enchantment with words that had never been used quite that way before. But he and his close friend James Madison could not make Washington see why they suspected Hamilton of wanting to create a monarchy in America. And they feared that one of the younger man's proposals could put him in a position to accomplish just that. Blocking Hamilton, however, seemed as dangerous as letting him win, for the clash might wreck the young country's financial standing in the world, which Jefferson called "the Ultimate Calamity." It would have stifled the nation's growth, mangled its future.

Then Jefferson gave a dinner—one of many that were notable for their elegance. But this one was a history-making event, because it appeared that he was putting all the firepower into Hamilton's hands. Even the host thought he might have given too much.

But the magic of Jefferson's touch—and a dash of luck—made it work out otherwise.

This Dinner-Table Compromise has been a plaything of historians ever since, with a variety of theories about what happened or whether it really happened at all.

It did, and I hope you will find it—and all that flowed from it— coming alive in these pages.

I
Before the Clash

THE THOMAS JEFFERSON WHO ARRIVED at Norfolk harbor in late November 1789 was not the same man who had left for France almost five years earlier. He had acquired a French suavity and polish, a different cut of hair, and an elegance of clothing. In place of the loose, shambling gait of a Virginia farmer, he walked with the more measured steps of a continental gentleman and held his head with little or no movement.

But he remembered his countrymen well. He knew that over 90 percent of them were farmers, and that this new version of himself would not do in America, not if he was to join the political world that President George Washington held out to him. He had not quite accepted, but he was already thinking of the style changes he would have to make. After all, his looks need not show in the letters he would write back to his French friends and near-conquests; there he could continue to show all the charm he thought they expected of him.

He wanted to hold on to those five years, for they had been like a second youth. He had gone abroad as a middle-aged widower, still grieving for his lost wife, and also as a semiretired politician who had to push himself to savor new experiences. But the magic of France had quickly enveloped him, making years that were his forties seem like an enchanted span from, say, twenty-five to thirty.

At the time, it had not mattered so very much that his flirtations had been platonic, though it took an effort to keep from seeing this as a series of defeats. His justified confidence in his writing skills blinded him from realizing that his love letters were ponderous and even tiresome, possibly spoiling the opportunities that might have been. But nonetheless, there had been moments of titillation in the relationships, and his mind returned to these euphorically.

Now, as he disembarked in Norfolk, he was startled to learn that newspaper accounts had already told the public that he was to be secretary of state. Everyone he met on the dock bowed and called him "Mr. Secretary." President Washington was so anxious to have him accept the job that he had sent several letters: One had been handed to him before he left the ship. One dated October 13 caught up with Jefferson when he reached the inland town of Eppington, Virginia, on December 11. Four days later, as he continued toward his Monticello home, a copy dated November 30, 1789, reached him in the town of Chesterfield.

Jefferson quickly responded, but with an unusual delaying tactic. He wrote that he was "truly flattered and honored by your nomination of me to the very dignified office of Secretary of State." This was followed by a dozen lines that stressed "how poorly qualified" he was, and the strangely predictive words that he foresaw "the possibility that this may end disagreeably for me." But he added, "It is not for an individual to choose his post . . . and my inclination must be no obstacle." By thus leaving the decision in Washington's hands, Jefferson caused the president to write another letter in January that would reach him at home early in February 1790.

Meanwhile, another bit of pressure had been exerted when Jefferson's friend James Madison came to welcome him home, but also to press Washington's case and urge Jefferson to accept, which he finally did on February 14. Seldom has anyone been pressed so hard to accept a highly desirable political office. And yet, Jefferson's foreboding was meaningful. The appointment would prove painful, both for him and for Washington.

To begin with, the president's offer had come as a mixed joy and sorrow to Jefferson. To be secretary of state and clearly the senior among Washington's advisers was a high honor, holding the unspoken possibility that it could lead to the presidential office in four or eight or twelve years. What a triumphant slap at those who persisted in claiming that his role as Virginia's governor had ended shamefully in fleeing from British raiders! If General Washington showed his approval, who could say a contrary word? Who else knew as much about the art of retreating?

But was this step back to politics the life he wanted? His inner voice probably cried "No!" many times, but just as often responded to a new and contrary ambition that said not "yes," but "perhaps."

Why this conflict? Jefferson had dreamed of returning to his beloved Monticello, improving the farms around it to strengthen his troublesome finances, altering the house according to the gracious neoclassical examples he had grown to love in Europe, living quietly with the books and friends that pleased him most. After five years of virtual freedom from supervision in France and the surrounding countries he had visited with such an avid appetite for learning and beauty, Washington's letter seemed more like a call to harsh duty than an invitation. It was a reminder that he would be expected to reside wherever the government might choose to set the still-undetermined capital, to attend meetings whenever someone else called them, and to think more about the advice he would owe to the president than about the much larger world he had seen whose main cities exceeded half a million in population.

But he must have been conflicted, for this newer thought taking his mind in the opposite direction had to be considered: *the presidency.*

He did not want it for personal aggrandizement, but for a chance to lead the nation toward the glowing future he had in mind and away from what he saw as a looming threat to the best hopes of mankind. It is curious that so little has been written about a Jefferson ambition to be president. Virtually every man in the upper ranks of American politics surely imagined a turn of fate that might propel him to the top. And this man, so often and so widely admired since his early twenties, could not have failed to encounter such an idea, if only because people at the many receptions that were thrown for him made remarks on the subject as they shook his hand. They all considered him special, as he had been used to hearing people say since his boyhood years. Why not presidential, then?

Nothing Jefferson wrote proves that such an ambition had struck him forcefully, but consigning the thought to paper was not to be expected. Yet his behavior in months to come pointed directly to a presidential goal, and at least one keenly interested observer later revealed that he was sure of it. Once the thought had touched Jefferson, it must have become very intrusive. What were his chances and what would it take? Would being Washington's secretary of state advance his cause? That would depend on how well their opinions matched, and he could not know this in advance. He and Washington had exchanged innumerable letters over the years, but most of them dealt with vast generalities, such as the possibility of opening the Potomac River to greater traffic or a Jeffersonian observation on facts discovered in his travels. They had seldom discussed anything that could be called politics. If he accepted the new post, a fresh set of subjects would engage them. It was regrettable that a secretary of state could not sign on for a trial period, for once begun, the term should continue at the pleasure of the president.

The very idea that he was now expected to proceed in haste, when Washington had already been president for nearly a year without a secretary of state, made him question the importance of the role. It was galling to be told that there was suddenly some urgency about coming to self-important little New York to set up a Department of State in a temporary capital that consisted of only thirty-three thousand souls. But there was no decent way to turn down the appointment—not without inventing a tale about having contracted some dreadful ailment. He would not stoop to that. But he would not be rushed. Even if he was compelled to agree that Washington's offer must be accepted, there could be no haste about settling down to work. This must have been the mood that led to the letter he sent, considerably less reverential than Washington was used to getting:

Feb. 14, 1790

Sir,

I have duly received the letter of 21st January with which you have honored me, and no longer hesitate to undertake the office to which you are pleased to call me. Your desire that I should come as quickly as possible is a sufficient reason for me to postpone every matter of business, however pressing, which admits postponement. Still it will be the close of the ensuing week before I can get away, and then I shall have to go by way of Richmond, which will lengthen my road. . . . I hope I shall have the honor of satisfying you that the circumstances which prevent my immediate departure are not under my control."

What it meant was that he would take his own good time to get to New York City and enter on his post. He would stay at Monticello for a reasonable week or so to rest from his ocean crossing, then attend the marriage of his younger daughter, Martha, to her cousin Thomas Mann Randolph. (This was one of "the circumstances" that prevented his "immediate departure.") Martha, barely seventeen, was not a beauty, but had a sweet look that accurately depicted her temperament. Jefferson was aware of how patiently she bore the end-less strictures he steadily wrote her to admonish more attention to household skills that would please her husband "on which your whole happiness will depend." Yes, he was trying to do the work of her absent mother, but how could such a great writer have composed such dreary words? No feminist he, but nothing in the world would have kept him away from her wedding.

After that event, he needed a few days in Richmond, the state capital, to work out new payment arrangements with his English creditors. His debt to them—some of it going back to the estate his wife had inherited from her father—had risen to £7,500, about half of which was from compounded interest charges. How he hated bankers and their hideous compounding! And now he would be borrowing even more to pay for a lavish gift of land and slaves to the new couple. After that depressing chore, he would proceed in the general direction of New York on a route that might take him to stops at the homes of various old friends, depending on weather and road conditions.

A decade later, Jefferson's trip could have been much swifter if he had wanted to go by stagecoach. A curious bit of litigation had interrupted a trend to speed travel between the states. This had started in 1785 when the first American turnpike began to take shape in Virginia (going between Alexandria and the lower Shenandoah). But a grand jury in Baltimore had shockingly ruled that country roads were "a public grievance," and the travel industry was traumatized for over a decade. Only in 1804, with a push from Alexander Hamilton near the end of his life, was there a surge of corporate ventures that began to create numerous turnpikes. The time it took to go between cities would plunge.

A stop Jefferson insisted on making was in Philadelphia, for he had heard that Benjamin Franklin was probably on his deathbed. A very touching last meeting took place between the fabled American representative to France and the man who had succeeded him. Enfeebled as he was, Franklin talked about the politics of Europe "with a rapidity and animation almost too much for his strength," Jefferson recalled. And Franklin also put into Jefferson's hands pages from the manuscript he was preparing of his own autobiography. His flair for the dramatic had not deserted the dying man, for part of these pages told of an attempt by Franklin in 1775 to avert the rebellion by the colonies through his friend Lord Howe, who would command British forces in America for a time. And Franklin had learned that it failed because—incredibly—Lord North, Britain's prime minister, actually wished to see a rebellion. This hidden fact was apparently suppressed in the final printing because of the explosive nature it would have had in Britain.

Sitting there and thinking of the unique life this person had lived, Jefferson found himself wondering whether a man so near death could still be thinking of the Revolution as Franklin had once called it—"a glorious task assigned to us by Providence."

After that, Jefferson's call on Benjamin Rush, a respected former legislator and a signer of the Declaration of Independence, made him feel that he knew the answer. For it was a joy to find themselves both as fixed on republican principles as they had been in their youth, and Jefferson emphasized again that "it is impossible not to be sensible that we are acting for all mankind." Ambitious as Jefferson still could be, he now treasured the freedom of private life. The right to be sitting with an old friend or the right to make his own plans as he had done in France now seemed vastly more attractive to him than the post he was about to undertake. Unless, of course, that post opened another door.

If he arrived in New York by mid-March, he thought, there should be time enough to pick up the threads of the young government that had been forming around George Washington. After a year in office, the general was still trying to learn what the presidency meant and how he was to use this recently invented job.

Even though he had sat through every minute of the Constitutional Convention, wielding the gavel as its presiding officer, Washington had not grasped all the subtle nuances of power that were created there. He was so aware of his deficiency in subjects of this kind that on one occasion he wrote James Madison a remarkable note, thanking him "for letting me peep behind the curtain" at the mysteries of Madison's attempt to create a new government.

So it goes without saying that Washington was a long way from fully understanding a far-reaching suggestion made by Connecticut's brilliant Roger Sherman at that Convention. It could have changed the nature of American government profoundly if enough of the delegates had been keeping up with the trends in British government, as Sherman had. When the delegates were discussing how America's chief executive was to be chosen and what his powers should be, Sherman suggested that the presidency was really "nothing more than an institution for carrying the will of the legislature into effect," and that he should therefore be appointed by the Congress, not selected by the people and made into a separate center of power, which could only make it a cause of constant jockeying for position.

Sherman had been reading about developments in Britain, and he knew that this line of reasoning had been gathering force there for half a century. It resulted in the long-standing fact that whoever heads the majority party is always prime minister, which is to say chief executive. And it was a way of quickly translating the will of the voters into a single unified power source, not necessarily related to monarchism. Since many of the delegates had a great respect for the British way of governing, it might have made a great difference in the decision about America's method of presidential choice if they had known this and realized that it was easily adaptable to republican government in America. But clearly no one was up to date on the subject, as Sherman was. And there was no sign that Washington had ever thought about such a precedent. As far as he knew, the presidency that he had stepped into was an unexplored mystery for him to adapt and shape.

Jefferson could not know that Vice President John Adams was being no help to Washington in shaping the presidency. This honest and dedicated vice president was given to exaggeration, and his advice in this case was a total failure. Adams had suggested that the president's every move be calculated to emphasize the grandeur of his position, "that a splendor and majesty be proportioned to the President's legal authority," and that he be addressed with almost monarchical titles (such as "His Highness, the President of the United States of America and Protector of Their Liberties"), all of which sickened the plainspoken general. And Adams's sudden new interest in elaborate hairstyle and bursts of emotion in his own new job led members of his party to say that he had "a half frantic mind." This was far from the truth. He had a superb mind, but it was so persistent that he could seem tiresome to those who disagreed with him.

Throughout his two terms, this first of America's vice presidents would be treated in a totally dismissive way; this was a pattern that would remain in place far into the future. Yet Adams would have a role to play, increasing with time. And the ambitious men who were disregarding him now would later wish they could replay the past.

Jefferson might have felt more of a sense of haste if he had realized that Washington was counting on him to join two much younger men as his chief advisers: James Madison, Jefferson's closest friend, now a leading member of the new Congress that he himself had created but often doing double duty because Washington prized him as a problem solver. The other was Alexander Hamilton, whom Jefferson had never met, though he knew of his dazzling reputation.

This young man, Jefferson had heard, had come from a Caribbean island and entered King's College in New York City at just about the time of the Boston Tea Party. He had become inflamed with the sheer, daring patriotism of the event and promptly wrote a political piece about it for the New-York Journal, praising the spirit of it and defending the natural right of the colonists. He had also given talks that held crowds of New Yorkers spellbound, especially because he looked younger than his nineteen years.

Jefferson, thinking mainly of the foreign affairs role he was to play, had in mind just one or two men whom he might recruit to assist him with running his new State Department. He had no inkling that

Hamilton, working eighteen hours a day, had already hired over thirty people to carry out his projects in the new Treasury Department, and planned to hire many more. Nor that even Jefferson's good friend Madison, as floor leader of the new House of Representatives, had become a martinet who urged fellow legislators to shorten their breakfasts and read fewer morning newspapers in order to push ahead with necessary legislation. Madison's performance during the opening session of the First Federal Congress was thought to have exceeded even his triumphs in the Constitutional Convention. He had molded the policies, forms, and procedures of the new government at a stage when nearly every action set a precedent.

Jefferson did not wonder at this, for he genuinely admired Madison and was often surprised to find himself adjusting his own thoughts because of a few quiet words Madison had said or written to him from an ocean away. Typically, while John Adams had doggedly insisted that pompous titles would strengthen the presidency and proposed that Washington at the very least be called "His Majesty, the President," Madison said in a speech to the House, "The more simple, the more republican we are in our manners, the more national dignity we shall acquire." His ability to reduce everything to an elegant simplicity was incomparable.

As for the other member of this trio of presidential advisers, Jefferson's early meetings with Hamilton would give no hint of the intense enemy the young man was to become. He knew, by reputation, that Hamilton had been a daring soldier before becoming General Washington's closest aide. It was known that he had once overridden the retreating general Charles Lee, rallied the fleeing men, and swept the British with a withering fire. There had been several such incidents, and his ambition for military glory would always struggle against his steadier skills of the mind.

Jefferson's words after his first introduction to Hamilton were very favorable, even laudatory. But it took only a few exposures for the suspicion to dawn that this younger man's head full of ideas and complex plans might become troublesome or deadly if one sought to alter them.

It was one of the worst moments in the new country's history for a clash of wills to strike the presidential office. The states were just trying to learn new forms of cooperation rather than competition with one another. The Constitution was supposed to remake the old relationships that had seen them as adversaries in every form of domestic and foreign endeavor. It was a time when a fragile nation called for the stability that Washington could well have provided if his aides had been more dedicated to him and less to their own interests.

Washington had frequently shown and openly expressed great confidence in each member of the trio: Jefferson, Madison, and Hamilton. The word *cabinet* had not yet been introduced, but these three plus Henry Knox, as secretary of war, and Edmund Randolph, as attorney general, would almost have fit the term. Only Madison, as a member of Congress, would have been an oddity, for unofficially he was a key figure in both the legislative and executive branches of government. The president's dependence on these men gave them something exceeding what would later be called cabinet status. But Washington seldom met with them as a group, preferring the clarity of a one-on-one talk with the man whose subject was being discussed.

The situation, however, was destined to be clouded by the fact that the president's clear favorite was the youngest of the group. The general hid that as well as he could, but the truth broke through his resolve. And this, Jefferson had to notice, could well become a factor in his own political ambition.

Washington had respect for Jefferson's learning, enormous reach of interests, and ability to express and deliver his views. He very correctly considered Madison a true genius at reducing the knottiest questions to their simplest level and quickly pointing to the most practical solutions. But in his own heart he clearly trusted young Hamilton most of all. He intensely disliked being forced to express this fact, but the seething complaints about Hamilton's aggressiveness that would inevitably arise sometimes forced Washington to remind an angry elder person of Hamilton's record of accomplishments.

For a man with no son of his own, a certain amount of affection may have been involved, but it was more than that. On almost every issue, Hamilton's position—and his ability to explain it clearly— struck Washington as exactly how he felt on the subject. Hamilton's

almost unbelievable combination of battlefield daring and intellectual brilliance must have seemed magical to a general who had to
work and ponder very hard to reach his impeccable conclusions.
One wonders whether the president secretly saw the treasury secretary not as a younger man, but instead as his senior in the ability
to propose a course of action on any given subject. It had been so
during the war, when Captain Hamilton's suggested responses to
incoming mail suited the general perfectly, and when Colonel
Hamilton's remarks on strategy often seemed wiser to Washington
than the opinions of his senior generals. It was noticed often enough
by the older officers to cause tight-lipped resentment. And it continued to be so in the political world that Washington was trying to fit
himself into. Hamilton was such a great help to him, yet such a cause
of widespread jealousy.

There had been no sign of Hamilton's national role on the day of
Washington's inauguration, April 30, 1789. Hardly daring to hope
for a high office, he was, for once, subdued and cautious, hiding the
massive ideas he wanted to introduce. With his private law practice
producing a handsome income and his rising stature in New York
State politics, he was unsure whether he wanted to leave that life at
age thirty-two for a period in the penury and uncertainty of public
office. But he knew that if the chance were offered to him, he would
certainly grasp it.

At that time, the country was not paying interest on its debts
and its bonds would have been called "junk" in today's terms.
Hamilton dreamed of overturning this situation in a series of bold
strokes. But it was three weeks before the lower house of Congress
proposed that a Department of Finance be established. The Congress seemed blind to the urgency of creating a powerful Treasury.
And for a time, because the danger of tax abuses was an overriding
fear, there was the deadly threat that the leadership of this controversial department would be given to a board, in order to avoid
handing any one individual great financial power. But strangely predictive was the fact that James Madison was the person who finally
rose and, in his peculiarly persuasive way, explained to the Congress
why one secretary should run the department. Thus he virtually
gave the man who would become his determined opponent the very

position—secretary of the treasury—that he had dreamed of years ago, even while the Revolutionary War was raging.

Hamilton was warned by many of his friends that this job was dangerous—sure to bring accusations of financial wrongdoing against anyone who accepted it. And he had to face the great personal sacrifice of giving up his lucrative law practice and trying to live on a $3,500 annual salary. But not for a moment did he consider passing up this opportunity to reach for the historic impact that he had in mind. He wanted to stamp the United States as the best managed nation in the world's history, a country that paid its war debts while others only blurred them by starting new wars. He was determined to make a dollar bill "as good as gold" anywhere in the world. He meant to add this form of greatness to the democratic opportunities that were already making *America* a magical word around the globe.

2

An Old Friend's Bombshell

WRITING TO HIS NEW SON-IN-LAW soon after arriving in New York City, Jefferson sounded like a dedicated member of the government who was setting an example for the young newlyweds:

> I arrived here on the 21st instant, after as laborious a journey of a fortnight from Richmond as I ever went through, resting only one day at Alexandria and another at Baltimore. . . . Much business had been put by for my arrival, so I found myself under an accumulation of it.

Actually, he had been greeted in New York with two solid weeks of dinner parties in his honor, and the accumulation of business that he mentioned consisted largely of reviewing the work that had been taken over and very capably handled by an enthusiastic substitute. Unfortunately for Jefferson, Alexander Hamilton had been all too willing to step in and help the president with questions that would normally have fallen to the secretary of state.

Washington was almost a full year into his presidency before the man he had chosen to organize and head a Department of State arrived in New York. Part of this delay had come because the president had deliberated about whom he should appoint to handle foreign affairs, and then Jefferson had to give up his post in Paris, cross the Atlantic Ocean, and finally consider whether to accept

Washington's offer. Jefferson's refusal to be hurried about traveling to the temporary capital city had only extended the lapse by a matter of weeks at most, but they were meaningful weeks that had special significance.

Because many diplomatic issues involved financial matters as well, it was natural for some of these to be referred to Hamilton in the absence of a secretary of state. So Hamilton had been led into a closer relationship than would have been the case otherwise with a British diplomat named Major George Beckwith. This man was part of the Canadian government, but he was taking an interest in American affairs while Britain was petulantly refusing to send an official diplomatic representative to the United States. Since both Hamilton and Beckwith were treading on unofficial turf and dealing with matters that had not been specifically assigned to them, they must have felt somewhat clandestine and perhaps even a little naughty at letting their talks stray beyond the usual limits in such unorthodox

This street scene shows a lively Tontine Coffee House, the Starbucks of its day, at the intersection of Wall and Water streets, and a glimpse of the harbor in the distance.

contacts. They were so aware of their questionable status that Beck-with assigned a secret code number to protect Hamilton's confidentiality. He was known as "Seventh" or "No. 7" in Beckwith's records.

As they became closer, they discussed an unusually wide range of important subjects that had not been mentioned since the United States and Britain had been at war, including extensive bargaining over rights to certain forts that England still retained in the Ohio Valley, and the possibility of a commercial treaty between the United States and Great Britain. This last was long overdue, considering the great volume of trade between the two nations. But it was a very touchy subject, with England feeling disinclined to pay their former colonies this much respect, and Americans reluctant to undertake negotiations in which they felt likely to be treated as inferiors. Hamilton and Beckwith, always chatting as equals, escaped that trap altogether.

Most of these talks Hamilton carried out very properly, despite showing his pro-British attitude in a way that a diplomatic bargainer should have avoided. He also favored Beckwith with some of his personal feelings that should not have been revealed to a foreigner, such as his personal preference for "a connection with England" and his belief that Congressman Madison, "though clever and incorruptible," was "very little acquainted with the world."

At the same time, Hamilton was making one mistake in his own Treasury Department that would haunt him. He had appointed as assistant secretary a bright and qualified but talkative and careless young friend, William Duer. Soon after taking office, this man had sent to contacts abroad secret details of Hamilton's funding plans that were bound to result in disruptive financial speculation. While Hamilton himself was leaning over backward to steer clear of personal involvement, he somehow failed to realize how disastrous this friend's appointment had been. He let Duer stay on much too long after he had been urged to be rid of him.

On the other hand, Hamilton's irregular "negotiations" with the British representative were well balanced, careful to avoid any major favoritism to the English, and so thoroughly cleared with President Washington that the latter agreed to send an American representative to England to extend these talks. This promised to be a new breakthrough in healing postwar British-American relations. The choice for this delicate role, also suggested by Hamilton, was an excellent one—Gouverneur Morris, who had been a key figure at the Constitutional Convention and who then had been chosen to actually write the final document. The choice of such a brilliant figure greatly increased the chance that these contacts were going to bear fruit and lead to normal and profitable relations between the United States and its old mother country. President Washington had to be pleased with this development and to realize that it had been crafted by Hamilton. Washington's tendency to favor the man who was accomplishing so much should hardly have been a surprise.

It is almost unimaginable that all this involvement in foreign affairs could have been carried on at a time when Hamilton was working feverishly on his *Report on Public Credit*, a complete financial plan that Congress had asked him to submit. He had been given about three months to prepare it, which would have been ample time for the paper that was expected. But instead, Hamilton did a massive and brilliant job that was called "herculean" by more than one critic. He searched through the economic history of the world, drew ideas from the greatest French and British thinkers, and did not hesitate to top them with new thoughts of his own.

The amount of overall debt that had to be considered was staggering. Apart from $25 million of old war debt owed by the states, there was over $50 million of national debt accumulated during the years when the weak national Confederation had been unable to collect taxes. Hamilton knew that he would not only have to borrow a huge additional amount from Europe to begin reducing this daunting sum, but also find a new way to raise money within the country. And with his intimate knowledge of how things had been done in England, he turned naturally to luxury taxes on tea and coffee and "sin taxes" on wines and spirits. These were bound to arouse heated emotions.

Knowing what a storm of conflicting reactions he was certain to set off, Hamilton was unusually nervous when his report was about to be made known to the public on January 14, 1790. And he was right to be, although he did not suspect who his most prominent attacker would be.

FEDERAL HALL
The Seat of CONGRESS
Printed & Sold by A. Doolittle New-Haven 1790

Having provided this beautiful site for George Washington's inauguration, New York City hoped it was preparing to be the nation's permanent capital. But the French architect Pierre L'Enfant, who idolized Washington, had bigger plans and left to design the new city of Washington, D.C.

Among the key conclusions Hamilton presented was that the states should all contribute to a fund that would be used to take over (or "assume") the $25 million of old state debt, turning it into a federal obligation. So *assumption* became a byword for making it clear to the world that all of America was resolved to honor its obligations. In fact, if Hamilton had his way, the government would also have a clear plan to reduce its total debt by some 5 percent each year, giving European lenders new reason for confidence. New money bor-rowed from Europe would be used to pay off the old bonds that had been issued during the Revolutionary War, and these bonds would be bought back from *whomever the current holders were, even if they had changed hands over the years.*

What? came the cry. Were the "little people" who had shown their patriotism and faith in the rebel cause to get no consideration? Many patriots had first bought these bonds during the darkest days, then had been forced by poverty to sell them for pennies on the dollar to speculators who made a business of such purchases. Would former soldiers who had accepted as little as fifteen dollars for a hundred-dollar bond get nothing more?

Exactly so, they would get nothing more, was Hamilton's reluc-tant answer. He tried to explain that there is no fair way to step in and make sudden discriminatory rules that give more to some bond owners and less to others. A bond, plus the stated interest, must be payable in full to the person who holds the certificate. There is no other way to preserve order and build respect in the financial world.

There were further knotty questions about the rate of interest that should be paid on these securities and the creation of a "sinking fund" composed partly of money from post office earnings, which would contribute to the ability to make yearly reductions of debt.

The report virtually exploded onto the American scene, noisily greeted with a combination of exaggerated reactions. For one thing, it set off a wild speculative craze among people of all economic levels, a mad lust to win profits by buying up old bonds cheaply and hoping to collect the full value when the federal government paid. Some succeeded, others did not. There were myriad questions and rumors, some with a slight validity, some sheer inventions. One rumor, rather insulting to southerners, theorized that the current owners of bonds—who would profit hugely—were northerners and that they had tricked the simple people of the south into selling their bonds for a pittance. Rumors were also spread about shiploads of northern speculators racing southward even at that moment to buy up the suddenly precious paper before the southern simpletons learned of the government's pernicious plan. And there were rumors about congressmen who made fortunes on the presumed basis of advance information. Other congressmen, having failed to make fortunes, thundered against the devilish secretary of the treasury.

The misunderstanding that infuriated Hamilton most was that opponents of his plan were able to trumpet the idea that he was advocating a perpetual public debt. Without careful study of the long document, which few attempted, this was easily believed. But in fact, an important passage in Hamilton's report had stressed that he wanted the plan to embody the means of extinguishing the debt. He even wrote about the progressive accumulation of debt as "a Disease of Government." This was what his proposed sinking fund was supposed to help avoid, but the false rumor had more staying power.

All this and much more had been heaped on Hamilton's plate, and he had put most of it there himself, willingly taking on more work than any other squadron of men could have dealt with. A major part of this had been handled with great finesse. He was embattled, but he seemed to have a chance of emerging triumphant. He had become a central figure in American foreign policy as well as in finance—while the secretary of state was visiting friends on his leisurely way to New York.

Now it would be up to Congress to consider all the pros and cons and decide whether it would support the treasury secretary's tremendous financial effort. And Hamilton optimistically assumed that James Madison, as the floor leader of the House, would be on his side. They had worked closely together to create the Constitution, even though it was not the document that Hamilton would have preferred, and then cooperated even more dramatically to get it ratified.

But in mid-February, just a month before Jefferson reached New York, Madison set off a bombshell of his own. Contrary to everything Hamilton had expected on the basis of Madison's former sentiments, Madison had reversed his position. He would not support Hamilton on the assumption plan. The date is important. Because of having come before Jefferson's arrival, it tends to contradict some theories that Madison was influenced by Jefferson. Because he was eight years younger and much less imposing in appearance than Jefferson, it was not generally recognized that Madison often took the lead in forming their joint opinion on a subject. On the issue of assumption, it is likelier that Madison's negative position eventually convinced

Jefferson that they must both find reasons to oppose Hamilton. And there could have been no doubt of Jefferson's opposition to Hamilton's plan for having all the state debts assumed by the federal government, for nothing could have been more distasteful to the states-rights-oriented Virginian.

But that was just one cause of disagreement. The greater underlying fact is that both Jefferson and Madison came to have a strong personal, political, and, they believed, patriotic motive to oppose Hamilton's plans.

This motive was a deep fear that the proposed financial scheme would create a sure and loyal following for Hamilton—a band of influential voters who had been given millions by his plan. This, together with their conviction that Hamilton was secretly a lover of

James Madison, the Father of the Constitution, while he was the floor leader of the nation's first Congress and an early opponent of Alexander Hamilton's plans for the country.

monarchical government, pointed in a grave direction. They thought it possible, even likely, that Alexander Hamilton could steer America toward becoming a monarchy, first with George Washington and eventually with himself as its head. Even short of that, Hamilton's potential power could far exceed anything called for by the Constitution. It seemed virtually a moral commandment for them to defeat anything that gave this man a permanent loyal following that he might then use to destroy democracy in America.

Finally, on March 21, 1790, a month after the Madison bombshell, Jefferson ferried across the Hudson River and arrived in New York. The city's population was less than half the number boasted by Philadelphia with all its suburbs. But the variety of businesses and the character of New Yorkers overcame the population differential and gave this city a vitality that had always been unique. As the visiting duc de Liancourt, a friend of kings who has been called as cynical as Machiavelli, said, "This is an area that is growing so fast that whatever is true today concerning its population, its establishments, its prices, its trade was different six months ago and will be different six months from now." He also added, in defiance of his French heritage, "There is probably not a more beautiful street than the Broad Way anywhere in the world. It is nearly a mile in length and over a hundred feet wide."

Where there is rapid growth there tends to be disorder; except for the few wide and beautiful streets, most were narrow and crowded, some with garbage in heaps and pigs roaming free. The odors can hardly be imagined, and the only available water had to be bought at one cent per pail from moving carts. But changes were on the way. The owners of pigs were ordered to move them out to the country, and a program of pipe installation was under way to start bringing fresh water into the city.

Remarkably, a number of charitable operations had been started, at great cost. There was a city hospital, where the poor could be treated at no charge. The capacity had begun with 60 beds, but it soon doubled to 120, with one paid surgeon and several physicians who donated part of their time. There was also a home for foundlings. And although there were inevitably some poor, most able-bodied people could find jobs at higher pay than in other cities.

New York had—and has never lost—a great sense of self-importance that had not been put down by the fact that it was occupied for so long a time by the British, from the very beginning of the Revolutionary War until November 25, 1783, when the last of the British occupiers left in defeat. On that very day, George Washington had come to New York personally, and the date is still known as Evacuation Day. Instead of feeling subjugated, the city had a certain pride about what it had endured.

That heritage had been further enhanced with the added excitement of being a temporary national capital. As Liancourt had observed, the city was growing rapidly. New York's east side extended a mile and a half up the river, while the west side was a mile long. But it had no great appeal for Jefferson, who had so recently left the elegance and multiple attractions of Paris.

A greater reason for his distaste was the decidedly close-minded tone of the dinner table conversations he heard. Jefferson began to realize that New York's long connection with occupying forces had left behind a certain amount of pro-British feeling. It was far from pleasing to come from a France that was wildly excited about the freshness of American politics to a New York that seemed to have limited liking for its new form of government. The talk he heard around him made it seem that some Americans were already tired of the new government. To find so many people who seemed to miss the old monarchy was a cultural shock he hadn't expected.

Could they really be tired of democracy already? he asked himself. This strong note of disapproval seems incongruent with what one would expect of a Jeffersonian mind. And especially as a presidential hopeful, should he not have asked himself what these people were missing that made them recall monarchy in a favorable way? In any case, he seems not to have asked these disappointed Americans to discuss their thoughts, but rather dismissed them all as a variety of lost sheep. It was almost like a forecast of Alexis de Tocqueville's harsh finding: "I know of no country in which there is so little independence of mind and real freedom of discussion as in America."

Jefferson would be in New York less than six months, from late March to September 1. Yet, although he knew that his stay there would probably be brief before he moved on to some other temporary or permanent capital, Jefferson gave full vent to his spendthrift ways by ordering home improvements that only a long-term tenant should have considered. Debt, a subject that would increasingly plague him for the rest of his life, was piling up without respite. Vice President John Adams, who had grown close to Jefferson when they were in Paris together, somehow had the mistaken impression that Jefferson "was pulling back from his habitual extravagances." He was wrong. The huge sum Jefferson owed to British creditors alone kept growing monthly. Although he had always had proper respect for public money whenever he dealt with it, he was totally unsound in handling his own and would not reform.

During the two weeks of dinner parties in Jefferson's honor that opened his stay, he devoted a part of each day to searching for a suitably fashionable house, especially one appropriate for entertaining guests, and preferably on "the Broad Way," which Liancourt had correctly named the most desirable street. But there was nothing to be found, so Jefferson had to settle for Maiden Lane, number 57. He thought it small, but the demand for housing was such that Jefferson felt fortunate to be able to rent it for a year.

While the place was being readied for him, he had to spend over five weeks in a boardinghouse, which was not unusual. During this time—on his own forty-seventh birthday—Jefferson wrote to an old friend that public employment was only "honorable exile from one's family and affairs." Most of the congressmen and senators were also "homeless," and after the parties in his honor abruptly ended, there should have been a certain enjoyment in the fraternal evening talk around the large dinner table. But it was not the sort of pleasure he might have hoped for. Jefferson had quickly found that he was encircled mostly by men whose thoughts were not at all like his own, and he struck the others as being very quiet.

For the barely three months that he was to occupy the Maiden Lane house, he had made changes and additions as if this were to be his home for life. For example, he had a gallery built onto the back of the house, and the amount he spent for cabinetwork alone was more than the cost of a full year's rent.

Being ready to entertain company was a must that he worked toward passionately, pressing everyone whose efforts might bring this about. As the move into the Maiden Lane house neared, he feared that Bob, one of the servants whom he had brought with him from

Monticello, was not up to the new standards he had acquired in France. So Bob was sent back to Virginia. In his place, Jefferson engaged two new servants who had more experience, but they too disappointed, being merely adequate.

James Hemings, who had been with him in France and who had studied French cooking there, was a mainstay in the kitchen and was also entrusted with buying most of the household supplies. Hemings had been very prompt and clever about finding New York's best suppliers for this purpose. Jefferson agreed with Hemings that his slavery should end, in view of his exceptional abilities, although he never freed Hemings's better-known sister, Sally. Jefferson granted Hemings his freedom on the condition that he would first train another chef in all the skills he had learned in Paris. This was successfully accomplished after James trained his capable brother, Peter Hemings, and then went on to remunerative employment as a free man.

But another form of expertise required international action to reach a solution. Jefferson's experience abroad had made him feel that life without a really fine maître d'hôtel was almost insupportable. The ones he tried to recruit locally failed utterly, so he sent off an urgent message asking André Petit, who had served him in Paris, to come at once to America.

These aftereffects of his Paris stay continued to resonate, and they had a day-to-day effect on his personal life and especially on his active entertaining on Maiden Lane. But it was not until the fall of 1791, a year after his forced move to the new temporary capital in Philadelphia, that Jefferson would finally feel his home life was falling into place for in addition to the expertise of André Petit and the growing skill of his chef, his own chariot and sulky finally arrived from France, just as a further shipment of champagnes and Bordeaux wines also appeared.

But meanwhile, even though he felt inadequately prepared for entertaining and was suffering from more of the mysterious headaches that occasionally plagued him, Jefferson vigorously pursued the gallant attempt to be an elegant short-term host in his temporary quarters in New York City. Even in that limited time, there was more than one dinner at Mr. Jefferson's that would affect the nation—and one that would reverberate in the history of the United States.

3
The Mounting Anger

AFTER HAVING BEEN INCORRECTLY called migraines for nearly two centuries, Jefferson's headaches are no longer a mystery. According to the latest science, Jefferson suffered from tension headaches. By correlating the spells of illness with Jefferson's work schedules and experiences, researchers have shown that the headaches clearly came on and worsened in accordance with the amount of work-related stress Jefferson imposed on himself. The final proof of this would come by analyzing the years after 1808, when his presidency ended: his headaches disappeared forever.

But during Jefferson's early months as Washington's secretary of state his headaches were in full force, for the drama that was to envelop Jefferson came on and intensified quickly. Little more than a month after his March arrival in New York, he felt that he and Hamilton were destined to be enemies. Worse yet, he sensed that George Washington leaned toward Hamilton's opinions on almost every issue.

Jefferson's only ally appeared to be his close friend James Madison, but the nature of their contest against Hamilton was elusive. It seemed unreasonable that a friendly relationship should have tumbled into serious enmity over a single piece of legislation. But it was more than that. It was Hamilton's hyperactive and all-conquering personality. For Jefferson and Madison, the image of Hamilton as a dangerous person—actually a threat to democracy—was a galloping force that increased by the day.

Before summer, an uneasy atmosphere pervaded the office of the president. There was a veneer of politeness in the many conversations that took place between Hamilton and the two men who increasingly suspected him. But it was clear that the courtesy was simply formal, with no mistaking the underlying tension. A careful observer would have detected that things were about to turn grim.

At a glance, it might be said that Hamilton started it all, but this would be only a half-truth. Because he was so active, he "started" a great many things, but most of these began as well-thought-out and highly constructive plans. As much now as when he was a young artillery captain while the Revolutionary War was raging, Hamilton kept thinking of ways to make America a great financial power. It was as though the boy who had written at age twelve "I would willingly risk my life, but not my character, to exalt my station" had come upon the magic garden where all things were possible. And he knew that finding even one such garden in a lifetime was a favor that few were granted—that he must make it bloom quickly or tumble back to being little more than a clerk on the island of Nevis. "Yes. Yes. Now," he always seemed to be telling himself.

Hamilton's colleagues became opponents as they saw themselves bested by a man whose ambitions and energies were far above normal. Even though it should have been clear that his contributions to the nation were indeed great, his opponents made each policy question into a personal accusation, partly because they genuinely feared his "monarchical" ideas but also because they had no better answer to his string of heady plans and his capacity for endless work.

What would America be like without this Hamilton? many of his contemporaries must have thought. It would surely have progressed, but at a far slower pace. Things that were accomplished in Washington's second year as president—the debt-repayment plan, the national bank, the new currency—might have been delayed until his sixth or seventh year. Some might have said it would have been a quieter and smoother kind of progress without Hamilton. Still others might have offered: "America without Hamilton? Well, what would France have been like without Napoleon?"

The comparison was not far-fetched. Napoleon, it was said, could work eighteen hours at a stretch, turn from subject to subject with total recall, and remember the whole face of France well enough to move regiments and approximate their stock of arms and their supply of ammunition. He would often say things like: "Last night, at two o'clock, I got up to examine the field reports sent in by the Minister of War. I found twenty mistakes."

Eighteen hours' work at a stretch was not unusual for Hamilton when he was preparing one of those massive studies, and he could turn his attention to another subject, discuss it fluently, and then pick up the original project where he had left off. All such stories, whether Napoleonic or Hamiltonian, are probably based on a few such incidents that admiring cohorts later speak of as their hero's routine behavior. But in both these cases, there is no doubt that they convey a real sense of the remarkable individual.

Comparing the two men is more than mere wordplay. Just as many rules that France still lives by derive from carefully detailed orders given by Napoleon Bonaparte; certain present-day U.S. government officials who are carrying out traditional duties—notably in customs offices and in the U.S. Coast Guard—still respect standards that Alexander Hamilton established. And Coast Guard officers, in turn, are among the most respected of all American officials, admired for their high principles and response to adversity. During Hurricane Katrina, when almost all services in New Orleans collapsed, it was said that the behavior of the Coast Guard was nearly perfect, saving many lives. The man who brought this about, clearly Washington's favorite, had been a genius from childhood on the Caribbean island of Nevis, going to work before he was eleven in a complex business that sold ships' supplies and learning to manage the baffling enterprise entirely alone. He seemed to learn everything without being taught—languages, fine writing, financial complexities, perfect social manners. And he wrote articles for the local newspaper that won him fame and enough financial support to give him a chance to study on the mainland.

He had been destined for Princeton University but needed some additional foreign language study to qualify, so he spent a short time at Elizabethtown Academy in New Jersey, then transferred to Kings College in New York City, where the excitement of the near-war moment pushed education into the background and inflamed him with a wish to take part in the fight for liberty. He discovered an unsuspected flair for oratory and gave astonishingly knowledgeable talks to explain why the colonies should adopt a policy of boycotting British goods. He also wrote brilliant political analyses that predicted how France would aid the American colonists to achieve victory, and even wrote perfectly reasoned military plans for the Americans to win battles against regular troops by using harassment tactics. All this was before he turned twenty.

When he enlisted to fight in America's war, he brashly exaggerated a little knowledge of weapons that he had learned from a friend, and he was made an officer. Ron Chernow's incomparable biography of Hamilton makes it plain that he did not simply have an accidental meeting that led him to become General Washington's aide in handling correspondence, as had long been the prevailing wisdom. As a twenty-one-year-old artillery captain, Hamilton had drilled his sixty-eight-man group well enough to draw the commanding general's notice, and then he had been observed in several battles to be perfectly composed and extremely daring. These traits, supplemented by his good looks and emphasis on careful military dress, had brought invitations to join the staffs of at least two other generals (for generals love to have smart-looking aides). But Hamilton had politely turned such offers down, until the magic invitation to join General Washington came.

Hamilton's remarkable ability to blend intellectually with older men was particularly in evidence at that point. As they became acquainted, Washington was astonished at the wisdom that came from this young man. He sounded clearer, more probing, and more keenly decisive to Washington than most of his top generals. This mental tie never wavered.

Washington was a man who constantly looked for clarity. In certain familiar subjects, he was marvelously clear-headed and made his own clarity. But he knew his limitations, and he cherished any associate who crisply and thoroughly summarized facts, touched certain key points, and suggested possible courses of action. Then Washington's own mind was keen enough to recognize the beauty of a perfect analysis, and he was a master decision maker who assessed the risk and knew when to move. In Hamilton, he had found the perfect associate.

What Washington had not realized during those wartime conversations was that he was seeing only one facet of the total Hamilton. Another part of the young man's remarkable mind had been dreaming far into the future, imagining the greatness that America could demonstrate if its financial affairs were properly handled. He found and hungrily studied books by leading European economic writers. And it was then—in midwar—that he had thought out a financial approach he would give this nation if he ever had the opportunity.

Robert Morris, the financial wizard who had done so much to provide funds for Washington's army throughout the war, had learned this through a few conversations with Hamilton. When personal problems forced Morris to refuse Washington's offer to give him control of the new government's finances, Morris told him, "But you have the best man for the job. Your Colonel Hamilton knows everything I do, and perhaps more." It was the first Washington had heard of it.

At war's end, although Hamilton had quickly qualified to practice law in New York and was making a resounding success both in the law and in New York politics, that original image of how to make America great had never been out of his mind. As a New York delegate, he had been at the Constitutional Convention, remaining unusually quiet for some weeks, then startling the assembly when he announced that he disagreed with much of what had been said. He appeared to have taken direct aim at Madison's plan, for he strongly praised the British constitution as the ideal form that the United States should be aspiring to. He received accolades for a great speech from many delegates, but none of them wanted to follow his lead, fearing the reaction from their constituents.

His speech had seemed to contradict one of James Madison's basic beliefs—that all great nations of the past had finally perished because their upper class had grown corrupt. Madison's main prescription for avoiding this fate was to give every citizen an equal vote, so that sheer size would overcome the influence of any corrupt group.

Hamilton had veered from Madison's views when he explained in Federalist Paper No. 76 that "any group of people will contain measures of vice and virtue. The supposition of venality in human nature is little less an error in political reasoning than the supposition of universal rectitude. A portion of virtue and honor has been found to exist in the most corrupt periods of the most corrupt governments." In praising the British form of government as an antidote to this condition, Hamilton did not necessarily advocate monarchy, but a system of senior officials who could override the possible errors of the common people. Such a system could have been achieved by having an upper house with veto power, consisting of older people with higher intellectual attainments who served for life, paralleling the selection and unlimited term of our Supreme Court justices.

Though he did not specifically approve or oppose suffrage for all citizens in selecting members of a lower house, it can be assumed that he would have approved it, as long as the lower house was balanced by an upper house that would have final control. For (as you will read in the next chapter) there was a moment in the Constitutional Convention when Madison was momentarily under attack on this very subject, and Hamilton had jumped to his feet, insisting on a vote by all the people to choose the lower house.

After realizing that his speech would have no effect on the Convention, Hamilton had quietly left the meeting and returned to his New York office. Then a pleading letter from George Washington asking him to return ("I am sorry you went away. I wish you were back.") coincided with second thoughts he was having. Madison's constitution, like it or not, offered the only possibility of seeing an American government that he might shape to fit his financial plan. If Madison failed, there might be no place for a Hamilton. He not only returned to the meeting, but became a strong advocate, convincing other delegates to sign.

Typical of his rush to be ahead of all others, Hamilton was the first to publish a letter in defense of the Constitution, on October 2, 1787, only two weeks after the signing. And then he was the hero in the tremendous fight to win ratification for the new document. The majority of the great Federalist Papers that won so many adherents were composed by Hamilton, almost on the run, while he tried to conduct his law practice. And his three-week struggle to win the approval of New York State was a classic with a dramatic ending.

A decade after his wartime meditations, he had plunged into his dream job as treasury secretary with incredible zest. On the day after his confirmation by the Senate, September 11, 1789, he set up a $50,000 loan from the Bank of New York, and on the very next day he asked a Philadelphia bank for another $50,000. Potential enemies had no time to intervene, for the Hamiltonian force was setting a pace that left all others behind. While the heads of other departments were beginning with two or three employees, Hamilton conceived of many new operations that could be logical offspring of the Treasury Department, each requiring dozens and then scores more workers. He was often spending long days writing job descriptions for the thirty-nine persons he had already hired and micromanaging how they were to correlate their work with the rest of the government.

Most of what he did was handled with a careful attention to detail that could be called perfectionism. When he started the Treasury Department's program of guard boats to detect smugglers along the East Coast—the Revenue Cutter Service, which proved to be the foundation of the U.S. Coast Guard—he studied many aspects of the boats that would be required, and quickly convinced Congress to provide funds for the first ten cutters. Hamilton also studied the type of cargo that would be searched for as well as designs for lighthouses. He devoted great attention to the training and discipline of the men who would make customs collection effective by identifying the merchandise to be taxed and the lawbreakers to be seized, making sure their methods were highly professional and their ethics were on the highest plane.

Dr. Robert M. Browning Jr., the historian of the U.S. Coast Guard, assures us that Hamilton's long letter of instructions, written in 1791 (see appendix B) is still carefully observed and is required reading for newly commissioned Coast Guard officers. There is not known to have been any existing set of instructions that would have served as the basis for this letter, so it is a perfect example of Hamilton's uncanny ability to create the most detailed solutions for each challenge that arose. And all the while he was skillfully putting together the basis of an American economy that would astonish the world. But while Hamilton's enemies were overrun, they were not to be underrated.

One decided enemy, who used the harshest words, sometimes even scatological, when speaking of Hamilton, was Vice President

John Adams, even though the two were of the same party and would normally have been political allies. Adams, for example, was four-square with Hamilton in admiration for the British constitution. But he simply detested the younger man. While most people found Hamilton unusually agreeable, impressive, and amiable, Adams saw him as "an insolent coxcomb" (then a popular term meaning "a showy but shallow person") and also described him with much stronger words that were far outside the polite dictionary. This dis-like was purely personal, not political, since the two men were both Federalists, meaning that they both believed in a strong national government, less power for state governments, and a measure of lib-eralism in approving change, as opposed to the relatively strict con-servatism of Jefferson's Republicans.

This visceral dislike for Hamilton was a grave misfortune. Adams had a powerful mind, even if its unnatural persistence sometimes had painful results. As a young man, just over thirty, Adams had composed a newspaper essay that Boston's senior pastor praised as one of the best things ever written. Another article of his, about taxation without rep-resentation, was adopted by forty towns—something that had never happened before. "Government is a plain, simple, intelligent thing, founded in nature and reason, quite comprehensible by common sense," he wrote in A Dissertation on the Canon and the Feudal Law.

> The true source of our suffering has been our timidity. We have been afraid to think. . . . Let us dare to read, think, speak, and write. . . . Let it be known that British liberties are not the grants of princes or parliaments . . . that many of our rights are inherent and essential, agreed on as maxims and established as preliminar-ies, even before Parliament existed.

Here was an inspiringly pro-British message that was entirely free of monarchism or royalist pretension, one that any Federalist might have agreed to. Yet, without reference to any political reasoning, its author and the young Hamilton could not stand the sight of each other.

Quite apart from politics, Adams and Jefferson, on the other hand, had been good friends for years. Adams's brilliant son and the president-to-be, John Quincy Adams, was unusually attached to

Thomas Jefferson during their period in Paris, and dined with him so often that Adams said with great pleasure, "I thought he was as much your son as mine." The young man had a more restrained view of Hamilton than his father did, but more to the point, observing quite rationally that "it was hard to get along with him if you disagreed with him."

In the time when they were together in the New York capital, Vice President Adams had little to do with the ruling circle around Washington, but his enmity toward the treasury secretary posed a potential threat to Hamilton's future that the latter seemed entirely unaware of.

A more immediate threat was James Madison, physically delicate, but pure steel within. He thrived on four hours of sleep per night and interrupted those hours by waking to jot ideas on his candlelit bedside notepad. Having a small voice and no natural speaking talents, he made it a point to have his pockets filled with notes on every possible aspect of any upcoming discussion. So even when he debated a great natural speaker with a clarion voice, like Patrick Henry, the advantage was usually Madison's. When he debated in Congress, he seldom lost.

Henry, the aging hero of pre-Revolutionary oratory, hated Madison because the latter had destroyed one of his favorite projects. In his later years, Henry had become a religious zealot, and he had a theory that all the ills in the society could be attacked if every citizen contributed to a Christian church. By this he meant literally that even nonbelievers and Jews should be required to contribute to Christianity. Madison and Jefferson both considered this to be an attack on freedom of thought. They both had respect for religion, but a firm belief that each person should have a free choice in the matter. (Jefferson himself showed his passive attitude when he wrote his own version of the Gospels omitting the miraculous parts, such as the Virgin birth and the Resurrection.) But Henry was Virginia's governor at the time, and was such an effective speaker that it seemed possible his odd proposal could be adopted. Because there was no constitution to bar the mingling of church and state, the weird measure could actually have become law.

Madison found an antidote for which Henry never forgave him.

He wrote a powerful message called "Memorial and Remonstrance against Religious Assessments," which, among fifteen major points, included the phrase "Rulers who leap the great barrier which defends the right of the people are tyrants, and those who submit to it are slaves." A supporter of Madison had great masses of this message distributed around the state, asking people to sign and mail it back to Richmond if they agreed. A mountain of these signed papers cascaded into the state government, some bearing up to a hundred signatures. Of course the bill was dead, and Madison told Jefferson he thought they had "extinguished forever the ambitious hope of making laws for the human mind."

A young John Marshall, who later became a great chief justice of the Supreme Court, was so impressed by Madison's debating method that he sat and listened to him whenever he had the chance, and then he rushed to find an opponent whom he could demolish by using Madison's technique.

Madison's close relationship to Jefferson was unique in American politics and also the linchpin of both their great careers. Here again, although the word *presidency* never appeared in the innumerable letters they exchanged, it is unimaginable that Madison's constantly questing mind did not foresee a presidential future for the man he knew so well. During the months when he tried to rouse Jefferson from his lethargy following the loss of his wife, and when he even created political openings for him (which Jefferson refused), he surely imagined that Jefferson's looks, mind, voice, and pen would easily fit him for the highest role, if only he could be brought back to a full life. And that was why, when Madison was the first to get word that Jefferson had been selected to replace Benjamin Franklin in Paris, he tore down the street breathlessly to bring him the news.

Madison was greatly admired by President Washington, partly for his aforementioned problem-solving skills, but also because he shared some of Washington's personal habits. Chief among these was punctuality. They both shared the agony of the on-time person who repeatedly suffers from the chronic tardiness of most others. Madison recalled, almost lovingly, the morning when the Constitutional Convention was scheduled to begin, although it had become clear that the gathering in Philadelphia was far short of a quorum. On Monday, May 14, 1787, exactly at the appointed hour of 10 A.M., General Washington joined Madison at the door of the State House, knowing that there would be no meeting that day, but determined to set his usual example. He did the same thing on every succeeding morning for nearly two weeks, causing many other delegates to start joining him, so that very useful informal meetings began to be held, even in the absence of a formal start.

More important was Washington's admiration for Madison's advance preparations and management of the deliberations that made him the unchallenged father of the Constitution. Madison had then joined brilliantly with Hamilton to assure that the document would be ratified. Though that had been only two years before, the memory of their cooperation had already dimmed. For when Madison had so quickly turned his congressional power to block his old partner's plans, it was hard to recall how close they had once been.

Madison's reason for opposing Hamilton appears to have been more personal than ideological. That is, Madison had little hard evidence for the charge that Hamilton was really aiming to move America away from democracy and eventually toward a monarchical government. But it was quite believable that his rival was driving toward much greater individual power than the Constitution had ever envisioned for any one official. Hamilton's bursts of energetic leadership too clearly hinted at a force that was capable of undermining the nation's democracy. Madison seemed convinced that Hamilton's rate of self-promotion and advancement might easily give such a man too great and lasting an excess of concentrated power, with effects ultimately reaching into every state, city, riverbank, factory, and farm. He might not become a king, but it was easy to envision the probability of a dictatorship.

There was no animosity in Madison's manner in the early spring of 1790, although bad feelings were bound to develop later, when all the parties in this political merry-go-round exchanged cutting words, some of them invented or expanded by their hired journalists.

At the start, however, Madison performed the whole anti-Hamilton operation with his usual veneer of politeness. Far from denouncing Hamilton's financial plan, he praised it faintly when speaking on the floor of Congress, but pretended to be overwhelmed by concern for poor war veterans who might have been forced to give up any bonds they had for a tiny part of their full value.

Around the same time, a letter he wrote to longtime friend Edmund Pendleton on March 4, 1790, put it in this delicate way: "The report of the Secretary of the Treasury is in general . . . supported by very able reasoning. It has not however met with universal concurrence in every part. I have myself been of the number who could not suppress objections. I have not been able to persuade myself that the transactions between the U.S. and those whose services were most instrumental in saving the country did in fact extinguish the claims of the latter . . . or that there must not be something radically wrong in suffering [them] to lose seven-eighths of what was due them and those who have no particular merit towards their country to gain seven or eight times as much as they advanced."

With a similarly velvet glove, Madison turned an iron fist against Hamilton's plan to have the federal government assume the entire war debt while forcing some states (and especially his beloved Virginia) to contribute more than a fair share in the repayment plan. "A simple unqualified assumption of the existing debts would bear peculiarly hard on Virginia," he wrote. "She has paid I believe a greater part of her quotas than Massachusetts since the peace. She suffered far more during the war. . . . If such an assumption were to take place, she would have to pay more . . . whilst Mass. would pay less. The case of S. Carolina is a still stronger contrast. . . . The payment of the balances among the states will be a fresh source of delays and difficulties."

Hamilton was so stunned by this change from the position that he and Madison had agreed on earlier that he was briefly silenced. He had not previously encountered such an unexplained change of attitude on anyone's part, nor such an opposite view of every point.

During Hamilton's unusual quiet period, other legislators began to follow Madison's lead and attack the treasury secretary's plan with more vehemence. An unusually long speech in the House by another Virginia congressman, the notably gentle and well-liked Theodoric Bland, brought a reminder of how completely many of the political figures were throwing themselves into the issues. Bland spoke more eloquently than he had ever been known to do about the exceptional wartime losses suffered by his state, which he said sadly distorted any calculation of what it might fairly be thought to owe. Then, exhausted, he begged pardon for having talked at such length, reminding his hearers how rare this was for him. He promised not to do it again. Shockingly, this promise struck a note of memento mori, for those proved to be virtually the last words he ever spoke. He was stricken, and a few days later, on June 1, 1790, Bland was dead. On Wednesday, June 2, the "History of Congress," as it was then called, had a note saying,

> Resolved unanimously, That the members of this House, from a sincere desire of showing every mark of respect due to the memory of Theodoric Bland, deceased, will go in mourning for him one month, by the usual mode of wearing a crape round the left arm.

But the shadow of death only seemed to deepen Hamilton's isolation.

4

The Radical
Conservative

JEFFERSON, HOWEVER REGRETFULLY he had come back to be secretary of state, had cemented his close alliance with Madison. No
two men could be more unalike, yet they were united in nearly every
political idea and instinct. And each was more ambitious for the
other than for himself.

Now that he had readapted to his own country, Jefferson's manner was what today would be described as "laid-back." Most of the
French ways he had taken on during his five years abroad had been
sternly suppressed. His posture and walk were loose and gangling; his
clothes were usually informal—sometimes to the point of giving
offense to persons who thought he was expressing a lower opinion of
them by not bothering to dress properly. But he still favored the
guarded French way of discussing affairs. By nature, he was more
suited to it than to the more outspoken British approach. He kept
his views to himself so much that Vice President John Adams, even
at a time when they were close friends, once called him "a shadow
man." A sad commentary, for after a life of unmatched dedication to
his country, Adams himself was discovering that a vice president
was, indeed, a shadow man.

Jefferson, guarded though he may have been, embodied far more
special features than an ordinary person is heir to. There was deep
intelligence, instant perceptiveness, a talent for assembling disparate

facts into firm conclusions, and an energetic determination that was almost too great for his physical strength. All of this was often translated into action by his fabulous command of language.

While the truth of Jefferson's words will be questioned on a number of these pages, it is important to note that this does not mean he habitually lied. Rather, it is part of what made him a remarkable writer. He often toyed with the truth or veered from it just enough to give his words more interest. But it would be an injustice to him and to the reader if one consistently regarded his account of events with great suspicion.

For example, he once said, "I read but a single newspaper, Ritchie's *Enquirer*, the best that is published or ever has been published in America." The truth is that he also subscribed to the *National Intelligencer* of Washington, D.C., the *Aurora* of Philadelphia, and the *Central Gazette* of Charlottesville. But in this case, he was trying to emphasize the excellence of Ritchie's, which was, in fact, a splendid source, and the untruth, though undoubtedly wrong, was no more than a form of emphasis.

In a sense, Jefferson was a born philosopher. His mind loved to ramble over intricate subjects and to find their basic inner workings. The great John Locke was the philosophical leader he naturally turned to, with his theory of a "natural law" based on the designs in nature. But just as Hamilton had the courage to improve on the works of the greatest economic writers, Jefferson did not hesitate to dispute Locke's conclusions. (What a pair Jefferson and Hamilton would have made if they had decided to work together.)

Jefferson had much too broad a mind to be simply a follower of any one thinker. Devoutly as he studied Locke's thoughts, for example, he was fascinated by the very different ideas of Thomas Hobbes and his *Leviathan*, in which Hobbes wrote that man's life without government is an endless war—"nasty, brutish, and short."

Bringing these beliefs down to the practical aspects of American life, Jefferson had put into the Declaration of Independence his conviction that all human beings have natural rights by their nature, not by a gift from society. And his felicitous use of the term "the pursuit of happiness" brought more adherents to the revolutionary cause than any other phrase. After that, he had a long success with the less dramatic but equally winning insistence that America's future lay in the hands of the simple farmers who were already pressing westward to occupy and cultivate the land that stretched toward the Mississippi. He did not intend that they should remain uneducated, for he had specific proposals of education for all. As he saw it, these guileless folk were the forerunners of a new breed of fine citizens, if their greater numbers could only fend off the evil Eastern money manipulators whom Hamilton considered his prime constituents.

Jefferson's dedication to this idea, even when he was still a young member of the Virginia Assembly, had made the assembly session that started in October 1776 one of the most eventful meetings in history. He was introducing the most democratic of ideas, presenting them with a sense of total certitude, and he made a powerful impact. Even if he had not succeeded in creating changes, the effort would have been historic and memorable. But he did succeed to an amazing degree, considering the fact that his seniors were essentially baffled and somewhat affronted by being told of all the changes that were needed in what they had thought was a settled society. He wanted to abolish entails of land and primogeniture, which tied up land ownership in a way that resulted in fewer families and fewer persons clustering "into a Patrician order," as he put it. He proposed "to annul this privilege" and "instead of an aristocracy of wealth, to make an opening for the aristocracy of virtue and talent . . . which nature has wisely . . . scattered with equal hand through all its conditions."

Through ALL its conditions! What more revolutionary thought than to insist that talents and even greatness might well be found among the poor? When, later in this book, Jefferson will be labeled a conservative, it will be a political term based largely on a wish to maintain the separate rights of individual states and to avoid the dangerous concentration of wealth that he feared would damage democracy. But "conservative" in the sense of suppressing change or opposing progress? No one could have been more anticonservative, more "liberal," in the struggle to open opportunities for the masses.

Jefferson's five years in Paris, much as some of the beauties of nature and the beauties he loved to be with enticed him, never made a dent in his passion for life in the United States of America. He saw the superiority of Europe's art and architecture, and the charms of life among the elegant, but whenever he summed up his comparative views of the Atlantic's two shores, there was no contest.

From France, he wrote a number of letters—one to George Washington—that were really exaggerations, declaring that not one European leader he met was intelligent enough to be a vestryman in a small New England church. More balanced and believable was a long letter he wrote from Europe to Charles Bellini, a William and Mary professor, who had become a friend. This missive exactly painted the conditions as he saw them. In this case, perhaps because the recipient was an Italian, Jefferson was careful not to write demeaningly of Europeans. A few sentences taken from it tell the story and also may invite interesting comparisons with present-day America:

> Behold me at length on the vaunted scene of Europe! . . . You are, perhaps, curious to know how this new scene has struck a savage of the mountains of America. Not advantageously, I assure you. I find the general fate of humanity here most deplorable. The truth of Voltaire's observation offers itself perpetually, that every man here must be either the hammer or the anvil. . . . While the great mass of the people are thus suffering under physical and moral oppression, I have endeavoured to examine more nearly the condition of the great, to appreciate the true value of the circumstances in their situation, which dazzle the bulk of spectators and, especially, to compare it with that degree of happiness which is enjoyed in America by every class of people. Intrigues of love occupy the younger, and those of ambition, the elder part of the great. Conjugal love having no existence among them, domestic happiness of which that is the basis, is utterly unknown. In lieu of this, are substituted pursuits which nourish and invigorate all our bad passions, and which offer only moments of ecstasy, amidst days and months of restlessness and torment.
>
> Much, very much inferior, this, to the tranquil permanent felicity with which domestic society in America blesses most of its inhabitants; leaving them to follow steadily those pursuits which health and reason approve, and rendering truly delicious the intervals of those pursuits.
>
> In science, the mass of the people are two centuries behind ours; their literati half a dozen years before us. . . . With respect to what are termed polite manners . . . I would wish my countrymen

to adopt just so much of European politeness . . . which really ren-
der European manners amiable, and relieve society from the disagreeable scenes to which rudeness often subjects it. Here, it seems
that a man might pass a life without encountering a single rudeness. In the pleasures of the table, they are far before us, because
with good taste, they unite temperance. They do not terminate the
most sociable meals by transforming themselves into brutes.

I have never seen a man drunk in France, even among the
lowest of the people. . . . It is in their arts that they shine. . . . I am
almost ready to say, it is the only thing which from my heart I envy
them.

Madison was receptive to Jefferson's belief in the farmer and his
wish for wider opportunities, although the former's independent
mind made him predict—with amazing accuracy—that the next
century would, like it or not, feature a great American swing to cities
full of workers who would leave their farms in favor of urban life.
There had been signs of this in England, but none at all in America
at the time, so Madison's insight is most impressive in its originality
and accuracy.

It is worth repeating that Jefferson's appearance of being the
leader who shaped Madison's ideas was inaccurate. Though Jefferson
cut a much more impressive figure, he sensed that Madison's mind
was often the first to reach shrewd conclusions, and he willingly
adjusted his opinions accordingly.

When he wrote from Paris about Madison's constitutional
decisions, Jefferson had been somewhat critical, especially about
the secrecy at the Convention. He said Madison was "tying up
the tongues of members." But he eventually agreed when Madison
explained in person that no secrecy would have meant no
Constitution.

A curious and long-running example of their frequent interplay
was a philosophical letter that Jefferson had addressed to Madison
while he was still in France. Calling it "The Earth Belongs To The
Living," he proudly built up an argument "proving" that it was a law
of nature that "the earth belongs always to the living generation"
and that "no society can make a perpetual constitution, or even a
perpetual law." The implication was that a living generation can
bind itself for only a limited number of years approximating the

average adult's working life span. So every act of a society and every declaration of public will would have to be expressly reenacted on that basis in order to be valid. Otherwise, the dead would be ruling over the living. Jefferson had forgotten to mail the letter and found it in his pocket when he got to America. He gave his masterpiece grandly to Madison, who promptly demolished Jefferson's main propositions. He showed that land ownership, debts, and other obligations often persist beyond the life span of the person who first undertook them, adding that many of these are not obligations, but positive investments that benefit the living long after the originator has died. To soften his attack, Madison said it would give him pleasure to see Jefferson's principle announced in federal legislation, to prevent the living generation from imposing unjust burdens on their successors, but he added, "This is a pleasure which I have little hope of enjoying." And he joked at how unwilling he would be to see the Constitution created anew every time Jefferson's fixed dates invalidated the old one.

Jefferson could afford to accept such corrections from Madison, for he was secure in a different form of leadership. He had an astonishing way of creating a political following with no apparent effort, and now Secretary Jefferson saw the start of a Republican party forming around him in opposition to Hamilton's Federalists.

There was a realistic basis for Jefferson's unique popularity. He had praised the common man—and especially the farmer—as no one ever had before. If he thought Hamilton was building a band of followers that would ensure his political power, it is not clear whether he saw any similarity in his own worshipful admirers. Even those who were not highly literate had heard his words that praised the ordinary Americans as the finest human society ever. And more specifically, he had written things—provable printed documents—asserting that states and people had almost unbelievable rights. The Kentucky Resolutions that Jefferson wrote when Virginia's Kentucky County was preparing for statehood plainly announced, "Resolved that the several states composing the United States of America are not united on the principle of unlimited submission to their general government. . . . That the government created by this compact was not made the exclusive or final judge of the extent of the [powers delegated to itself]. . . . Each party has the equal right to judge for itself." In these phrases, and in this sense, we are stunned to realize that this towering American figure had not really accepted and internalized the Constitution's unitary concept of the United States of America. The sanctity of states somehow blended with the love of individual liberty, and the latter rose above any other consideration.

But wasn't putting individual liberty first an outright threat to the solidity of the nation? It had no such effect in Jefferson's world, for the situation was more like a loving family that repeatedly insists on each member's individual rights, yet venerates family unity. When it came to actions rather than words, Jefferson was dedicated to the nation. For he had followed up his startling language with specific proposals that helped adventurous Americans to buy and finance new farms. People had read his writings. They knew this was a politician who added practical action to his words. They repeatedly drank toasts to Jefferson, and never questioned that this man was truly on their side.

With only impromptu planning, much of it done on the run by Hamilton and Adams on one hand, and by Jefferson and Madison on the other, two combative political parties were born. The Federalists had taken shape first, starting even before Jefferson came home from France, and the Republicans later formed around Jefferson, but with little more than hints and suggestions on his part. Jefferson's Republicans later came to be known as the Democratic-Republican Party, then split in the late 1820s, giving birth to the present Democratic Party. Today's Republican Party was organized in 1854 to oppose the extension of slavery.

It should be noted that neither side took any pride in declaring itself a political party. Too many persons thought of the term as a symbol of participation in something low, as one might not wish to be called a gang member. And the sorry fact, of course, was that parties have all too often deserved such a reputation.

Hamilton was the great symbol of the Federalists, the writer and speaker they looked to without question, although he had an ambiguous role. He had not formally set himself up as the party leader because he wanted to continue to devote time to his law practice, hoping to become independently wealthy. Then he had to give up the law in order to become secretary of the treasury, so he still allowed lesser lights to perform some of the functions of party leader, while no one doubted that he was its primary contributor of ideas.

Jefferson was the unquestioned leader of the Republicans, and his life was less complicated because, unlike a Treasury official, no one thought he was enriching himself when he went to work each day. Then as now, political parties—whether rough or genteel—had blurred edges and were hard to define because they tried to appeal to followers who agreed on some points and not others. But to simplify their general alignment, it might be said that the Republicans were strongest in the center of the country, popular with the farming people, and with conservative defenders of states' rights. The Federalists dominated in the Northeast, were backed by the leading financial interests, and favored innovations that led toward greater power for the national government. They were very strong in New York City, and Jefferson, nearly twenty years afterward, still found himself unable to describe "the wonder and mortification" he felt on first encountering those previously mentioned dinner-table conversations in that city where he was "for the most part, the only advocate on the Republican side of any question."

In only a few years, it would become clear that most of the new challenges facing a growing nation favored the Federalist willingness to espouse change, especially in the form of federal government expansion. Jefferson's personal popularity kept him in the leadership picture, but he would sometimes find it necessary, in order to see progress that he favored, to accept changes that he considered unconstitutional.

Even when he had written to Madison from Paris, trying to comment as gently as he could about the latter's new Constitution, Jefferson could not refrain from reminding, "I own I am not a friend to a very energetic government. It is always oppressive." But indeed, there would be a time only a few years ahead when he was cheered by the whole nation for the most "energetic" move in American history, but privately groaned that it was a violation of his firmest belief. This was the purchase of Louisiana from France, which would double the size of the country, even though President Jefferson secretly felt that the Constitution gave him no right to make such an acquisition.

President Washington, struggling to maintain order while dealing with his disparate aides, never spoke of being aligned with either party. It was assumed, however, that he felt more like a Federalist. This was not only because of his clear preference for Hamiltonian ideas—which Jefferson had quickly learned, to his sorrow—but also because the president was much more attracted to logic than to emotions. When Hamilton showed a preference for Britain, as opposed to France, Washington agreed, but not because of any emotional attraction and certainly not from a preference for monarchy. He was influenced by knowing that nearly 80 percent of America's foreign sales were to the British and that nearly all the U.S. government's income came from customs duties that were charged on imports from England. He was very ready to praise Benjamin Franklin for having brought France around to helping America win its independence. But even on the day the Treaty of Peace was being signed, the American government could not have functioned without the customs duties being collected on goods arriving from Britain. In this, as in everything else, Washington was a realist.

In dealing with this tempest-tossed executive branch of government, the House of Representatives, rather than bringing the political leaders together, tended to separate them more brusquely. This "lower chamber" and voice of the people soon developed into the sort of bumptious debating society that it has been ever since. The language and the legalistic terminology sounded little different from what it grew to be in the succeeding centuries. And then, as now, there were moments of special excitement, raised voices, threats that one group was planning to consider stronger measures . . . and always exaggeration.

This time in 1790 was an especially aggravated one, and men who were highly respected representatives of their own states were trying to assert that no splendid Hamilton or Madison, even if he was destined to be a centerpiece of the nation's history, was going to sell them the idea of saddling their people back home with debt to suit the great men of Virginia or the great city of New York. The chamber was regularly resounding with raised voices.

Madison, now the floor leader of that House, must have recalled —and probably with mixed emotions—the critical day at the Constitutional Convention when this kind of Congress had been invented. He had asked in too casual a voice "whether members of the national legislature should be selected by the people?" This was the key point in his whole hope for popular government, and in trying to sound reasonable, he had somehow said it offhandedly.

Then, trying to strengthen his approach without sounding too eager, he said, "This would surely put the government on firmer ground." But again, the tone was uncertain, and it seemed to invite comment. The result was that several opposing voices started up, saying, "No, they are not wise enough to make the choice," and "The people are wayward," and "They are too often the dupes of pretended patriots." Madison was oddly off base, somehow not himself, and America's future hung in the balance.

It was Hamilton whose lightning-fast brain had first noticed this and, in the surprising way in which he often did the unexpected, came to the rescue, saying firmly, "It is essential to the democratic rights of the community that the first branch, at least, must be directly elected by the people." The remark was subtly self-serving, for he had decided to go along with Madison's plan as a way of reaching his own goal. But it came as a surprise that proved effective. It led to follow-up remarks along the same line by George Mason of Virginia and James Wilson of Pennsylvania, giving Madison time to gather his thoughts and carry the day. The popular vote for Congress had been saved. But if Madison remembered that critical intervention of Hamilton's, it made no difference. The new politics did not give points for grateful memories.

5
Aggressive Lobbying

EVEN BEFORE ITS PROVISIONS became known, Hamilton's *Report on Public Credit* had set off waves of speculation in the country's primitive financial markets. The outlook for this dramatic legislation was doubtful in any case, because state loyalties still played a major part in the decisions that were waiting to be made. And it was clear that many states would be loudly for or against Hamilton's plan, while none would be passive or neutral.

Because something of Hamilton's amazing work habits and massive output had already been a subject of interest to many Americans, there was an expectation that something great would emerge. This optimism had begun to waver in February when it became known that Madison, the Father of the Constitution and now the floor leader of the House, had given a speech that appeared to find fault with Hamilton's project.

Hamilton was laying down a plan for the union to assume the debts of all the individual states, to combine this with debts already owed by the federal government, making all of these into federal debt—that is, $54 million in national debt, plus $25 million in state debt, for a total of $79 million. The government would then issue bonds, enabling investors to earn interest while effortlessly helping to finance the government.

The possibilities for profiting in a variety of ways was obvious. People who already held or who could speedily buy old government bonds that had fallen to very low prices would now see them soar in value, as it became clear that an active national government was backing them for 100 percent of their value. Even newly issued government bonds, paid for at full price, might provide good rates of interest—over 6 percent—plus the security of being backed by a sound government.

Most southern states were known to be strongly opposed to any such agreement. They claimed to have already paid more heavily in the course of the war, so they maintained that having to pay a share of this new debt burden would load an unfair cost onto their citizens. New England states, such as Massachusetts, New Hampshire, and Rhode Island, tended to favor Hamilton's bill, but were especially insistent on special terms, making their payments proportionately less, as a way of recognizing that they had suffered more than most other states during and after the war.

States that depended heavily on maritime business had indeed been crippled during the long periods when war had prevented normal shipping. Then it had taken years to restore the formerly healthy maritime trade. Meanwhile, as in the case of Rhode Island, the slack period had made it impossible for the state to meet its obligations to the Articles of Confederation. The resulting unpaid debt had given Rhode Island a terrible reputation in the eyes of its neighbors. Some of that was deserved, because the people had repeatedly voted for a bad government that consistently tried to live on paper money and showed no sign of ever bringing the state back to normalcy. But beyond doubt, Rhode Island was simply unable to meet its inevitable financial obligations. Some newspapers routinely referred to the state as "Rogue Island." And this miserable reputation would take years to repair.

In the House chamber, the atmosphere was volatile, with states easily jumping to regard each other as real enemies, bringing on an eruption of vivid and often angry speeches. The House's sergeant at arms was notably active in calling for order. Every state was deeply involved—some because they still owed larger than normal war debts (making them happy to see the burden shared by others) or because they had worked to reduce their war debt (making them shrink from agreeing to take on a share of the overall national debt).

"How much do we gain? How much do we lose?" was the calculation each state was making.

Despite all these warning signs, Hamilton's chance for victory with his assumption plan had looked favorable until Madison's unexpected opposition surfaced, portending a chilling fight between the floor leader of the House and the Treasury Secretary, both of whom were already legends in the making. Among other advantages, Hamilton had an unusual relationship with the House of Representatives: the House regularly requested reports from the secretary of the treasury on matters it was considering. This was specifically approved by the act that had created the Treasury Department, for it was assumed that many of the Treasury's subjects would contain technical aspects that congressmen needed help in understanding. But the habit of relying on such help had a substantial effect on the legislation that resulted. Simply put, the Treasury almost always got its way. At one point this practice was intensely debated by the House, with some Republican opponents saying that the House should be able to draft a revenue bill without calling on Hamilton. (They considered this a surrender of their constitutional authority to originate money bills. What kind of origination is it if you have to ask someone else what to do? they wondered.) The Federalists, being pro-Hamilton, simply brushed this aside, saying that the House was free to accept or reject whatever the secretary might recommend.

Another of Hamilton's regular work habits added fuel to this issue. He might be somewhat loosely called the first active lobbyist, although the term being used at that time was "references by the legislature to heads of departments." He went directly to the offices and cloakrooms of the congressmen to make personal appeals for their favorable votes. Although seeming minor at first, this assumed great importance in the eyes of Madison and some other congressmen. Hamilton could often be seen on the floor of the Congress or going into the surrounding rooms, talking with legislators to explain some of his points about pending bills. At those times, he was literally more like a modern lobbyist than a cabinet minister. He was clearly observed talking emphatically with small groups of congressmen or senators, to explain his aims and urge certain votes.

The liberties Hamilton took in speaking with congressmen were more than a mere annoyance to Madison, who felt that such actions should at least have required his permission as floor leader. If he could have rewritten the Constitution, he would probably have tried to include a paragraph barring cabinet officers from the area reserved for the congressmen—perhaps calling it "separation of legislative and executive activities." (But this would have called into question why Madison himself, a leader in the House, also had quarters in the president's office.) As things stood, there was no constitutional provision for Madison to prevent this lobbying habit—and he was reluctant to propose a specific House rule against the practice, since everyone would recognize it as a clear shot fired at Hamilton. So the latter had considerable success at influencing the congressional votes in the direction he preferred.

Jefferson wrote unfavorably about this practice. But there is at least one striking example of how he himself used a "dinner at Mr. Jefferson's" in effect to lobby against the practice of lobbying, and thereby advance his own political agenda. In this case, he wrote that after a dinner he had given, "Messrs. Fitzsimons and Gerry (among others), having dined with me, staid with a Mr. Learned, of Connecticut, after the company was gone. We got on the subject of references by the legislature to the heads of departments, considering their mischief in every direction. Gerry and Fitzsimons (both Massachusetts legislators) clearly opposed to them."

The effect was swift. Soon after this dinner, the subject of such consultations between congressmen and heads of departments was taken up on the floor of Congress—mirroring the after-dinner talk at Jefferson's. An animated debate took place on "the practice of department heads having direct contact with members of Congress." It seemed, at first, that a great majority would be against such activity. But the Treasury was said to have been so alarmed by the controversy that "much industry was supposed to be used before the next morning" (in other words, Hamilton and some of his staff spent much of the night contacting congressmen to influence their votes). Then it was brought on again and debated through the day. And when a vote was taken, the Treasury carried it by 31 to 27.

A Maryland legislator, Michael Jenifer Stone, spoke out bluntly, saying that this very small majority seemed inadequate, even though this was only a minor bill related to a larger one, "whereas in such momentous concerns, a large majority is necessary to satisfy the public." He reminded the House that some states were totally opposed to having the federal government take over the war debts, and a four-vote difference, even on a small aspect of this subject, did not convince them that they were wrong. This, he said, was an example of how a close vote meant that the states that had barely lost were feeling ill used. And he added warningly that opinions might change suddenly if a new light were thrown upon the matter.

Stone predicted that the Treasury would be deeply wounded by this close vote, by which he meant loss of respect. And indeed, many shifts of positions had occurred among the congressmen, some of whom had even absented themselves in order to avoid participating in the argument. It was something new and ominous for Hamilton to find some legislators preferring to steer clear of sharing in his schemes. And it is especially pertinent to our subject in showing how much influence Jefferson could have when he simply held a dinner at home and then exchanged ideas with a few guests afterward.

Anyone who reads the "Debates of the First Federal Congress" can detect that the Treasury's aggressiveness was beginning to tire some of the House members, for after another vote on a different Treasury Department issue, one finds the stenographer's remark, "This brought on a long and desultory conversation before at length it was agreed to, 29–27." *Desultory* is an editorial word that the stenographer should not have allowed himself to use, but it was useful in conveying the message that "Hamilton won, but not with his usual dominance."

Jefferson had quickly turned against assumption, owing to his conservative desire to protect the power of the states from being overcome by federalism. Then, over and above the issue of how much each state was to pay and the separate question of who would get the bond money, Madison and Jefferson had come together in their serious concern that assumption was a mass of endless evil possibilities. They suspected that Hamilton foresaw a dazzling career for himself in the bill he hoped to pass. But where he doubtless saw his future as a sparkling diamond, his grim adversaries saw a dark stone whose facets reflected the ugliest warnings.

They were determined to oppose the glittering personal prestige that Hamilton would win among the nation's wealthier folk, who had the most to gain as holders of federal bonds. For Madison strongly suspected that Hamilton still had the pro-British, pro-monarchy leanings he had once referred to in his memorable speech at the Constitutional Convention. And they thought he might well be planning a move toward an American form of monarchy for President Washington, with the subsidiary notion that the childless Washington might then declare Hamilton to be the heir to the throne. If he had already won the admiration of the wealthiest Americans, they felt, this shift to royal grandeur might be a natural step.

It was possibly an unfair thought, and could even be called mad in view of Washington's total dedication to democracy. But fairness makes it essential to recall that Jefferson and Madison were encountering remarkable signs that devotion to the recently defeated British monarchy was stunningly high in New York. Apparently, many New Yorkers had been secret Tories who had hidden their views during the war, but now were daring to show their real feelings. And so it seemed wise to assume that the area harbored large pockets of Americans with similar sentiments.

Lorenzo Sabine, the leader of the American Loyalists (a club consisting of Americans who had opposed the Revolution and felt themselves to be still loyal to the king), thought it "beyond all doubt that the Royal Party had the preponderance in all of New York state." And he was considered a responsible person whose words should not be dismissed.

Listening to the conversations around him at every dinner, Jefferson had ample reason to believe Sabine's claim. The table talk he described as mortifying had politics as its main topic, he said, "and there was a clear preference for kingly over republican government." Even at the height of the Revolutionary War, some said, a huge number of Americans who lived within the British lines had danced at "the enemy's" parties and balls. They neither knew nor cared about the suffering that was going on a few miles away or about the horror of the prison ships in the East River.

Putting such pieces of information together made Jefferson and Madison feel that they had a clear duty to take this threat seriously, for it was as if they were hearing the Revolutionary War revived, with the old issue in doubt again. Without wanting to overreact, they felt the need to be actively on their guard.

Jefferson was not an innocent, so he had heard shreds of such talk before coming to New York. But now, being here in the center of it made it much more vivid. And he had heard Hamilton quoted as saying that "The people are gradually ripening in their opinions of government. They begin to be tired of an excess of democracy."

Anyone subjected to such bursts of undemocratic feelings would naturally begin to wonder, "Did we really win that war? Or is it still ahead of us?" But didn't the nature of democratic government—the very fact that people were supposedly allowed to express their opinions—make it proper for them to be tired of democracy when they saw rowdyism in the streets or other disorderly behavior that had been less in evidence when they were ruled by a king? Or if they were not free to express such feelings, did America's freedom of speech have certain limits? Understandably, because they were practical politicians, Jefferson and Madison appear to have been untroubled by the inconvenient questions.

Even apart from any current monarchist opinions, Jefferson and Madison may have thought Hamilton quite capable of contriving an apparent governmental crisis at a later date to convince the aging president that he needed to transform himself into some stronger form of chief executive, without going as far as the word *king*. They never said this was so, just that it was possible. And if that great a threat was possible, then every action to guard against it appeared reasonable.

The very notion seemed wild, but the astonishment about Hamilton's amazing career can be seen as the impetus, for it did seem at times that literally nothing was impossible for this man. Jefferson and Madison may have been wrong, but they were not irrational in sensing a great danger. If there was one thing Hamilton forgot in his careful planning, it was the need to avoid sending danger signals to potential rivals.

Even though Hamilton's ambition did appear excessive at several points in his career, his part in getting the Constitution ratified and his writings in the *Federalist Papers* clearly appeared to be major arguments in his favor. As Ron Chernow has written, "Inviolable property rights lay at the heart of the captalist culture that Hamilton wished to enshrine in America," and that was a far cry from monarchy. Whenever those excellent *Federalist Papers* he wrote seemed to plead for liberal executive powers, stressing the importance of energetic executive performance, Hamilton balanced the thought with careful reminders of the need for caution to be sure the rights of the people were uppermost.

As a result, he was sometimes so even-handed in those *Papers* that the question of whether he was a potentionally dangerous man or a paragon will never be laid to rest. But we should not leave it without making an effort.

Alexander Hamilton, treasury secretary and President Washington's closest associate.

If forced to seek help in deciding, one could do worse than to rely on the admiration of Hamilton's fast friend the brilliant Gouverneur Morris, who ranks just behind James Madison in responsibility for the U.S. Constitution. Morris played a major role at nearly every important moment of the Convention, then wrote the masterful final document. He had his own opinion of each Convention issue, scarcely ever fully agreeing with any one person; but as a moderate conservative, he could reach accords with many of the leaders, including Hamilton. The two deeply respected each other, and Morris praised Hamilton's controversial speech at the Convention, in spite of his reservations.

Morris later expressed an intricate thought, which seems to narrow the gap between his position and Hamilton's: "When a general abuse of the right of election shall have robbed our government of respect, and its imbecility having involved it in difficulties, the people will feel what our friend once said: That they want something to protect them against themselves. And then, excess being their predominant quality, it may be a patriotic duty to prevent them from going too far the other way."

This sounds like a forecast, meaning, in plainer language: the electoral system is going to be violated at some point, and people will then lose respect for our government, which will be in trouble owing to foolish mistakes. They will have lost confidence and so will wish they had wiser heads to protect them against themselves (as Hamilton once proposed). But because the people always move to excess, we must hope some source of wisdom that is not too extreme will prevent them from going too far in that other (monarchical) direction.

Not only does Morris's respect for Hamilton imply a strong vote in his favor; it also makes clear that he has no doubt about Hamilton's steadfast belief in the principle of democracy that the nation was embarked on.

But he is recalling Hamilton's never-to-be-forgotten warning that "excess is the predominant quality of the people," so great wisdom is needed to keep them from going too far in that other direction (that is, to avoid giving away their freedom to a monarch).

Thus, Gouverneur Morris, the man who also worked closely with

Thomas Jefferson to design America's new money, and who would make a huge contribution to the support of Hamilton's family after he was killed, gives us a substantial vote in Hamilton's favor. That Hamilton had a strong attachment to the British principles of government is unquestionable. But the odds are that he merely wanted to see the United States build on that structure—and see it surpass everything that Britain's system had achieved, not to copy it entirely and not to be ruled by a monarch. George Washington would be pleased with this conclusion.

6

Thoughts of
Breaking Up

Near the end of May, less than two months after his arrival in
New York, Jefferson knew as a certainty that he had done the wrong
thing—politically—in becoming secretary of state. Serving George
Washington, with his clear preference for Hamilton's ideas, would be
a deadening experience that he could hardly bear to face. He was
beginning to realize that even without the Hamilton influence,
Washington had a strong wish to see the states firmly welded into a
single unit. And this took the president as far as one could go from
the Jeffersonian wish to see the states as independent as possible.

Moreover, being part of an office that would sponsor ideas to
exalt the federal government and diminish the role of individual
states might well confuse the public's image of the real Thomas
Jefferson. He faced at least a year and probably more before he could
decently withdraw from this hopelessly wedged position. Meanwhile,
he would keep struggling to make Washington "see the light," as he
saw it. But already, the strain of living this divided life had put him
into a tense, apprehensive, and weakened condition that would perhaps be recognized as depression in our day.

Apart from his own woes, Jefferson saw that a very real threat to
the nation's unity was in the air again. The notion of separating
some of the states was an old thought, but one that was coming
closer to the surface now. And to a man verging on a depressed state,

this threat to a country that he loved passionately was almost unbearable. The interest in politics might be more or less like a game to some of his contemporariés. But to Jefferson, love of country was nearly as powerful as love of a cherished person.

The recently elected congressmen, still conducting their first session and already approaching new elections, were getting repeated warnings from worried constituents that key people in a number of states had serious thoughts of wanting to quit the union.

John Adams, the excitable New Englander who was vice president, feared that some of his "old friends in Virginia and Massachusetts hold not in horror as much as I do a division of this Continent into two or three nations and have not an equal dread of civil war." The North-South divide was undoubtedly real, as shown by Virginia's Henry Lee, the legendary "Light-Horse Harry" whose son would become General Robert E. Lee. He wrote to James Madison, "I would rather myself submit to all the hazards of war and risk the loss of everything dear to me in Life, than to live under the rule of a fixed insolent northern majority." The bitterness of those words showed what a grim sense of enmity there was between states that should have been firmly bound by all they had been through together.

A civil war was seventy years away, yet the talk was as if America's attempt to create a model nation was about to fail. Signs of growth—interstate roads, turnpike corporations, and factories that signaled the Industrial Revolution—gave a sense of healthy activity, but the very leaders who had the energy to make this growth happen were suddenly focusing on destructive politics as their prime interest.

The idea of the thirteen states staying together or breaking up into separate groups had been very fluid in 1776. But they quickly saw that they all had to be together to fight a common oppresser. What would happen after that war ended was an open question. The states that had formed the union were not all alike. They had different origins and different customs. It was not at all unthinkable to suggest a separation and a new scattering into two, three, or more nations that had a great deal in common, once their basic freedom had been won.

Russel Blaine Nye, in his 1960 book, *The Cultural Life of the New*

Nation, pointed out that for several decades Americans "declared themselves free agents, exempt from the forces of the past that played on other nations. . . . [T]here were to be no dead hands laid on American society." And this unique sensation of beginning anew did not make them feel locked into a thirteen-state structure that must be kept exactly that way. On the contrary, it gave the sensation that all things were possible.

As the years went on, and especially after there was a Constitution, the possibility of dividing, while thinkable, was not a thing usually heard in polite conversation. After 1776, most people stopped describing themselves with the term "British American," and then for a time it became a point of pride to call oneself simply "American." It was still true, however, that a person was likelier to identify himself or herself as being from a certain state. Rather than just saying, "I'm an American," they would be likelier to say, "I'm a New Yorker," or "I'm from Maryland." But it was generally taken for granted that anyone in one of the thirteen states who spoke or tried to speak English was at least getting ready to be an American. So the idea of becoming anything other than a single nation began to be disturbing.

But now, as literate Americans heard about the disagreements in Washington's inner circle, they recalled times when the possibility of separating had been openly discussed. The issues being argued did not sound like the normal problems of a newly reborn nation. A disturbing number of influential citizens who read widely and discussed political issues made comments to friends in other state capitals and clearly thought some of the differences at the top were seriously threatening the unity of the United States.

When it became rumored that men close to the president were unable to agree on the most important issues, people began to wonder, "Is a country as big as this just too clumsy to ever march in step? Would we be better off if the states were grouped into three or more separate nations?"

The year 1790 marked the third time in as many decades that Americans talked openly about the possible collapse of the single united nation they wanted to build. In the 1770s, they had stared disaster in the face until France helped General Washington to trap

Lord Cornwallis, effectively ending Britain's grip. In the 1780s, the young country staggered under the weakest of governments (the Articles of Confederation) with a bankrupt treasury; yet it went on to close that decade with a great new Constitution and soaring spirits because the same Washington had agreed to be its president. But now, when this great man's first term in office was still new, the leaders who were his principal advisers had moved from petty skirmishing to signs of outright war against one another.

There was, in fact, no sound reason to talk of a breakup, for the main problem now was not one of size or of different backgrounds. It was chiefly a hunger for political power, affecting state politicians as well as federal leaders. True, the question of federal power versus state power was real and daunting. But this was precisely the kind of difference that these intelligent men should have skillfully examined and sought to resolve in a series of reasonable steps. It was not so much that it was impossible to reach an agreement on the issues, nor the size of the United States that made it hard to work together. It was the determination of these leading men to gain stature, promote party superiority, and win the right to rule. Like a massive plant large enough to be viewed from thirteen parts of the continent, the terrible force of American politics had blossomed overnight in full view of all the states, and the issue of which group should rule had become even more pressing than what ruling would mean, what the rulers proposed to do.

Strangely, this division into political parties was contrary to the early views of the founders, who considered them an affront to the principles of a true republic. "Factions," as they were first called, had been flatly denounced by both Jefferson and Hamilton. Both of them claimed to dislike this divisive turn and the combative approach to politics, although Hamilton was better at it and actually derived some pleasure from it, while Jefferson was telling the truth when he told John Adams, "I do not love difficulties." But Hamilton had written in the *Federalist* that factions would ruin us. He had written of political parties as a fatal disease. There is no way to be sure whether this was intentionally misleading or really showed a duality in his thought.

From Jefferson's point of view, even the public's interest in

America's political problems, which he might normally have wanted to encourage, were bound up with his own misfortune. He could not explain to the public why he was working for an administration that took a course so different from his own.

The ugliness of the situation was enhanced by a war of printed words that Hamilton started. Jefferson and Madison were incensed to find that Hamilton was backing a newspaper called *Gazette of the United States*, which a Bostonian named John Fenno produced for the purpose of glorifying the treasury secretary, and often carried Hamilton's own articles under assumed names. These habitually knocked the men who were his colleagues on President Washington's staff.

It was a case of attack and counterattack. For Jefferson's response was to select a journalist and poet named Philip Freneau and appoint him to be the State Department's translator, a job for which he was hardly qualified. But that made no difference, because, in reality, this man's modest salary was to encourage him to start a Republican newspaper, carrying the combative anti-Hamiltonian articles that Jefferson and Madison wished to see.

Neither of the competing papers had much journalistic merit. They carried little news, and both contented themselves and their sponsors mainly with trading rival opinions and attacks on the opposite party. But they did gather enough readership to rouse public attention, and they managed to expose and enlarge on issues that led to bad feeling between certain states that competed with one another for trade opportunities. The men who had first championed freedom of speech and of the press were now misusing these rights to bedevil and undercut each other.

In the course of this, they actually harmed the nation, for the states were easily goaded into unhealthy competition. The people of New Jersey and Delaware could be roused by hearing how New York stole their deals with European customers and imposed heavy charges on any shipments that touched their territory. And a surprising number recalled an inflammatory remark by a Delaware delegate that had leaked from the Constitutional Convention less than two years earlier: "Rather than let ourselves be ruined, there are foreign powers who will take us by the hand." The hushed moments following that remark had led to cold reproaches and a deep apology from the speaker, as from a boy who had said a naughty word. But it was only the idea of linking up with foreigners that had been shocking—not the notion of breaking up the United States. "Dividing the country is worth considering," they seemed to say, "but joining with Europe? Never!"

So it was surprisingly easy to generate thoughts about dividing the country into pieces. And Hamilton's massive plan for federal assumption of all the war debts overhanging the states was just the sort of initiative to trigger such thoughts. Because every state was intensely interested and deeply committed, in favor of assumption or against it, the mere word became a battle cry.

Unlike some complex issues that the general public more or less ignored, the subject of Hamilton's debt proposal was steadily in the public eye. Most Americans were able to understand that if their state had to contribute, some of that money was going to be their own. And the thousands of Americans who had once owned bonds or who still did own them were quite clear about whether they were expecting to collect or to be passed over. So while the sharpest disagreement was right inside President Washington's office, it was an all-American problem, and all the states were humming with the competing points of view.

The plan might have made its way through both houses of Congress if Madison had worked hard in its favor, as Hamilton had expected. The latter knew that the small, intense "Father of the Constitution" had an unusual ability to make followers do his bidding. When they had walked together and discussed the debt in Philadelphia during the Constitutional Convention, Madison had entirely agreed with Hamilton that there was no way they could find the original holders of old bonds issued by the revolutionary wartime government. They would simply have to pay the money to anyone who held the certificates.

More than that, Hamilton knew that even earlier, in April 1783, Madison had written an "address to the states" for the old Confederate Congress strictly ruling out any discrimination among the several classes of creditors, which meant no favoritism for the original investors. Having the document in hand was the only test of ownership. Now Madison was saying just the opposite, insisting that the poor who had sold their bonds early should get most of the money. It was a political ploy, since there are more poor than rich people, so the original news would please a larger number. But the full truth about ownership of each old bond would have been hard to find. Like many government promises, it sounded pleasing, but would probably never have been carried out.

The fact that there were contradictory opinions was not surprising, but politically alert Americans found it disturbing to know that the president's own advisers had not tried to iron them out in advance—and especially that the arguments were often becoming quite heated. The situation was worse than the public realized, for Jefferson, Hamilton, and Madison—each in his different style—took their complaints to President Washington, and the unfortunate man was infuriated by their tendency to present him with what he considered irreconcilable points of view. He must have wondered what had happened to the great problem-solving skills they had shown before.

It may come as a surprise to some to learn that George Washington had a delicate nervous system that behaved badly under certain types of stress. He could walk placidly through a hail of gunfire and go back to a happy dinner. But receiving a complaining letter from his troublesome mother, and having to sit and write her a response that explained why she should not consider moving to Mount Vernon, invariably gave him shoulder pains bad enough to force him to bed. Martha had observed this so many times that she ordered his bed prepared whenever an envelope from his mother appeared.

The dedicated president, knowing himself—knowing that the stresses of this job were ill suited to his temperament—had taken it on with the unspoken but clear assurance that these three trusted aides could be counted on to counsel him at every turn. When he realized that their personal feuds could make them talk of resigning, he was deeply disappointed and often infuriated at seeing them put personal rancor ahead of the nation's future.

It may also seem surprising that a man like Washington, who had kept his spirits high and had outwitted the British so often during a bitter war, now felt so desperately in need of support from advisers who were not even considered his equals. But Washington was now an aging man who had been handed an assignment different from any that he had ever attempted and, in fact, different from any that anyone had ever encountered. The military life was one that he had known well, and whenever it had presented new challenges, they had been within the scope of his former experiences. Becoming chief executive of one nation would also have been an understandable assignment, probably one with a precedent that could be followed. But to become the first president of a complex group made up of thir-teen diverse states meant considering new rules for each of them and for himself every day of this new life.

Hamilton, Jefferson, and Madison had exceptional personalities and skills that would have made them ideal helpers in this learning experience. The fact that they stopped making the effort to help—that they made what seemed like petty squabbles their first priority—not only left Washington feeling deserted, but also filled him with a real fury. When each of the three great Americans who did this to Washington are remembered and rightfully praised for many of their contributions to the new nation, all three should have a small black mark beside their names for their petty behavior and desertion of a man they should have felt privileged to serve.

Washington was personally affronted by remarks that Jefferson made about Hamilton's influence over him. It was genuinely aston-ishing how bluntly Jefferson addressed the man who had become accustomed to the most courteous treatment from the entire world. And the secretary of state often combined these comments with the suggestion that he was on the point of resigning. On one occasion, later in 1790, when Jefferson had just restated his old belief that Hamilton had caused the president to follow a wrong course, Wash-ington spoke up to say, "You appear to feel that I am either too old or too stupid to judge Mr. Hamilton's advice for myself." And he made it very plain that he did not at all take Hamilton's side on every issue. He actually produced papers and showed Jefferson the evidence of how many times he had gone against Hamilton's view. The president had been keeping score!

Jefferson also kept interjecting strong remarks about Hamilton's "preference for monarchical government" and implying that fear of this was the root cause of their disagreement. This was an idea that

Washington totally rejected. He had probably heard Hamilton speak of "the ordinary depravity of human nature" as a reason for needing strict rules that checked the behavior of these unruly creatures. But Washington could not imagine why that implied a need for monarchy. Hamilton was not out of step when he talked about people being unprincipled, for most educated men thought and talked that way about the common man.

Quite simply, the democratic United States of America were held in line by a secret class consciousness. The much admired Fisher Ames of Massachusetts, perhaps the greatest of all speakers, who died at a very young age, considered man to be "the most ferocious of all animals," and he defined democracy as "government by the passions of the multitude." John Adams had said flatly that "All men are men, and not angels. Whoever would found a state . . . must presume that all men are bad by nature."

Jefferson and Madison stood apart, known to have an exceptionally high opinion of mankind's possibilities. The latter in Federalist Paper No. 55 had mentioned "the infirmities and depravities of the human character," but then softened it by writing about "other qualities which justify a certain portion of esteem and self-confidence." And Jefferson wrote that men could be "habituated to think for themselves and to follow reason as their guides." But this was advanced thinking that was not to be expected of every worthy person.

The eminently practical President Washington, who wrote to his friend the Marquis de Lafayette "that as the world is much less barbarous than it has been, its melioration must still be progressive," was showing that he was open to the possibility of future improvement. But he was no dreamer who saw the people of his own time as nearly finished products. So it was Jefferson and Madison, rather than Hamilton, who appeared out of step to Washington.

Nothing made Washington seem quite as seriously affronted as the occasion when Jefferson dared to tell him half-seriously, "Mr. Madison and I have wondered whether we should resign, since Mr. Hamilton is taking over both our jobs." In other words, the practical aspect of staying on the job and getting work done was of more moment to the president than the debate over democracy versus monarchy, which Washington did not find worth discussing. The president kept pointing out what great contributions to America's power and prestige were being made—stopping just short of saying that Hamilton was achieving more than everyone else combined—which silenced Jefferson without mollifying him.

But what could have come over Jefferson to make him constantly challenge the greatest American in a way that was almost rude? It might be kind to ascribe it to excessive sincerity. That is, to be as dedicated as Jefferson was to a certain image of America must have made it appear unthinkable for an intelligent person to believe the opposite. It would seem to have created a desperation about failing to budge the president from his pro-Federalist position. Perhaps the fact that Washington had habitually relied on opinions and other help from a few people close to him had given Jefferson the impression that his mind was rather malleable, so that he fully expected his own views to sway the president more than those of the younger Hamilton. When he found the case to be just the reverse, it doubtless made him angry. And this made him all the more determined to prevail.

But any such explanation boils down to meaning that such determination to control the outcome was basically about the blow to Jefferson's personal plan, that is, his quest for the presidency. Nothing else comes as close to explaining the agony that Washington's political position was causing Jefferson. In any other case, he could easily have taken a light attitude of, "All right, Mr. President. Have it your way." But if he found himself virtually wearing a badge of "Federalist" just for serving a Federalist president, how could he ever become a credible anti-Federalist candidate?

Apart from whatever degree of depression Jefferson was suffering, perhaps he even had a premonition of the great sacrifice that was about to force itself upon him, though the details of it were not yet clear.

Meanwhile, sympathy might also be extended to George Washington, who was on the receiving end of Jefferson's despair, for he continued for months to read notes he could not understand from his secretary of state. One of them read: "Alexander Hamilton's system at the Treasury flowed from principles adverse to Liberty and was calculated to undermine and demolish the Republic, by creating an influence of his department over the members of the Legislature."

Washington was simply bewildered by this. "Adverse to Liberty?" "Undermine and demolish the Republic?" He understood the words, but not the sentiments, which seemed to him wildly exaggerated.

As men surrounding the president and others in Congress wrote letters to their own friends and relatives in various states, a hazy idea of the dispute became common knowledge. Interested citizens were inclined to take sides, choosing their favorites among the contestants. The hunger for power was not just the whole nation watching a few prominent men with a political appetite. A large and growing number of persons who looked on with interest began to take part in local gatherings. The newly formed political parties were being energized and strengthened by this, but not the nation. The fact that it was intensifying competition between the states awakened an old fear the Americans had—the possibility of falling into habitual disputes among neighboring states and seeing them turn into wars, as the Europeans had done. This was something they had vowed to keep out of the New World.

All these concerns were blotted out for two weeks in May 1790, when terror struck. No illness has ever caused such a fright as this period when George Washington was suddenly taken ill with pneumonia. It was horrifying because it was almost immediately pronounced to be very serious and "probably fatal." It is likely that doctors made such findings in order to protect their own reputations. If a patient died, the doctor was proved right; if he survived, the doctor was admired. But the idea of political life going on without a Washington to stabilize it was a cause for panic. A succession of doctors kept coming to the mansion on Broadway (which had replaced the original smaller house on Cherry Street).

Aside from real concern for the man himself, there was virtual terror about the notion of having a new president. For anyone else to take over the presidency seemed unthinkable. John Adams himself, never a pretender, made no show of rising calmly to the occasion. Instead, he admitted to extreme anxiety. Even his wife, the loyal Abigail, said a strange thing, considering the fact that her beloved husband was the subject: "The prospect of anyone succeeding to Washington's place was unthinkable." And she added, "Most assuredly I do not wish for the highest spot."

Although Washington would be well enough to go to Mount Vernon by June, the recollection of this scare left a constant reminder that Washington would not be president forever, and that the group of possible successors had done more to destroy confidence than to build it. Knowing that the threat they had just lived through would inevitably turn real, perhaps at any moment, had created a steady feeling of uneasiness.

Even without direct evidence, it is reasonable to conclude that the shock of Washington's illness played a part in making Jefferson suddenly realize the heavy responsibility of being secretary of state.

He had been thinking for some weeks, and had talked with his protégé, James Monroe, about the gathering danger that European bankers would begin to fear the many signs of an American breakup. Men who had loaned millions willingly to states that were part of a cooperative union could easily become distraught at the idea of seeing the young nation fall into separate pieces. Europe's bankers, avid readers of American newspapers, weighed every new indicator. If they heard about Washington's illness at the same time as a rumor of disunity in America, the flow of loans would not only end, it could become a demand for repayment.

Why had Washington or Adams not thought about this? Jefferson wondered. Wouldn't Washington at least have asked Hamilton about the threat? Yes, and Hamilton would almost certainly have told him that the one certain way to reassure the lenders was to pass his Assumption Bill, and Mr. Madison had decided to make that impossible.

But even if Washington—or Adams—had thought about this credit problem and failed to fashion an answer, what about Mr. Jefferson, whom many considered the nation's Third Man? The presidential succession, after the vice president, had originally gone to a series of congressional leaders because they had been chosen by the people. But almost a century later, the Presidential Succession Act of 1886 recognized the practical fact that only one congressional leader, James K. Polk, had risen to the presidency, while six former secretaries of state had done so. So even before this act designated the secretary of state as first in the succession after the vice president, Americans had clearly been thinking of this officeholder as the nation's third-highest person. And Jefferson knew it to be so. (Today, the Presidential Succession Act of 1947 makes the Speaker of the House first in line after the vice president, followed by the President of the Senate pro tempore. The secretary of state is next, in fourth place.)

Did this leader have an answer to the credit problem? He did, and it was one that turned the blood cold in his veins. He wasn't well enough for this.

7
Jefferson's Awakening

THE NEW THOUGHT THAT HAD GRIPPED the ailing Thomas Jefferson in late May was almost as jolting as if someone had announced: "You have just been given an entirely new job. You are now responsible for the nation's financial health."

At the same moment, Jefferson realized that being secretary of state did not involve only diplomatic affairs, and we know that he talked to close friends about this, probably during Washington's illness. In a practical sense, although it was not yet the law of the land, his position put him immediately next to the president and vice president in overall responsibility for the protection of the nation's welfare. If they had not moved to counter the threat he saw, it was up to him to act.

Sick as he felt and agonized by tension headaches, he was struck by the thought the United States was in great danger simply because it was *threatening* to break up. Even if nothing of the kind happened, the uncertainty alone could wreck America's credit. And once credit is questioned, nothing is ever the same.

Much more serious than domestic politics was the suspicion of a creeping international danger that George Washington's office should have responded to promptly, even before the president's illness. "The Americans will never stay together," some foreign observers were beginning to think, without clearly understanding the issues. "Every few years, they are ready to break apart."

This thought was good news to the English, for they had not expected the Americans to make a success of their separation from the mother country, and they looked forward to winning "their colonies" back. But it was painful to other Europeans who saw the Americans as good customers. And it was even more critical to foreign bankers who had been lending major money to the fast-growing states, but now began to take their instability much more seriously.

Much of the country's hope depended on its credit rating in Europe, and by giving the impression of a country prone to crisis, it was on the point of shattering confidence. The money to develop the vast new nation could only come from European lenders—notably Britain, Switzerland, and the Netherlands—and those grim critics were undoubtedly having waves of stop-and-go emotions. Recall that even the money to fund Hamilton's disputed financial plan would have to rely on borrowing from abroad. In these early 1790s, the Europeans were undoubtedly questioning the outlook for the unpredictable colonials more intently than ever before. The bankers saw massive amounts of interest to be earned, but they would also be seeing danger signals at every turn.

This threat alone might be as destructive as the fact itself, Jefferson knew. When Europe's bankers began to fear it, they would act—probably asking some of the smaller states first to liquidate what today would be called "subprime loans." If the states stalled or admitted outright that they were unable to pay, the bankers might even allow partial settlements to be made at a discount, accepting less than full payment in order to get a portion of their cash back. The spreading action would develop rapidly to get at least partial repayments from larger borrowers. The lenders knew that full repayment was impossible, nor did they even want it. Just reducing their exposure to this shaky market would be considered smart practice. But the effect on America would be stultifying. Its growing business world would stall like a climbing airplane that lost its power. Even if an actual breakup of the states were avoided, it would be the death knell of the nation's astonishing growth, for mere rumors would be enough to keep Europe's bankers away from the liberal credit policies that had fueled the new country's surge.

Just the fact that this question was being talked about abroad had already put America in danger. No one could know at what moment the European money centers, from which most of America's vital loans came, might start denying any new credit. All the new immigrants who were now on ships headed for America might find that the great job market they had heard about had disappeared.

The more he thought about it, the surer Jefferson became that the president and Hamilton had surely discussed this danger, and that the latter had stressed how the passage of his assumption plan would have been the perfect answer. But he would have added that it was out of his control because "James Madison is holding the nation hostage by his refusal to let it pass."

"Am I making too much of this?" Jefferson must have wondered. But he knew at once that this would have been wishful thinking. The answer was no.

So, the suffering man asked himself, was it up to him to take action? He knew the answer was yes. If the president and vice president made no move to counter the danger, many serious people would consider the secretary of state as responsible as if he were number one, and the country's fate was in his hands.

It was a challenge he didn't feel well enough to confront. He tried to think of ways to pass the job on to another. Madison himself, perhaps?

But that would be asking his best friend to suffer a humiliating reversal and defeat in his place. To enlist Madison in his own effort, and to share the personal sacrifice with him, was another matter. Painful, but not unthinkable.

Any distant threat to democracy posed by Hamilton would have to be addressed later, as would Jefferson's own political hopes. Europe's view of America must come first, for if its credit standing were to erode, all the rest would crumble.

The more Jefferson thought about this, the more imminent he knew the danger to be. The nation was facing total, disgraceful failure, for he saw that European lenders had reasons to distrust the United States as a borrower. The nation's credit rating could well be near the point where no banker would want to advance more funds and all bankers would then press for repayment as promptly as possible. The United States of America would be like a great plant drying up, unable to make jobs even for those already here, much less for the new ones who were even now waiting to become new Americans.

Jefferson did not write this in just these words, but several of his notes and remarks to confidants combine to show beyond any doubt the impact of such a sudden realization that his position in the government involved an urgent duty in this regard. The thought apparently assumed a form and a force that made this seem a very specific obligation, one that he could not evade. It meant that this essentially self-centered man had to steel himself to pursue a hard and unselfish course.

He hinted at this in one note, and his resolve is proved by comments that he made about two months after his arrival in New York. These combine to show how soon and how seriously he suddenly took the need to find a compromise that would serve the one great purpose of preserving America's credit standing in the eyes of Europeans.

On one occasion, during that spring of 1790, Jefferson told Senator James Monroe that he had realized more pointedly than ever that "Credit was an essential element in the conduct of foreign policy." And he later told Monroe that he "saw the necessity of yielding to the cries of creditors in certain parts of the Union . . . to save us from the greatest of all calamities—the total extinction of our credit in Europe."

It is strange, in a sense, that something as fine as the struggle to keep democracy alive, to keep improving human life, should have depended on the crude instruments of commerce and finance. But considering the fact that man had once depended entirely on brute force to improve his life, this did represent a distinct step forward.

For the first time since Washington had asked him to be secretary of state, Jefferson's thoughts went far beyond the questions of his personal comfort or his future. He was only concerned about staying well enough to accomplish what must be done. The fact that any action he took to reach some form of agreement with Hamilton would surely affect, and might well wreck, his presidential ambition had to be ignored for a time. At the moment when he was feeling poorly, when his brutal headaches were particularly oppressive, he felt the weight of that title, secretary of state, and he realized, with no spark of pleasure, how much now depended on the person who carried it

He felt, more than he ever had before, a direct responsibility to take action. It was not the kind of diplomatic move that a secretary of state is usually called on to make, although, in a sense, it was the quintessence of foreign policy that he would be dealing with now. But it would have to start with a political move at home—a move that told Europe's bankers: this young country is stronger than you ever hoped or imagined. To do this, he must first—quietly and persuasively—sell the idea to his closest friend, who might well think he had lost his mind. He had to convince James Madison that Hamilton's assumption plan must be approved. It was the only way to show Europe that this government would stay together.

It must have been a strange feeling to have known in his heart that he was probably planning the most unselfish act of his entire life. He would be handing a great victory to a potential enemy of democracy, and undoubtedly disappointing his own closest associate, while en route to embittering all his followers. There would be no glory in it for him. But if the title *secretary of state* stood for anything, it was for the security of America. And if security in this case was spelled C-R-E-D-I-T-W-O-R-T-H-I-N-E-S-S, so be it. It was his job to spell it in capital letters.

All the emotions he had on returning from France must have recurred to him at this time: Conflicted thoughts about becoming secretary of state. Other plans that had to be laid aside. A courteous response about serving President Washington in any way, despite sadness over the shelving of his own plans. Those broken plans seemed so glorious now. If he could have had a restful period at Monticello, it might have refreshed him enough to make presidential politics truly appealing.

He had been really conflicted about saying yes to George Washington for those two reasons—because the longing for Monticello and private life had become a constant obsession, and because the presidential possibility had appeal as well. This conflict might have been simplified if he had found the road to higher power wide open. When, instead, he found the younger and dynamic Hamilton so much hungrier for power, he was half-inclined to withdraw from the competition, for Jefferson knew himself well enough to realize that he was repelled by the price to be paid for power.

But that low-burning flame inside him fired a genuine insistence on the preservation of the nation's future. Jefferson was sometimes capable of duplicity, but not on this subject, this vision of what America could be. This was a man who had once written from Europe to the distinguished jurist George Wythe, his former law professor, "A thousand years would not place the people of Europe on that high ground, on which our common people are now setting out." The glowing conviction that a democratic nation made up mainly of well-schooled landholders could become the finest society ever known would not let him carelessly lose America's future to the moneylenders of Europe.

Against this, the secondary threat that Hamilton might sell this nation to his own group of money-grubbing financiers who might even move toward monarchy filled Jefferson with a rare animosity. But that struggle would have to wait its turn.

Now, to protect America, he had to face up to a sacrifice that would hand the dangerous Hamilton exactly what he wanted—a passkey to a political future with unlimited possibilities. And only one small consoling thought might have made Jefferson smile a little to himself: he would be making the same sort of sacrifice that Hamilton had been forced to make in Philadelphia. Hamilton probably had not liked Madison's Constitution at all. When he had said, "The people are turbulent and changing," he had meant it with all his heart. Surely they were not to be trusted with so much power. But after walking out, Hamilton had returned to the Convention and fought desperately for ratification because he knew there must be a new American government before a place in that government could make him great. In the same way, Jefferson now knew that he and Madison would have to do an about-face and give Hamilton the interim political victory he wanted before—he hoped—they could arrange to defeat him in the end.

It would be war, but Europe must think it was only politics as usual.

For now, in view of Jefferson's new concern for America's stand-ing with moneylenders, all this had to be laid aside. He and Madison did not have to pretend to any great liking for Hamilton, but they had to allow his assumption plan to pass and thus reassure the foreign bankers that their investments in America were safe. Why the "financial hash" that Hamilton had put together should give any creditor confidence, Jefferson had not a clue. But early reports showed some sophisticated Europeans rather favorably disposed toward it. Puzzling, but helpful for the moment.

Convincing Madison to accept his new reasoning was not at all the challenge that Jefferson had doubtless imagined. Madison's quick response showed that he had not been surprised, and might easily mean that he had been thinking along similar lines. Agreeing on a joint policy for appearing to work with and compromise with the person they distrusted would not be pleasant for them, but Madison now showed how much he had grown while Jefferson was in Europe. He had demonstrated a rare flair for painful compromises at some of the most difficult moments in the Constitutional Convention. Because he had carefully taken time, before the Convention began, to sound out a number of state delegates as a way of preparing for the worst, Madison had known that some of the southern delegations— especially South Carolina—had orders to quit and go home if there was any strong attempt to interfere with their policy of slavery. Their demand was not only a continuation of slavery, but even a continu-ing right to keep importing more slaves. Otherwise, they would urge several states to quit the Convention. This would have meant the collapse of any meaningful federal government, leaving the slaves as hopeless prisoners of their white masters. So Madison had steered around any mention of slavery, even infuriating such an important Virginian as George Mason, who left the Convention and refused to sign the final document because he had been stifled on this subject.

In the same deceptive way, Madison had once appeared to deliver a strong blow against states' rights (which, of course, he and Jefferson strongly supported) by asserting in a Convention debate that the American states had never had the essential right of sover-eignty. It was like saying that they had never been real governments at all, which he did not in the least believe. But it served to win a point at the given moment, and later he revised his own notes to make it seem that he never said anything of the sort. The deceptively small man had learned to make instant changes of direction, turning his apparent weakness into an all-purpose weapon that overpowered most opponents. He had become the kind of brilliant performer who could climb aboard a moving vehicle, regardless of its direction or speed.

So now when Jefferson explained his reason to propose a sharp change of direction—a sudden move to support Hamilton's debt plan—Madison had no problem adjusting to it. Jefferson realized why Madison had given America a Constitution against all odds. He saw that his friend had become the master negotiator, tacking with every change in the wind, compromising as a matter of course. Together, they were the team that would outfox Napoleon Bonaparte and take a third of the American continent from him ten years hence.

Jefferson's own thoughts on how he and Madison were to accomplish their surrender were well advanced. They would not simply tell Hamilton that he could have his way and get the assumption plan passed. Far from it. To win without paying a price would make Hamilton suspicious. He might understand too well, take undue advantage of their haste, and press hard to keep this assumption victory, while also continuing to pursue attempts to make New York the capital city.

Instead, Jefferson's mind had jumped at once to the idea of a compromise, meaning that Hamilton would have to give up one favorite plan in order to win on another front. He was clear about the two issues that would form the basis of this trade, apparently allowing Hamilton to win on one issue while agreeing to lose on another one. And fortunately, Jefferson was hopeful that the issue Hamilton would insist on winning was exactly the one that Jefferson wanted him to win—assumption. But these choices must not be put forward too hastily. Hamilton must be made to think that he was developing and defending the ideas on his own. And he must never be allowed to know how determined Jefferson was to safeguard America's financial standing, for that also would make him fight to win on both issues. Jefferson would have to act as if he had given only a little thought to the idea, and let Hamilton enlarge it for himself. It was as though he were inviting Hamilton to join him for a ride on his coach without describing the intended journey.

It would not be enough to make Hamilton alone reach the right conclusions. The agreement would then have to involve a good many other players—making enough legislators change their votes to achieve the desired double result. This, he thought, was going to take a good while and a certain amount of good luck

Instead, a simpler picture emerged. It would soon turn out that the lightning-fast Hamilton had done much more than go along with Jefferson's unspoken plan. He had contrived to become a partner in the whole project.

8

A Country without a Capital

Normal people who find themselves in trouble do not usually cheer when they are told of still another great problem crying for attention. But high-level politicians often feel their pulses stirring when such a thing appears. The arithmetic of their craft tells them that one problem plus one problem may not equal two problems. It sometimes equals one solution.

In addition to the assumption wrangle, a second big problem hanging over these conflicted Americans was that their country, which was trying so hard to become a major player in the world, had no capital city. The selection of a location, which had been festering for some years, was another unresolved debate. And now Jefferson's new plan to reach a compromise with Hamilton would surely aim to settle that question, along with approving the Assumption Bill.

The location of the nation's capital was so touchy a subject that not even the adventurous fifty-five men who had argued and decided the Constitution's many complexities in 1787 dared to name a spot or even an approximate area for this purpose. In their great document, they had timidly said only that there should be a capital city and that it should be ten miles square, leaving the details for some later date. The thought of that unfilled promise kept haunting them, and suggestions were regularly submitted in

Congress. "The Residence Bill" was what they called it, for it was a little less touchy to suggest "where the Congress would reside" than to say, "I want to see the nation's capital in my state—or at least in my part of the country."

One reason for this nervous approach dated back to the spring of 1783, when an angry band of Pennsylvania militiamen whose pay was long overdue marched on the State House in Philadelphia, where the weak Continental Congress was meeting, and threatened to hold the lawmakers hostage unless they got their back pay. The state's leaders were not sure they had enough cash to make such a payment, and they refused to marshal other troops to rescue the besieged legislators. Hamilton and several other members of the Congress were disgusted by this poor-spirited response, and they arranged for their entire meeting to escape the alcoholic soldiers and to move, first to Princeton, New Jersey, where the quarters were unbearably cramped, then to Trenton, and later to Annapolis, Maryland.

The chief importance of this comic-opera incident was a general belief among the leaders that the national capital must be located in an area that was not part of any state, so that no state government or militia could ever take legislators hostage or otherwise interfere with the workings of the national government.

But in the years that had passed, a whole different set of theories had arisen about where the ideal national capital should be located. Such major northern cities as Boston, New York, and Philadelphia all felt themselves to be the natural choices because of age, supposedly higher educational and intellectual standards, and even more sophisticated commercial development. But this pretension or arrogance, as seen by the South, made many southerners swear that they would not tolerate any northern location. A southern site, they felt, deserved to be chosen as the only way to strike a balance against all the years when temporary capitals had almost always been in the North.

One thing in the South's favor was that George Washington was known to like an area near the Potomac River. As a commerce-minded man, a developer by nature, Washington felt that the Potomac area was central enough to promise a great deal of future contact with much of the nation's heartland, and that the Potomac River itself could probably be opened up enough to become an ideal conduit between the Atlantic Ocean and the central part of the growing United States. Jefferson and Madison, two loyal Virginians who also imagined that anything Washington sponsored would already be off to a superior start, had exchanged notes for years that were more and more enthusiastic about the Potomac.

The area had many enemies, repelled by the crude and primitive conditions that seemed to have none of the refinements needed for an agreeable capital. There were so many sunken areas in the proposed site that there was much exaggerated talk of a "wilderness," "full of mudholes," and "fit to be a hunting ground, not a city." Many of those who were looking into this subject with a serious attitude found it more interesting as a study of ancient history than as a hopeful look into modern history.

It was the sort of area that had far more appeal to persons who, like President Washington, were accustomed to passing it in the course of nearby travels. Washington had often passed it while taking shipments of tobacco to the nearby seaport of Alexandria, Virginia. Seeing wild birds and the occasional mudhole along the way seemed quite natural and agreeable to him. To the total stranger, it had nothing to offer.

An Englishman named Ebeneezer Cooke who had made a three-month study of North America in the previous century was convinced that the original homeland of this area's American Indians was somewhere in Eurasia. But his unconsciously humorous theory was that those ancients were not sufficiently advanced as sailors to have crossed the ocean. So he eulogized them in a long poem implying that the Eurasians had teamed up with Phoenicians in order to make the trip that somehow turned them into American Indians. But he concluded his verse with his own theory of why these Eurasians were no longer to be found along the Potomac:

They could not on the ocean float,
Or plant their sunburnt colonies,
in regions parted by the seas:
I thence inferr'd Phoenicians old,

Discovered first with vessels bold
These western shoars, and planted here,
returning once or twice a year,
with naval stoars and lasses kind,
to comfort those were left behind;
Till by the winds and tempest toar,
From their intended golden shoar;
They suffer'd ship-wreck, or were drown'd,
And lost the world so newly found.

Later scholarly researchers found more credible signs of ancient inhabitants, dating back nine thousand or more years to the Paleoindian age, in what was to become the District of Columbia. Certain types of fluted spear points, used in hunting woolly mammoth mastodons, were much in evidence. And other findings suggest that human groups from the end of the Pleistocene era ten thousand to twenty thousand years ago occupied nearby areas within a short distance of what was to become the nation's capital.

Most of the ancient facts about the area were learned in the earliest days of interest in the Potomac. Once the capital city actually grew there, those who were trying to research the past lost hope, for the rapid moves to prepare for all the needed buildings quickly blotted out evidence of the past. Some early archaeologists were able to learn that important cultural innovations occurred there in the first millennium B.C.E.—the widespread manufacture of pottery; the domestication of native plants such as the sunflower and the introduction of gourds, squash, and maize from Mexico; and the development of distinctive mortuary practices.

By the time American politicians were considering the choice of a possible capital city, there was little sign of the ancient occupants. An Indian group known as the Conoy, who were related to the Iroquois, had moved into the area that was to be part of Washington, D.C. But by then the tribe numbered only fifty people, suffering from the dread inability of many Native Americans to survive the diseases and other pressures of that period. Small tribes like these were being absorbed into the Mohican and Delaware tribes.

Indian families with some of the same names were interviewed in

Washington, D.C., as late as 1925, but distinctive as they had once been, these people were being absorbed into the general mix of Americans—a cause of some regret to them; but in a sense it is interesting that Native Americans, who can hardly be called immigrants, had pioneered the direction that would later be taken by Italians, Irish, Germans, and Latin Americans.

It is no surprise that Thomas Jefferson, sometimes called America's first archaeologist, conducted such researches closer to his Monticello home. He found a small burial mound in that immediate vicinity, and left astute comments on its contents in his book *Notes on the State of Virginia*, written in 1785. As a policymaker, however, Jefferson was extremely hard on the American Indians. Not out of cruelty, but out of an unchecked determination to make room for the inevitable spread of the white inhabitants, he conceived of numerous plans whereby tribes exchanged some of their vast lands for much smaller areas, with a promise to provide protection and a certain amount of advanced help—often with very generous land grants to the chief, if he was willing to sell his followers on the plan while enriching himself. It was understandable, for the whites needed the land for expansion, but it was ignoble.

Meanwhile, George Washington was troubled by something more than simply pushing the Potomac area—and this was a form of trouble that was virtually unknown to him: it was the rare charge that President Washington was trying to feather his own nest, that he talked up the Potomac area because it was just a few miles from his own Mount Vernon estate, and because he knew that the development of a national capital nearby would send all his own land skyrocketing in value.

It happened that this kind of reasoning on the president's part would not have seemed outrageous in that day. Many would have thought a person who had made such sacrifices for his country had a right to improve his real estate holdings. People whispered such suspicions, but there was little of the journalistic interest or talk of illegality that might have been the case in later years. But to the rigidly correct president, a single article in the *Daily Advertiser* of July 13, 1790, bearing the pen name Junius Americanus, raising the issue of Washington's personal reasons for pressing the Potomac area, was an attack that made him repeatedly question Jefferson about who this Junius might be and whether he simply represented enemies of the Potomac site or was flatly questioning the president's integrity. The point about integrity was especially explosive in Washington's mind, but not for the usual reasons of financial correctness. The worst accusation he could imagine was a challenge to his own devotion to constitutional government. If anyone was implying that he wanted to embellish his own neighborhood in order to make it grand enough to be the site where American democracy might be replaced by a monarchical government, his fury would have been incendiary.

Washington directed searching questions to both Jefferson and Madison: "Who is this Junius, and what is his game?" And they collaborated in a response intended to mollify his feelings. The president may have been trying to sound out their own true position because six years earlier, these two had worked together in trying to move thoughts about a capital westward to a more central position.

As time passed, they went back to talking most favorably about the Potomac area (which was often referred to as "Georgetown," a small section of Maryland land that abutted the Potomac River). Madison, however, was in an uncomfortable position in the matter because he had seemed to shift sharply. At one time, he had been so keen about the Potomac area as a capital site that he had made a substantial investment in land there. Because his finances were limited and his investments usually quite small, this seemed especially meaningful. But later, he had written in praise of another area, more toward the center of the country. Washington could not have been very pleased about that, so he may have been inquiring as much about Madison himself as about the unknown Junius. It was the beginning of Washington's distrust of a man he had once trusted implicitly.

This issue was being followed by a great many people, including the ever-alert French, whose chargé d'affaires had said in early 1790 that he thought the eternal discussions about the seat of government would one day give the country a perceptible shock. Indeed it did, and promptly, for it was fanned into new flame by Virginia's offer of land on the Potomac, by her plans to improve navigation of the river, by her pledge of $120,000 for construction of buildings in the federal district, and by her invitation to Maryland to join in the gesture—all this in the first few months of 1790. The debate on the residence issue reached a peak six months later, and then it would be with the serious threat of disunion, as by then the almost unthinkable idea of the country breaking into parts would be clear and ominous.

Secretive letters exchanged much earlier between men who were not participants in the search for a national capital but were extremely interested bystanders show that very specific and pointed discussions were under way—almost as if steps toward the eventual deal were already well known. William Grayson, a Virginia legislator, traded letters with Madison that sounded like wartime secrets and spoke of plans "that could not be put into writing." As early as May 24, 1787, Grayson had written to Madison: "A little flurry has been kicked up about Philadelphia. . . . The enemy wanted to raise a mutiny in our camp by proposing to go to Georgetown at a certain time. . . . Since the matter has blown over, some particular gentlemen have offered to join us in getting Georgetown fixed as the capital of the Federal Empire." Grayson's letter then wrote of several key points that were actually occurring at the Constitutional Convention, which was then just getting started. This showed that he had exact inside information from a meeting that was supposedly airtight, for he ended by writing, "I shall see Gerry and Johnson as they pass [two Convention delegates], and perhaps give you a hint."

The fact that Grayson's letter was some four months ahead of several Convention events to come shows that his points about the choice of a capital—although the writing sounds almost like code—were based on real inside information. In short, such talk had been circulating in an uncounted number of places—and all this before the Constitution was half-written.

Even more to the point is the fact that on Sunday, June 13, 1790, Jefferson, the man who would insist at every turn that he "really knew nothing about these matters," informed friends in Virginia that the old issue of "residence"—meaning the location of the capital—would come up in the next day's session of the Congress. And he added that the assumption of debt would come up in some form. Both these events did come up just as Jefferson said, so he was clearly and accurately linking the two, thinking in terms of compromise.

But he added, "I'm only a passenger on these voyages, and therefore I meddle not." Sure.

In letters to Virginia about a week later, Jefferson wrote bluntly that Congress was faced with "two of the most irritating questions that ever can be raised." And further, he wrote, no funding bill would be adopted "unless some plan of compromise could be agreed upon." He wrote, too, of "some mutual sacrifices."

> Whereupon The Secretary of State in him rose to the surface and put the nation above partisanship, fairly crying out again, "The greatest of all calamities would be the total extinction of our credit in Europe."

The man who repeatedly said he "knew little about these matters" and who so often struck Washington as putting his personal feuds above the welfare of the United States had made it clear in that one sentence that he would sacrifice anything to prevent this ultimate calamity.

Then, like a family doctor, Jefferson began to write his prescription to ward off such a deadly attack: "What is needed is something to displease and something to soothe every part of the Union but New York, which must be contented with what she has."

The medication will become a bit harsher and a lot more specific, but remembering this one sentence will make it easy and exciting to follow the progress toward Dr. Jefferson's cure.

The two pieces of legislation, assumption and residence—if they could only be balanced against each other—would be all that was necessary to set America on the course to greatness. But there are many occasions in medicine, in politics, in matters of war and peace, when a compromise is clearly needed, but where the elements that could give something to displease and something to soothe each party are maddeningly elusive. Only rarely does a good compromise emerge, because that "something to displease" is too distasteful for at least one of the contending parties to swallow. One party may be too small or weak to absorb anything that is at all displeasing. So it literally cannot afford to take part in an expedient compromise. It will choose a spirited last-ditch fight—and consciously elect to be gallantly defeated. Fortunately, Jefferson's prescription was not that harsh and—equally important—he would be up against a rare bargainer who could swallow a bitter pill with a smile if there was also something to smile about.

In the early spring of 1790, the competition for land that might become the seat of government grew really fierce. People sensed that decision time was coming, and the lure of quick profits was great. Citizens were bidding for land along a stretch of the Potomac sixty miles from the site that would eventually be chosen. Robert Morris, tumbling into serious financial trouble as his massive domestic and foreign investments lost their luster, kept hoping to be saved by having the capital surprisingly come to Philadelphia. Senator William Maclay, seeming to care more for money than for Pennsylvania (but probably jesting), pronounced himself ready to sell half his acreage in Harrisburg to buy in Maryland and Virginia.

George Washington, experienced in land bargaining, deepened the secrecy by touring the Potomac area, but saying nothing. He tried in every way to support and cheer the efforts that James Madison and Henry Lee were now making to bring the federal district to the Potomac.

The pensive Roger Sherman of Connecticut said grandly, "I think the growing west should be considered as a factor making the Potomac a central location. I wish the seat of government to be fixed there because I think the interest, the honor, and the greatness of the country require it. From thence, it appears to me, the rays of government will most naturally diverge to the extremities of the Union." The fine words sound as if the wily Sherman had already invested his own cash in the project, but he was also being a patriot—a man from New England who could point southward for a compromise capital city.

One resolution that clearly aimed in the Potomac's favor urged the selection of "a place as nearly central as a convenient water communication with the Atlantic Ocean and an easy access to the Western territory will permit."

It was relatively easy to put such prescriptions down on paper, but it was extremely hard to convert them into real place names, for as soon as that process was tried, the names offended more people than they pleased. The process began over and over again, raising short bursts of enthusiasm followed by long sighs.

9
Doubters and Believers

THE CHANGES PACKED INTO a ninety-day burst of time were almost breathtaking: the joy of having a meaningful currency, the money magic that was being practiced by a wizard in the Treasury, the search for new ways to invest, the narrowing choices for a new capital city. They seemed to represent years of activity, but in fact they were a series of successive flashes packed into the first few months of 1790. And bear in mind that 1790 had been less than three years after the great Constitutional Convention of 1787. It is little wonder that some very intelligent citizens were confused enough to talk about the country's possible breakdown and its exciting new money in the same breath.

The effect, even on ordinary people who only half understood the implications of each event, was almost electrical. Many more Americans felt themselves gripped by a new excitement about the nation's future. It was an epidemic of people taking an interest in things beyond their normal scope. A surprising number of citizens who could hardly envision the huge national debt were nonetheless trying to understand whether their state should take part in paying it off. Even more had opinions on where to place the national capital. Both of these questions had persisted for years and had always seemed like subjects to be put off until another day. Now there was impatience to get them decided.

Even before this, the difference between the America of 1787 and the America of 1789 had been like a revolution in itself. The thousands of people who had attended all the state-by-state meetings to consider and pass judgment on the new Constitution represented a great new number of citizens who felt far more involved in judging their leaders' words and ideas.

And when Americans saw that their new nation had actually replaced the limp old Articles of Confederation with a strong Constitution, a new note had sounded. The fact that a meeting in Philadelphia had suddenly ended that nagging weakness acted as a wake-up call. It proclaimed that questions could be answered after all. Riddles could be solved. Feeling the pressure of this, more politicians were becoming activists, taking up strong positions. Their remarks at meetings and festivities roused other interested citizens to take sides in the issues, especially about where the national capital should reside, an issue that was easier to comprehend than the complexities of debt.

Significantly, George Washington's cabinet did not entirely reflect this mood change, and its slack ways left the field open to Hamilton's dominance. The group's most frustrating member was the attorney general, Edmund Randolph. He had started as a remarkable young man because he made the courageous decision to stay in Virginia as a patriot when most of his family opted to give up their American status and sail to England. Anybody who could calmly wave good-bye to his folks and decide that he knew best would seem to be a most decisive person. But far from it, this man turned out to become famous for changing his mind.

Randolph had studied law, practiced as a lawyer, and also went into politics seriously enough to become governor of Virginia. James Madison had made use of Randolph as the person who would present his Virginia Plan to the Constitutional Convention, feeling that the prestige of a governor would be stronger than his own. Randolph had cooperated by first pretending to propose a mere adjustment of the existing Articles of Confederation, then converting to Madison's totally new form of government. But at the end of the Convention, Randolph had refused to sign the new Constitution because he felt that too many compromises had been made with slave states. Then, after this principled stand, he completely reversed position and took a hand in fighting for ratification of the new Constitution. This strange series of zigzags proved to be a sign of how he would continue to vacillate. It has been said that Randolph, both as a lawyer and as an official, usually reversed his stand whenever a difficult question had to be judged. "He was so analytical that he often weakened his own position," one biographer wrote.

As George Washington's attorney general, Randolph showed the same tendencies, so Washington's almost pathetic hope for guidance drew little support from this corner. The president had heard of the circulating talk about his relying too much on Hamilton, but he was at a loss to find a balancing source who was genuinely even-handed and still firm enough to make his position clear. Left adrift, Washington was increasingly angered by the thought that Jefferson and Madison, whom he had once admired, no longer made much positive contribution to his government; they now seemed dedicated to the negative path of simply opposing Hamilton.

Quite the reverse can be said of the secretary of war, Henry Knox, who had been known as a hero of the Revolutionary War, having won the admiration and friendship of George Washington for one incredible exploit. Now, as a retired general who was prominent in the Society of Cincinnati, the club of former officers who, like the Roman Cincinnatus, retired to peaceful pursuits after saving their country in battle, Knox roamed the nation a great deal, sending innumerable letters to the retired General Washington about his impressions. Reporting on his travel findings was his forte, not deliberations in the office. In 1786 and 1787, his warnings about the rebellions of northern farmers had suddenly turned very forceful. He was the first to alert the general to the seriousness of financial crises in many of the states. And this had marked the great change in Washington's attitude that had underpinned James Madison's drive to create a Constitution.

Henry Knox had gone to work in a Boston bookstore before age twelve because of his father's death. The overweight lad had fallen in love with books, studying without formal schooling, and became one of the rarest of birds—an uneducated intellectual. He had also fallen in love with young Lucy, who was built along the same generous lines, and they foiled her disapproving father by eloping. The two of them would grow to weigh nearly three hundred pounds each.

Henry opened his own bookshop, and also thought a lot about freedom from the oppressive British military rule that had been initiated after the Boston Tea Party. Four regiments had settled in Boston to enforce the rules against popular assemblies. Knox began plotting to undermine this incursion with a frequent customer named Paul Revere, and they often pretended to be arguing if a stranger came in. Another customer named John Adams, who had a special affinity for young people, showed his own superior judgment when he noticed Henry Knox and suggested to General Washington that the young man's book learning about artillery might make him useful.

The impressively large Knox had a strange first meeting with Washington. An officious officer kept telling him that he could not simply walk in and see the commanding general. He must start by telling all about himself to a lower officer. But John Adams had told him to "go and see General Washington," and he would not settle for an intermediary. Washington, who was just upstairs, heard the commotion and called down, "Send the young man up." It was a typically good decision by Washington. For Knox had an idea about rescuing and using fifty-nine cannons that he knew to be languishing at Fort Ticonderoga, some three hundred miles northwest of Boston. Washington knew they were there, but he had never heard a suggestion for their use, and he liked the sound of Knox's plan. He gave Knox a new title, then waited several months for the incredible project to develop. Knox devised the idea of hiring carpenters to make wooden sleds to hold the cannons, then procuring enough oxen to pull them over the winter snow and ice. The steep hills in the Berkshires were daunting. And there were times when one or more cannons fell through the ice of a frozen lake and had to be rescued, times when it seemed impossible to go on until a few passing Americans saw the struggle and volunteered to help move the project along. Even when angry people complained about what the ponderous cannons were doing to their lands, Knox usually managed to talk them into a better humor. And at last—cannons and all—he arrived at Dorchester Hill, near Washington's headquarters in Cambridge. On the night of March 2, 1776, General Washington bombarded the British position to divert attention, then assembled teams of men with barrels full of stones, which were chained together and rolled down a hill to create havoc among the redcoats, who were in formal ranks. The British general Howe saw the implacable cannons set to fire on his men. He made one vain attempt to attack, failed, then moved to evacuate. Soon Boston was free. The months of captivity were over. Washington never forgot that it was young Henry Knox (now Colonel Knox) who had made it possible, and he entrusted him with a series of difficult assignments. By the time the war ended, he was a general.

Henry and Lucy, generally referred to as "the biggest couple in America," gave great parties, with more courses and more varied specialties than any other table. Their unfailing good humor did even more to make people prize their invitations. Because of the laughter that always seemed to surround Henry, people were unsure of how seriously to take him. But Washington's respect for his judgment made them great friends and proved what a serious man the bulbous general really was.

Because Knox's friendship with George Washington was well known, the weight of his ideas had often been multiplied. But one of the things that drew them together was not known and had to remain secret, lest it cause a political uproar: a strong hatred of slavery. This may seem to be contradicted by Washington's aggressive attempts to recover two slaves who had escaped. But as a tough businessman, he was only responding to the loss of "his property." His hatred of the institution of slavery was in a separate compartment of his mind.

It would have created a disastrous collision with the southern states to learn that Knox and Washington had often stayed up together into the early morning hours, trying to think of financially practical ways of reducing and finally eliminating slavery. One of the ideas they considered was to start training young blacks as apprentices in various trades until they were twenty-one years old, at which point they would be freed to find paid employment. Obviously, for lack of money, this never went beyond the conceptual stage.

Washington was especially hampered in the matter because his own slaves were hopelessly entangled, making liberation virtually impossible. Some of them had been inherited by his wife, Martha, but they were "entailed," which meant they were already destined to be passed on to her relatives. She had no legal right to sell or to free them. To make it worse, the Washingtons were great believers in encouraging their slaves to marry and form settled families. This had caused some of George's slaves to marry some of Martha's entailed slaves, forming new families. Since the Washingtons also opposed any sales or other arrangements that would break up such families, which they considered tragic, it meant that even George's slaves were in a tangled state that could not be sorted out humanely.

In a sense, Knox had a role in starting the process that led to the Constitutional Convention, for in 1786 his words to Washington on what was going wrong with so many states had a powerful political effect. Washington had been trying to avoid facing the nation's wobbly condition for months. He knew of financial unrest, especially in several northern states. But he hesitated because he needed to restore his own lands, which he had neglected during the war years. And he had promised Martha that he would not be drawn into public affairs again. Only when he received Knox's vivid accounts of Shays's Rebellion—war veterans' attacks on courthouses that had been sending many of their number to debtor's prisons—had Washington been roused to agree with James Madison's plan to organize a meeting that would promote a stronger federal government. He gave Madison the signal he had been hoping for—to call all the states together for a meeting that would discuss ways to "strengthen" the spineless government. It turned out to be the 1787 Constitutional Convention.

Bear in mind that Madison, a young man without a job at the time and living on an allowance from his father, was working to create a new revolution. Washington later wrote his thanks to Madison "for allowing me to peep behind the curtain" and to understand what was really taking place. When Madison's Virginia Plan was made known, the fifty-five men who had convened in Philadelphia gradually realized that they were, in effect, asked to be revolutionaries. They had briefly pretended that the meeting would simply discuss changes in the existing Confederation. But it soon became clear that replacing it with a new government was the real goal. Although they were committed to making it a peaceful move, destroying an existing government and creating a new one was, indeed, a revolution.

Note how part of the president's greatness had been wonderfully built on the shoulders of men with special traits who had appeared at critical moments. These and many other examples that could be given may have seemed to be happy accidents, but, in fact, they reflected Washington's own skill at selecting assistants, building their loyalty, and making the most of their innate abilities. The staff problems he was having as president were so different from his earlier experience that they must have been seriously disorienting to him. For he had surely been aware that he had sometimes even earned respect and a certain amount of support from persons who had begun as opponents. How could his own chosen assistants have become less disciplined than political foes who found it impossible to ignore the excellence of his goals?

One unusual example of such a tamed opponent was William Maclay, a doughty legislator who has been mentioned before. He had only two years in the Pennsylvania Senate, yet his name frequently appears in history because of a written record he kept that tells with great frankness of numerous persons and events that would otherwise be forgotten.

During his period as a senator, from 1789 to 1791, Maclay made tart observations and remarks that help to illuminate some of the more famous political characters of his time. In a Pennsylvania group that was almost entirely Federalist, Maclay stood out as the only conservative, states' rights–oriented voice. This has led him to be called "the First Jeffersonian." So he obviously wrote favorably of Jefferson and rather dismissively of Hamilton. But although this made him a natural political foe of George Washington, he could never bring himself to write unfavorably of the president.

Maclay was just over fifty years old when he entered the Senate for only a two-year term (because the first senators drew terms of two, four, or six years in order to start the rotation that would later give all senators staggered six-year terms.) Every night, he faithfully and trenchantly recorded what he thought of the day's proceedings—and of the colleagues he had encountered. Few of them came away unscathed, for his natural style was aggressive and sarcastic.

But the closest he came to touching the godlike George Washington was when he scoffed at those who praised him endlessly. He wrote wearily, "No Virginian can talk on any subject, but the perfection of General Washington interweaves itself into every conversation."

At every turn, more even than Jefferson himself, Maclay skewered the monarchical pretensions of the Federalists. He was shocked by the royalist punctilio with which the Federalist majority wished to deck the new government. He winced at the affected elegance of a motion to thank Washington for his "most gracious" address. Why not call him "His elective Majesty," he asked sarcastically—using a term he claimed to have borrowed from Poland. But he would not for a moment accuse Washington of having encouraged this. On the contrary, he said, "It is already impossible to add to the respect entertained for him."

Like Jefferson, Maclay sounded a note of applause for the revolution that was raging in France, ending with an attack on the nearby royalists he felt himself surrounded by. "France seems travailing in the birth of freedom. Her throes and pangs of labor are violent. God give her a happy delivery! Royalty, nobility, and vile pageantry, by which a few of the human race lord it over and tread on the necks of their fellow mortals, seem like to be demolished with their kindred Bastille, which is said to be laid in ashes. Ye gods, with what indignation do I review the late attempt of some creatures among us to revive the vile machinery." (In other words, he—like Jefferson and Madison—considered many of his fellow lawmakers to be working toward a revival of monarchy.)

The period during which many persons were trying to think of titles that might be devised for President Washington gave Maclay a great deal of opportunity for making fun of his fellow politicians. And since Maclay had a very low opinion of John Adams, the vice president's unfortunate belief that titles with overtones of greatness would translate into more respect for the presidency was, almost by definition, a good joke. Because he wrongly thought the vice president a silly person, he said that seeing him preside over the Senate made him "think of a monkey just put into breeches." Adams failed to see that he was making himself look foolish by insistently proposing grandiloquent titles for George Washington. Maclay could denounce these flights without criticizing Washington personally. He even rose to address the Senate, which he was not often prone to do, on this richly rewarding subject. "Read the Constitution," he commanded his fellow senators, and then he quoted from the document: "No title of nobility shall be granted by the United States!"

The truth was that Washington, in trying very hard to find a level of formality that would suit the greatest number of people, got sucked into more royal behavior than he would have liked. His attendants seemed to feel that it was safer to err on the side of formality than to be too informal in their manner, and the grand behavior gradually escalated. Washington even spoke of this quite frankly to Jefferson in one rare talk they had when the question of monarchical behavior was discussed.

But while most of Maclay's remarks about fellow senators show that he was no respecter of persons, his words about Washington can barely conceal an inner struggle to hide his respect. As a dedicated Republican and a states'-rights Jeffersonian, he was theoretically opposed to Washington. But his written words show that he wanted to feel free to write about the president without saying a word against him.

Maclay was completely honest, and noticeably a bit agonized, in reporting very kind personal treatment from the president. "At eleven in the morning," he writes a bit pompously at one point, "the Senate waits on President Washington at his home in Cherry Street." On another occasion, when he went there to dinner, he says: "It was a great dinner—all in the taste of high life. I considered it my duty as a senator to submit to it, but am glad it is over. The President is a cold formal man; but I must declare that he treated me with great attention. I was the first person with whom he drank a glass of wine. I was often spoken to by him. Yet he knows how rigid a republican I am." (One wonders whether the president was hoping to please Jefferson by singling out his fellow Republican.)

It was a real loss when, at the end of his two-year term, Maclay seemed quite content to find that no one had any inclination to extend his stay in the Senate. He gladly withdrew, because he had never been much impressed with himself for being a member. There would be no more of the humorous sallies, as when Maclay looked sharply at individual colleagues around him in the Senate, questioning whether a Connecticut senator had "a particle of integrity," but concluding that "perhaps such a quality is useless in Connecticut."

Nor like the time when, looking at the New York legislators sitting around him, he observed, "These Yorkers are the vilest of people. . . . They resemble bad schoolboys who are unfortunate at play. They revenge themselves by telling enormous thumpers."

More seriously, one of his first combative comments had been a well-deserved slap at the much-admired *Federalist Papers*. He said, justifiably, that their authors had been instrumental in procuring the adoption of the Constitution by talking of "enumerated powers" and "limited government" in order to win ratification, but then finding "all manner of implied powers" and loose verbiage once they had their victory.

Some of the acts of the Congress itself drew a scornful assessment. He considered the Judiciary Act to be "inquisitorial" in requiring a defendant, under oath, to disclose his or her knowledge of events. "The conscience was to be put on the rack," Maclay said, by exercising a torturous tyranny from which the mind could not escape. He thought it left no way out between telling excusable lies and willful perjury, with the two combined being clearly a form of torture.

Brief as his federal career was, he is remembered partly because he recorded so lively a picture of his two years as a legislator, but also because his opinionated comments so often contained thoughts that deserved to be heard.

Believing, as he insisted, in republican simplicity and staying out of unnecessary trouble, Maclay considered it "a mad act when a Secretary of War was appointed in time of peace. For a War Secretary would necessarily want an army and would soon find employment for one."

Maclay was wrong on this point, as Henry Knox was no warmonger.

Noting that it cost some $40,000 to send an ambassador overseas, Maclay said, "I consider the money as worse than thrown away, for I know not a single thing that we have for a minister to do at a single court in Europe." He was strictly a noninterventionist. "The less we have to do with them the better," he insisted. "Our business is to pay them what we owe, and the less political connection with any European the better."

When Maclay commented on the states, he had little but scorn for most of them. But strangely, he defended the unlikeliest one. That was Rhode Island, the very state that was being attacked by the whole nation for its refusal to collect taxes and pay the funds into the hands of a federal government. In fact, Maclay had a good point in saying that Rhode Island, as an independent state, had an absolute right to spurn this "obligation" that it had never agreed to, and that it was being coerced and vilified for acting like the independent entity that it was.

Although he saw great dangers and flaws in Hamilton's funding plan, he also told the diminutive James Madison that he found a serious defect in his alternative plan. And then Maclay added, "This hurt His Littleness."

This unique gadfly was watching every slightest movement in the recurrent question of what capital city to choose and how the old war debt was to be paid. He highlighted the fact that Hamilton was "running from place to place among the members" in his intense program of lobbying for his proposals.

In rare instances, Maclay's daily reports were simply informative without being contentious. While the South, in its opposition to assumption, was vituperative and full of threats to break up the union, Maclay simply reported the plain fact that the disagreement hanging over them prevented Congress from doing anything at all. "Congress met and adjourned from day to day without doing anything," he wrote, "the parties being too much out of temper to do business together." It was one of the rare moments when Maclay felt no sense of direction.

Breaking out of that petrified condition, he finally was the first to say: "The New Yorkers are now busy in the scheme of bargaining with the Virginians, offering the permanent seat on the Potomac for the temporary one in New York."

Maclay has been noticed and cheered mainly because his reports on so many subjects from an insider's point of view have been most useful to historians. But more than just a source of information, he was also a witness to the amazing openness that America was bringing into the world. Some of the remarks he made against the ruling powers, even poking mild fun at those who venerated George Washington, came to be known in his lifetime. Even if his writings were personal, he made his feelings known to any number of persons. Yet there was never any suggestion that he should suffer any punishment or even the slightest reprimand. It was a gentle denial of the charge that Americans had abandoned the true political freedom to speak out on any subject. And one did not have to be royalist to acknowledge that this freedom had been born in England.

IO

Nearing a Decision
on the Capital

THE EXCITEMENT OF THOSE EARLY MONTHS in 1790 reached its peak in the last-minute attempts to guess the location of the capital city that clearly was about to be chosen. Far from being just a senti- mental issue that made people feel warmly about one location and coolly toward another, the debate over the capital location had become a desperate matter to many. It was a major financial issue that could rescue some from ruin or make others rich for life.

Robert Morris, the Pennsylvanian who had done so much to finance General Washington in the Revolutionary War, was one of the most concerned. As we have noted earlier, his finances had fallen into dire straits, and his hope of seeing his struggling invest- ments rescued by the selection of Philadelphia as the nation's capital showed how desperation had overcome his judgment, for it was the flimsiest of hopes. Many legislators had long been opposed to nam- ing any capital that was part of a state because they recalled how the whims of a single governor or his militia could hold a national con- gress hostage. And the competition among several major northern cities made it nearly impossible for any one of them to be singled out as a permanent capital.

The Pennsylvania senator William Maclay, whose humorous remark about buying land in Maryland and Virginia we saw earlier, happened to be right on target, as he so often was. For bits of land from both Maryland and Virginia would, indeed, be used to create a capital city. Yet when the competition was at its height, people were bidding for land in highly improbable places, often buying unlikely tracts of land for minor sums because they were long-shot investments, merely finger-snappers if they failed, but potentially worth a fortune.

Also at work during this time was a reminder of how keenly the large and small states felt themselves to be competitors. The issue had nearly broken up the Constitutional Convention in its opening weeks. New Jersey had spoken for several other small states when it announced that there would be no deal if the large states thought they could simply dominate Congress by claiming that their greater population entitled them to far more seats and voting power. Although the compromise that gave all states equal numbers in the Senate had solved that problem, the ongoing complaints of small states continued to be a lively part of American life.

The largest states managed to set up arrangements for receiving their imported goods faster and more efficiently; then they made life even harder for their smaller neighbors by making them pay heavily for rights to transship their own imports through the other states' territory. Worse yet, the problems this imposed on the small states often killed some of their foreign business altogether. So when the hyperactive Hamilton learned that New Jersey's governor, William Livingston, might be supporting Philadelphia as temporary capital, he tried a new twist. Forget Philadelphia, he urged Livingston, and support New York City as the temporary capital. In return, he would endorse Trenton, New Jersey, as the permanent capital.

This bold idea was never thoroughly considered. But it had a slim chance, and Trenton continued to warrant consideration until the very end because many politicians remembered it kindly as the place where they had taken refuge after fleeing from the drunken Pennsylvania militia. The extra bit of attraction in the idea was that it would keep any part of Pennsylvania from becoming capital. As one of the largest and most aggressive trading states, Pennsylvania was also the most feared as a possible capital, whether temporary or permanent. Once it became any kind of capital, many people thought, it would probably find ways to make the arrangement permanent. And that, combined with the state's industries, might make Pennsylvania into a global trading giant that no other state could compete with.

Having the capital in one's own state had one very practical advantage that appealed even to those who were not looking for great wealth or influence. It was the simple fact that you could go and talk with the officials more easily if the capital was nearby. If you had questions to ask about a personal or business problem that required government help, you might actually be able to make contact with an official person who knew the answer or who might refer you to the right colleague. Or if you had been promised information or a payment from the federal government, the advantage of being able to visit and even to pester the proper office was obvious. If the capital was hundreds of miles away, you might very well be forced to drop the subject.

And apart from the immediacy of this angle, there was the tendency to have good or bad feelings about certain cities, based on impulses that could not easily be suppressed, even if they were unfair. New York, for instance, had already acquired the reputation for "fast" living, so that a citizen of Virginia or North Carolina would doubt his own ability to negotiate successfully with a fast-talking New York–based federal official. Such a thought would never have occurred to him if the official were located in, say, Maryland. Rather wispy points like this one had impact because they caused many people to think uneasily, "Why does everything have to happen in New York or Philadelphia? Why can't our officials make some of these things happen near where I live?"

And there was a deeper psychological aspect to the decision, apart from trade matters and personal comfort. Southerners believed a capital in their part of the country would signal that agrarian life was the nation's first priority, just as Jefferson said it should be; and it would sound a call for expansion to the West, which southerners found much more natural and attractive than the northeasterners did. By the same token, a northern capital would imply that the moneyed interests were in command. They tended to look down on the South and to be disinterested in westward expansion. So the idea of choosing a northern city was so totally unacceptable to many in the South that they were ready to fight or to make a clean break rather than accept it. It seems almost mindless that sensible people would think of dividing a nation simply for the relatively few annoy-ances or conveniences that have been cited, but bear in mind that this was not a long-standing nation. All the adult people of that time had been born when there was no nation—only their own state. And that was still number one in the minds of all but a handful.

One of Hamilton's great advantages was in being free of these emotional hang-ups on the subject. He would have preferred to win at least the temporary capital for New York City, because it would please his New York political backers, but several other cities had seemed almost equally acceptable to him at various times. It was his own power that seemed to count most, outweighing these soulful questions that preoccupied others. So he had more potential choices than anyone else in the game. He was like a poker player who has several different winning combinations in his hand.

There was a great difference in the behavior of Hamilton and Jefferson during these tremulous days. Hamilton seemed to be every-where at once; Jefferson apparently was quiet in his office, giving no sign of his planning on the issue that was undoubtedly dominating his thoughts.

While every day was scarred by fear about a possible European demand for early repayment, Jefferson would also have been troubled by thoughts of the many people who would have to be persuaded in order to effect the compromise that was building in his mind. And none of that would bring the desired result unless it led to the choice of a capital city on which, Jefferson could exult, he and Washington were blessedly in agreement.

This momentous decision would be up to Congress, but no one person would carry as much weight as George Washington, not sim-ply because he was a much-respected president, but largely because he was experienced in land bargaining. He had bought many acres for himself when he was a young surveyor, and he knew many of the feints and shifts that were used to depress prices before making a purchase offer or to prevent speculators from bidding prices to unreasonable levels.

In this case, Washington prodded the interest by touring up the Potomac, but deepened the secrecy by saying nothing at all. He watched intently as James Madison and Henry Lee cooperated in moves to bring the Federal District to the Potomac, and they knew that his sympathies were entirely with them. As president, he said not a word publicly on the subject. But when Madison told him that he and Lee had bought shares in a large purchase of acreage at the scenic spot known as Great Falls, Virginia, he got a rousing response from Washington. Among other things, the president thought factories of all sorts would soon want to settle at the site—probably because the waterfalls would provide energy.

Madison acted like an aggressive businessman at this point. He quickly prepared a prospectus featuring Washington's glowing words, which he mailed to European capitalists. By also pointing out the Potomac area's contacts with the fertile Ohio region and the lakes beyond, Madison produced a sales document that had a powerful impact. It was noteworthy that people of great wealth, who were looked at askance when Hamilton favored them, looked much more appealing to Madison when he had something to sell.

In person, however, Madison began to be what one observer called "coquettish" on the subject of Great Falls. As the value of his own property rose, he became so confident of its future that he apparently wanted to limit it to a steady climb, rather than risk an unsustainable surge, for he avoided mentioning the good omens that appeared and concentrated on recounting unfavorable signs. He actually went out of his way to publicize Morris's threat to block the Potomac area's chances of winning the capital. And this uncertain behavior made Washington distrust Madison's motives even more. Step by step, the president's former great trust in Madison declined, just as his regard for Jefferson eroded. And every one of these steps moved Hamilton higher in Washington's esteem.

More and more indicants—a congressional resolution, and remarks by respected political figures—pointed toward the Potomac area as the favorite. Roger Sherman's emphasis on access to the growing West as a factor in favor of the Potomac found more adherents, as Sherman's arguments usually did. He was the Connecticut delegate who had saved the Constitutional Convention from collapse by working out a masterful compromise during a crucial weekend. No one was surprised, because his skill at bringing disputants together had first been noticed in 1776, when he also became inaccurately known as "the only shoemaker who signed the Declaration of Independence." The term was based on summertime work he had done in his teenage years, and his relatives laughed it off by saying, "Roger never made a whole pair of shoes in his life." True, but he made a great deal of money from his profitable writing and many business ventures. His formula for success was a simple one: once he had established a reputation for good judgment, all he had to do was keep being right most of the time.

Strangely, all these encomiums for the Potomac did not at all make the wiser observers believe the issue was about to be settled. The Potomac area could not win unless it had broad enough support to make the Massachusetts, New York, and Pennsylvania forces at least grudgingly agree. Any attempt to name a capital that could not command the adherence of all three of those would be doomed.

So fearsome did this hurdle appear that the big issue among all the decision-makers on both sides was whether to take the risk of presenting the Potomac plan to Congress again. If the vote was lost—however narrowly—the momentum for the Potomac might never be regained. And if agreement on a capital city could not be reached, that old danger of deciding to split the nation into two or three parts could well surface again. So days of waiting passed, and *breathlessly* is not too strong a word to describe how they passed.

It is surprising to find how much value many of the negotiators saw in winning a promise of becoming a temporary capital for this or that location. At one point in early June 1790, Hamilton made a date to meet Robert Morris on a morning walk for a discussion of a possible deal of just that kind—to make Philadelphia the temporary capital before allowing the Potomac location to become the permanent capital. That failed because a deal along that line, set up by others, was already pending. Virginia and Pennsylvania groups had tentatively arranged for Philadelphia to be the temporary capital before passing the permanent status on to the Potomac. But that arrangement was not yet commanding enough other support to win.

At another point, Hamilton made a proposal to Morris that combined the national capital problem with the issue of assumption in a new and ingenious way. Namely, if Morris could produce enough new Senate and House votes to pass the Assumption Bill, Hamilton would work to place the permanent capital in either Trenton or Germantown. These were so close to Philadelphia that either one would give the great city most of the advantages it could hope for. Apparently Morris doubted that he could provide the necessary votes, for nothing came of the idea.

Any number of temporary capital schemes were tried, presumably because businessmen believed they could develop large and lasting advantages if much of the nation turned to their city as its capital during a period of just five to ten years. Other than Philadelphia, two other cities that, for a time, appeared to have a real chance as temporaries were Trenton and Baltimore. But in all such cases, the local excitement was not matched by sufficiently widespread acceptance.

How great an issue it was to win even the status of temporary capital helps to envision how important the final decision naming a permanent capital city could be. In simply giving up the role of temporary capital for New York, Hamilton drew the angry fire of many New Yorkers, led by Rufus King, a prominent New York senator. And any number of Pennsylvania politicians were nearly desperate in discussions that finally won the ten-year period as a temporary capital for Philadelphia. It was as though a certain number of millions of dollars per year in business opportunities could be foreseen for even a temporary capital status. And the fact that results of each year as a capital could be measured in such a confident way says a great deal about the swift pace of business growth in America as the eighteenth century was closing.

But this time the usually canny Senator Maclay was off the mark in his assessment of Hamilton's priorities. He felt sure that Hamilton would not allow New York to lose the capital. "I have attended in the minutest manner to the motions of Hamilton and the Yorkers," he wrote boldly. "Sincerity is not with them. They will never consent to part with Congress." Of course they did, for Hamilton had bigger fish to fry than Senator Maclay had envisioned.

The United States had an especially compelling reason for wanting to establish itself as securely as possible in that particular period. The outside world seemed to be going mad, and distant as Europe was, it was frightening to hear that centuries-old arrangments were being pulled apart, centuries-old kingdoms were crumbling. Was there a danger that such an infection would spread, even across a great ocean? It was good to have the sea there, but the uncertainty now seemed even deeper than the Atlantic Ocean.

At such a time, the importance of avoiding war with any European power was paramount. War too often causes combatants to copy each other's worst excesses. So when John Adams later succeeded Washington as president, his steadfast behavior throughout in balancing relations with France and England would not only vindicate his insistence on diplomacy, rather than saber-rattling; it almost entirely wiped his image clean of his former erratic actions and insistence on grand titles. All that had become trifling.

Meanwhile, the secretary of state and the floor leader of Congress—Jefferson and Madison—showed signs of a new confidence on the subject of a capital city. Nothing that others were attempting seemed to account for this positive turn. But whenever these two men teamed up, they invariably made things happen. And in this case, it developed that they were actually starting to plan the Federal District on the Potomac, based on their considerable knowledge of what the president would want to see—the method of buying up property in the area, the city's size, the style of its architecture, the approximate dates when construction should reach certain points.

Was this somehow related to Jefferson's new plan to approve Hamilton's Assumption Bill, which might promptly determine the capital?

Nothing that was said or written has provided a clue. But it is logical to suppose that the compromise in Jefferson's mind made him increasingly confident that the capital would be on the Potomac River. Beyond that, he knew that a firm decision on a permanent capital would in itself be received as a welcome sign of solidity by those nervous European bankers.

Jefferson and Madison reviewed innumerable thoughts about the kind of capital city they knew Washington wanted. It was as if they were hearing it from his own lips, even though the president had not specifically called for any such action on their part. Surprisingly, they also added many ideas that others—even some of the disliked

Federalists—had uttered in the long hours of conversations. These had a balancing effect, as if a large meeting were being held to discuss an action plan. In the end, they retained chiefly the thoughts that they knew Washington would have favored, more for their true merit than because of their source. In this sense, it might be said that the Federal District was a truly democratic creation of that era when the future United States was being shaped, because the two men who put this together were—for the most part—thinking broad-mindedly. It is heartening to find that even though they clearly had personal interests, they were trying hard to capture the combined wishes of others as well as their own preferences on this one contentious subject.

The sense of fairness that seemed so lacking in the approach to other subjects recalled words that Jefferson, as America's secretary of state, had written earlier in 1790: "It rests now with ourselves to enjoy in peace and concord the blessings of self-government so long denied to mankind, to shew by example the sufficiency of human reason for the care of human affairs, and that the will of the majority . . . is the only sure guardian of the rights of man." The man who had said this, and the ideal he had embodied, had seemed hidden for a time by a wave of adversity. But now Jefferson's voice and his judgment could be recognized again.

For a moment, this spirit made all things seem possible. The wonder of majority rule was recalled, more highly prized than ever. The stability of a great Constitution was heartening; the power of a steady judiciary that could override government was deeply reassuring. And the belatedly added Bill of Rights seemed like a personal guarantee bestowed on each individual citizen. How exciting it would be if they found themselves with a real capital city—a permanent capital at last.

II

That Day on the Street

PICTURE THE MENTAL TURMOIL that Jefferson had endured since his arrival in New York on March 21. He had quickly suspected that his agreement to become secretary of state might have been a mistake, and this thought kept gathering force by the day. He found that Washington's politics were opposite to his own, and that the president was almost taking orders from a young man of unquestionable brilliance, but very questionable respect for democracy. Jefferson had learned that his close confidant, James Madison, had turned against this powerful Hamilton, and had already led a vote against the man's dazzling financial plan on which America's future was said to depend. And while trying to pull himself through an almost crippling depression, Jefferson had been struck by the realization that the United States was in imminent danger of losing the foreign sources of credit that were essential to its survival.

Now he was realist enough to see that there was no way of averting this menace that he would previously have considered even remotely acceptable. If he was to demonstrate American unity to the moneylenders, it must be by promptly giving Hamilton the victory that might propel him toward limitless political power and perhaps even monarchy. At best, Jefferson hoped to do this as part of a compromise that would place the country's permanent capital in his and the president's preferred Potomac location. Madison had agreed to cooperate in the arrangement, and now Jefferson was

only waiting for a propitious moment to engage Hamilton in conversation, hopefully without seeming to show any sign of eagerness
to negotiate.

In order to make it a compromise, with Hamilton also giving in
on some major point, Jefferson could not be seen as the pursuer. He
hoped for an opportunity whereby Hamilton could initiate the subject, and it must have seemed eons to him as he waited for the right
moment.

At last, on June 19, 1790, the moment Jefferson had been waiting for arrived. Since it later became clear that Jefferson and Hamilton both wanted this to happen, the meeting may have been
arranged by either of them—or in a sense by both of them, because
making frequent outings to pass in front of the president's house
would have invited such a meeting. But when Jefferson later wrote
his lively account of the encounter, he pretended that it was entirely
accidental.

This meeting and its very successful result have often been questioned or even disbelieved, which is odd, because, as we have seen,
Jefferson sometimes shaded the truth for effect, but he did not invent
truthless facts. What he wrote, entirely in his own handwriting in
1792, was longer than what is reproduced below. But the key sentences are all included herewith.

> Going to the President's one day I met Hamilton as I approached
> the door. His look was sombre, haggard, and dejected beyond
> description. Even his dress uncouth and neglected. He asked to
> speak with me. We stood in the street near the door. He opened
> the subject of the assumption of the state debts, the necessity of it
> in the general fiscal arrangement and its indispensable necessity
> towards a preservation of the Union: and particularly of the New
> England states, who had made great expenditures during the war
> . . . which were for the common cause . . . that they considered the
> assumption of these by the Union so just . . . that they would make
> it a *sine qua non* of the continuance of the Union. . . . That if he
> had not credit enough to carry such a measure as that, he could be
> of no use, and was determined to resign.
>
> He observed at the same time, that though our particular busi-
> ness laid in separate departments, yet the administration and its
> success was a common concern, and that we should make common

cause in supporting one another. He added his wish that I would interest my friends from the South, who were those most opposed to it. I answered that I had been so long absent from my country that I had lost a familiarity with its affairs. . . .

I had not yet undertaken to consider and understand it, that the assumption had struck me in an unfavorable light . . . but that I would revolve what he had urged in my mind. It was a real fact that the Eastern and Southern members (S. Carolina however was with the former) had got into the most extreme ill humor with one another. . . . On considering the situation of things, I thought the first step towards some conciliation of views would be to bring Mr. Madison and Col. Hamilton to a friendly discussion of the subject. I immediately wrote to each to come and dine with me the next day, mentioned that we should be alone . . . and that I was persuaded that men of sound heads and honest views needed nothing more than mutual understanding to enable them to unite in some measures which might enable us to get along.

Based on what is known of Jefferson's tendency to dramatize or exaggerate in order to give his words more force, we are justified in imagining that Hamilton was probably not quite as shabby or distressed as the account insists. The Pennsylvania senator William Maclay, who called Hamilton "a damnable villain" for having packed the gallery at Federal Hall with his supporters, wrote about the gloom of Hamilton's followers, saying, "I never observed so drooping an aspect, so turbid and forlorn an appearance as overspread the partisans of the Secretary in our House this afternoon," for the house was about to vote down the assumption plan. That Hamilton's look was somber is very likely in view of his reverses. It has been confirmed by others that he was looking noticeably upset during this whole period when his assumption plan was hanging fire. But that "his dress was uncouth and neglected" must be questioned. Hamilton was habitually a very neat dresser, and no one else has reported seeing him looking poorly dressed or disarranged. So we can assume that Hamilton's look of dejection was real, while his dress may have seemed "neglected" only because he was slumping in a way that allowed his clothing to seem shapeless. The recent attempts to get Congress to pass his bill had fallen several votes short, and he had been known to talk of making compromises of a different kind from what Jefferson had in mind—namely, introducing new and reduced figures, changing the arithmetic enough to induce a few more legislators to switch to the positive side. But such refiguring would have been a partial defeat, and it is not hard to believe that Hamilton was very distressed.

Reduced to basics, then, and to more modern language, the unquestionable facts were these: Jefferson, walking to pay a visit to President Washington, happened to meet Alexander Hamilton almost exactly in front of the president's house on June 19, 1790. According to Jefferson, Hamilton looked like a man in despair. His expression was extremely troubled. He simply did not seem himself. He quickly brought up the subject of assumption, painting pathetically the temper into which the legislature had been thrown, the disgust of those who were called the "creditor states," the danger of the secession of their members, and the separation of states.

With his whole great future appearing to be at stake, it is reasonable to imagine that Hamilton was not looking or acting quite himself on that morning. But it is also possible that he was playacting because this meeting with Jefferson seemed a rare opportunity to make the strongest possible argument to a man who clearly had the ear of that other key figure, James Madison. So a bit of extra drama in Hamilton's remarks can be considered quite likely.

It is totally believable that Jefferson, as he says, mainly just listened, telling Hamilton that he really was not very well informed on the subject, having so recently come from France. This is pure Thomas Jefferson. He was very well informed, and he denied it. We would know it to be so even if he had not written it. And of course it was true that he sounded in full agreement when Hamilton said the two of them should really work together to find a solution. This was not only common courtesy; it was also the course Jefferson had decided on as the only way to avoid the catastrophe of losing the confidence of Europe's bankers.

Jefferson's clear statement that he then invited only Hamilton and Madison to come and dine with him on the following day makes it very odd that so many historians have insisted on suggesting that there might have been several other legislators present at the dinner.

They may have thought it natural to have on hand the men who had to be persuaded to change their votes. Or perhaps the idea of greater attendance has seemed to aggrandize the event, yet it is totally wrong.

It is important to know that Jefferson added (without writing whether he actually said this to Hamilton or only thought it) that swallowing the pill of assumption would require that "some con-comitant measures be adopted to sweeten it a little." The "con-comitant measure," of course, would have to do with the capital city. And it is apparent that Hamilton raised no objection to the unspoken idea.

Another minor discrepancy is that Jefferson's written account makes no mention of a verbal dinner invitation to Hamilton, while most observers have somehow had the impression that Jefferson did make such an immediate gesture there on the street, followed up by the written notes that he mentions. But the basic fact that Jefferson quickly invited both men to come on the following day is clear, and there is no reason to question Jefferson's account. Those who have insisted on doing so have given too little weight to "the greatest of all Calamities" that had dominated Jefferson's thoughts.

No letters from him to Hamilton and Madison during that week have been found, but as they would have been little more than short notes, confirming the verbal invitation, they may not have seemed worth recording.

But do notice this significant fact: clearly, both Jefferson and Hamilton (and probably Madison) had been hoping for such an event to take place. The chance of an occasion like this was the reason that Jefferson had spent so freely in his attempt to have the Maiden Lane house ready to receive company, because he had an exceptional faith in his ability to make things go his way when his carefully planned dinners morphed into carefully planned after-dinner discussions. But as often as such dinners had occurred, there had never been one so ardently desired and so fully anticipated by all parties. So Jefferson's chance meeting with Hamilton seemed almost like a contrived event, perfectly suited to the circumstances, and the rest would appear to be a fair account of the action of the following afternoon and evening.

It is worth noting how sensibly and commendably both men talked during that session on the street. Here was Hamilton, desperate because his tremendous effort was apparently headed for failure. He must have felt like grasping Jefferson's lapels and shouting, "How can you fail to see how much is at stake? Do you really not care if America's credit in the world collapses?" But he limited himself to the friendly reminder that "the administration and its success was a common concern, and that we should make common cause in supporting one another." How could a more reasonable approach be imagined?

And Jefferson's equally measured words: "Considering the situation of things, I thought the first step towards conciliation of views . . . friendly discussion of the subject."

Admittedly, these soothing phrases are only symbols of good manners. We know that each man represented numberless others who would rather fight than contribute to another state's war debts or accept the other state's capital city. But those others were wrong in their intransigence. The honeyed words that Hamilton and Jefferson used to hide their positions are closer to the civilized approach that was needed. Whatever they might say later, or what they felt impelled to say for the delectation of their followers, they were already moving toward compromise when they faced the need to make common cause in dealing with each other.

One thing more: to say that the meeting on the street may not have been truly an accident is an understatement. Jefferson and Hamilton both were very anxious for the chance to meet, and both were feeling the pressure of time, so it seems most unlikely that they would both have merely waited for an accidental encounter. It does not seem typical of Jefferson that he arranged to be at a place where he expected to find Hamilton, but "ultimate calamities" call for unusual measures, so we cannot rule it out. Hamilton, on the other hand, was given to inventive moves, and he had often arranged to have a crucial meeting at an unusual time or place with someone who could be useful to him. It seems quite likely that, as anxious as he was, and with time for a new congressional vote growing short, he reasoned that he had a good chance of meeting the secretary of state in the area of the president's house around that time of day. He may have been there several times in preceding days, walking past, hoping for a meeting, finding nothing, and trying again the next day. There is absolutely nothing to prove or even to hint at this. But the odds would seem to favor it.

In any case, the die was cast. Both these men must have felt an excitement, a quickening in their chests, at knowing that a major moment in the game was only hours away. Whatever happened the next day, it would be decisive.

12

Dinner at Secretary Jefferson's

JEFFERSON'S DECISION TO LIMIT the number at dinner to just three people shows that he gave great weight to the importance of this night. Much as he had come to dislike Hamilton's rise, he was—perhaps more than he has been given credit for—an American determined to safeguard his country. Arranging for Madison and Hamilton to reach a compromise that would reassure European lenders was all that Jefferson was aiming for on this occasion. He had a remarkable ability to focus on a single objective, and preventing the European lenders from turning against these unpredictable Americans had taken first place in his mind, for the thought kept recurring that credit, once damaged, would never be the same again. His onrushing sense of responsibility, as secretary of state, came to the fore. Not even the excitable and ambitious Hamilton was any more determined to save America's reputation than this host was.

Jefferson left Hamilton with no doubt about how many would attend the dinner. He later wrote that his letter of invitation "mentioned that we should be alone," for this was a sign of seriousness. As he reflected on the arrangement, Jefferson must have realized that just the three of them had a smoother road to reaching agreement. Any other legislators would certainly realize that they were about to be pressed into service as sacrificial lambs who would be asked to vote against their own inclination—and perhaps to be reviled by their own states—all for the sake of helping the three great men to make their deal. The task of making those others agree on the spot would only muddy the waters. Besides, the presence of other congressmen (which modern writers have suggested) would have meant that those other men would have to be approached and persuaded on the spot. Much better that this should come later. Madison and Hamilton, if they agreed at all, could decide between them how they would divide the secondary tasks of making others fall into line.

Finally, the small number of guests was exactly in keeping with the words of Margaret Bayard Smith, the wife of the editor of the Washington *National Intelligencer*. She often helped with Jefferson's social planning, and she left memoirs of her many contacts with him that were published after her death. One of her firmest recollections was, "When he dined with persons with whom he wished to enjoy a free and unrestricted flow of conversation, the number of persons at table never exceeded four—each with a dumbwaiter beside him containing all the utensils and most of the foods needed for the entire dinner. Not only did the intervention of servants disturb the conversation, Jefferson felt, but much of the public discord that often followed was produced by the mutilated and misconstructed repetition of remarks that were heard by servants or by unnecessary guests." Notice that the apparently easygoing Jefferson, who never appeared to be focusing hard on business, actually had a specific objective in mind on most such occasions. And every part of the planning had a specific reason.

So at four o'clock on the day after his hectic talk with Hamilton, Thomas Jefferson stood in his newly appointed drawing room and waited for just two guests. He was still suffering from a tension headache that had threatened to force him into bed earlier in the day. But now it had eased enough to make the planned dinner seem possible, and even somewhat enjoyable. As he waited, he was able to read from one of several books that he always kept in the room for this purpose, for he had a great ability to use every free moment to acquire more knowledge. He was even a great consumer of novels, believing that reading fiction induced "a strong desire in ourselves of doing charitable acts."

He knew that he would not need to direct the flow of talk during dinner, because Alexander Hamilton would initiate much of the conversation. And it would be pleasurable to note the cleverness of James Madison in riposting most of Hamilton's flashing sallies as lightly as a fencing master who parried an enemy's blade with the smallest of moves.

Although Jefferson alone wrote a few lines to describe the dinner—and those lines may be somewhat imprecise—it is possible to reconstruct the likely flow of the event. One thing Hamilton probably wondered about was whether he was going to witness an entirely French meal, since Patrick Henry, a rival of Jefferson's in so many ways, had charged that Jefferson "has abjured his native victuals in favor of French cuisine." This was supposed to be almost an accusation of treason. But there was little chance of its being borne out on this occasion, for although Jefferson had admired meals prepared by Frenchmen at the Governor's Palace even during his student days in Williamsburg, and he loved the more advanced touches of French cookery that he and James Hemings had learned in Paris, the idea that he totally deserted American foods was a great myth. He never ceased praising the vegetables and fruits available in the New World, and they often won top honors when he compared them with similar items found in France.

"They have no apple here to compare with our Newtown Pippin," was just one example of his praise for American produce. He had asked James Madison to send fifty to a hundred grafts of these beauties to see whether they might become established in France. And in addition to growing Indian corn for his own table while he was abroad, he asked that seeds for canteloupe, watermelon, and sweet potatoes be sent to him. Virginia ham was another item that he found to be unmatched in Europe, and this, too, had to be shipped to him. So this evening's invited guests were more likely to dine as if they were at Monticello than as if they were in Paris.

The two guests happened to arrive at the same time—Madison because he was always a little early, and Hamilton because he was obviously most anxious for this meeting. The latter looked around him for a moment, as if expecting to see what other guests were on hand. And he fell a bit quieter than usual as he realized that there really were to be no other guests, meaning that a session of heavy bargaining might be ahead. He knew exactly how much he was prepared to back down in order to reach a compromise, but he was not sure how severe a price the others planned to make him pay. He would have enjoyed his dinner more if he had realized that they were very nearly as anxious as he was to reach an agreement.

Because Jefferson often liked pouring the wine, he poured for his two guests before taking just half a glass for himself. This white wine was, he explained, Hermitage, a wine made in the hills near the village of Tains and one of the esteemed whites. This, he said, "was made from the first light pressing, for subsequent harder pressings become darker and eventually red. I feel sure you will find this a pleasant way to begin." He described it with an expert's terminology as a wine that was usually drier than this, but these present bottles happened to be full-bodied and rather silky, which the French chose to describe as *doux et liquoreux*. We can assume that his guests looked interested at this modestly impressive explanation, Hamilton because he really wanted to master every subject that came his way, and Madison because he was polite, but quite ready to dismiss it with a nod and a kind word.

Hamilton, always hyperattentive on every subject, doubtless noted that Jefferson poured only a half-glass for himself. He looked pensive, as if wondering whether the host was intentionally trying to have a clearer head than his guests. This would be worth watching as the dinner progressed toward the discussion stage, when a clearer head might be decisive. (In fact, the half-glass was typical of Jefferson when his headache was troubling him. Otherwise, as he once wrote to a friend, "My measure is a perfectly sober 3 or 4 glasses at dinner, and not a drop at any other time. But of those 3 or 4 glasses I am very fond.") It should be noted that those were smaller than the wineglasses of today, more like what are now used as sherry or port glasses.

It is unlikely that anything related to the night's business was even mentioned at this drawing-room stage. The effort to make polite conversation probably centered on Jefferson's mention of France and took the form of asking him about his experiences, but without touching on his views of the revolution that was virtually remaking the French nation, for Hamilton knew they differed sharply on that subject. Jefferson had been surprisingly shallow in his willingness to blame Marie Antoinette for the revolution and cruel in hailing the wave of guillotinings. Anything that overthrew a monarchy was all to the good, he seemed to feel. Hamilton was quite the reverse, anti-French on most questions and inclined to be sympathetic to the victims of cruelty. Madison had received such a flow of letters from Jefferson during those French years that he could take considerable part in the polite chatter, while Hamilton had a genuine desire to listen to one who had traveled so extensively. Every chance to learn was of interest to him, as long as the talk was factual and not contentious.

A little more of the white wine was poured for each man as they chatted for a bit over a half hour in order to give a suitable impression of gentlemanly leisure. Despite the passion that Jefferson reported in Hamilton's manner on the previous day, the man was now calm, composed, obviously determined to contain his anxiety.

On that note, they strolled together to the dining room. Jefferson had the curious practice of letting his guests sit wherever they liked—sitting pell-mell, it was called, especially by the many proper persons who disliked it. Those who ended up in less preferred positions than they were used to felt slighted; those seated above their normal station felt uncomfortable. Most people much preferred the usual custom of carefully seating each guest on the basis of his or her social standing, for the uncertainty of the pell-mell approach made for stress rather than relaxation. The traditional host would have placed Hamilton on his right hand, for as a department head he outranked Madison. But Jefferson undoubtedly just motioned to his guests to set themselves as they pleased, then took the remaining chair himself. Even so, Madison probably tried to do the "proper" thing by putting himself to the left of the seat he guessed would be Jefferson's, and so letting the higher-ranked treasury secretary end up on the host's right.

Two servants came in quickly, placed the simple square four-shelved dumbwaiters beside each guest, placed the salad course on the top shelf, and deftly arranged the silver that would be needed for the entire meal. These dumbwaiters were common in England and

France, but most unusual in America. Jefferson had begun using them during his stay in Paris, from 1784 to 1789. These freestanding tables were not in good enough condition to be shipped home from France. So a member of the Hemings family—John, who was the head joiner—had made a group of them from walnut, with straight legs, slightly tapering at the foot. Servants would put them beside dinner guests, loaded with food, dishes, and silver. After that, the guests were largely on their own for a time. Jefferson's main goal was to promote a free and unrestricted flow of conversation.

On this occasion, as they all took the salad course from the dumbwaiters they found beside them, Jefferson undoubtedly said apologetically, "How I do wish I had the wonderful Virginia field greens that I would have offered if we were at Monticello." There, as the others knew, he grew some 250 varieties of greens, including some so exotic that guests often wondered if they might be poison-ous. "I can, however, serve this poor salad with some of my own wine jelly, made exactly as if we were there," we can be sure the host explained. This jelly was based on a gelatin made by boiling calves' feet and hooves, and it featured Madeira wine, milk, lemon juice, and sugar.

Because Jefferson much preferred white wines to reds, another French white, adequately identified by the host, accompanied the salad course. This wine he described as "a 1786 Bordeaux from the canton of Grave [sic]." This specific one, which he lauded as highly esteemed, he called Carbonnieux: "I had come upon it on a side trip which I had made through the Duchy of Anjou while returning to Paris from a wine-tasting visit to Bordeaux. There is very good wine on these hills, and I am partial to the whites," he informed his guests. "Not equal to wines of the very highest quality perhaps, but we shall come to that a bit later."

As soon as they saw that the salads had been disposed of, two servants were quick to bring in helpings of the first course that had been kept warming just outside the door. In keeping with the Mon-ticello custom, there were two main courses. The first was a capon stuffed with Virginia ham and chestnut purée, artichoke bottoms, and truffles, with a bit of cream, white wine, and chicken stock added. It was served with a Calvados sauce, made with the great apple brandy of Normandy that Jefferson had brought back from his travels.

"Because such a sauce might overpower a fine French wine," Jefferson said, "I take the liberty of serving an Italian favorite of mine—a Montepulciano from Tuscany." And the guests seemed to take well to this departure from French dominance.

As time passed, the second main course would prove to be the New York version of the famed boeuf à la mode, without which no Monticello dinner was considered complete. This was really an elegant beef stew that was a universal favorite. James Hemings had made it before going to France with Jefferson. He had added certain flavoring touches that he learned in France, and now the beef was a masterpiece that Hamilton praised extravagantly. They briefly fell silent while doing it justice with genuine enjoyment. Jefferson wisely refrained from describing the great red wine that was now served, saying only that it was a Chambertin, but saying it reverently enough to hint that this was a pearl beyond price.

We cannot be sure of the guests' response, but it is not hard to imagine Hamilton standing as if in a toast to his host and saying, "I must lift my glass in praise of the man who brought this incomparable wine all the way from France for our enjoyment!" Hamilton was as aggressive and brilliant in the art and science of being a guest as he was in every other activity. He undoubtedly also complimented Jefferson "for having so quickly made this residence not only so congenial, but so ready to make guests feel that they were in a home as gracious as all the fine things I have heard about Monticello."

The host smiled, but in fact, the perfectionist in Jefferson was dissatisfied at not having found a way to set up the revolving service doors that he had at Monticello, for those made it the work of only an instant to transfer hot foods to the dumbwaiters so smoothly that their appearance at each guest's side seemed like the work of a magician.

Nevertheless, Jefferson added an unusually friendly note by saying, "Until you spoke of Monticello just now, Mr. Hamilton, I had forgotten that you have never been to my real home. This is something you must plan to do at no distant date, and you are hereby warmly invited." Jefferson may have wondered whether he was being friendlier than was necessary or appropriate, considering their cool relationship. But he usually found this happening whenever he was the host, and he enjoyed it for the moment.

Hamilton recognized that these were the friendliest words he had heard from the secretary of state since the date of their first meeting. "And I hereby accept, with only the precise date left to further discussion," he said jovially, turning to attack the innumerable small delicacies that had appeared at his place, but with his mind working to decide what this friendly spirit portended for the negotiation that lay ahead.

There were meringues, macaroons, bell fritters, and other small sweets in endless varieties in front of each man, waiting to be consumed before the dessert. And these required no Jeffersonian apology, for New York's growing array of importers and specialty shops had enabled Hemings to arrange a dazzling display even beyond what he had done at Monticello. Great guest that he was, Hamilton chortled and made happy sounds as if he were a boy with a childish appreciation of sweets.

At the same time, Hamilton kept talking with a fluency that the host had to admire. He was able to talk of Monticello with the most perfect taste—and with never a gauche word to betray what their true relationship was.

"Everything I have heard about your architecture gives me such a longing to see it, for the neo-classical style building I have seen in pictures is so enchanting that it must be hard for one to leave such a home." It was, Jefferson must have thought, a bravura performance for a man with an insecure background, and, moreover, one who regularly vilified him in his newspaper articles. But the aura of the dinner made the outside world seem unreal, which was just the enchantment that this host consciously strived for.

And then, at the precise moment when the evening was approaching perfection, came the universally favorite dessert—the delicious vanilla ice cream that still seemed like a miracle, for it was enclosed within a warm pastry, like a cream puff, giving the illusion that the ice cream had come straight from the oven. It never failed to elicit cries from the groups of diners at Monticello, and it did not fail now. Even Madison gave a small squeal, and Hamilton positively exulted, as if his Assumption Bill had just passed by a huge vote.

And an added feature that required description appeared in their wineglasses. It looked like a slightly cloudy white wine, but Jefferson informed them that this was indeed champagne. Only there were no bubbles, for this was the precious *champagne non-mousseux*, meaning nonsparkling. Without quite saying it, the host implied that real connoisseurs disdained any display of bubbles, while enjoying the wonder of the champagne grape free of such pretension. Both the guests looked thoughtful as they weighed this new information. Madison already knew that Jefferson was the only person in America who was importing bubble-free champagne, and that one of his few victories over the president was that Washington had been captivated by this lack of pretension and had asked Jefferson to import quantities of the *non-mousseux* for his account.

We can turn again to Jefferson's own words—suitably rearranged —for the second part of the evening's event, the business part that came next:

> I opened the subject to them, acknowledged that my situation had not permitted me to understand it sufficiently but encouraged them to consider the thing together. They did so.
>
> After some discussion, which was not prolonged, [showing that these men were already set for the compromise in their own minds], Madison extended his remarks by saying that Assumption was a bitter pill to Virginia and other states that had already paid most of their wartime debts. Hamilton responded by indicating that he understood Virginia's unusual position, but wondered whether a reasonable adjustment of the amount that Virginia would be assessed might enable it to support Asssumption? To which Madison responded that such an adjustment would be a step in the right direction, but that considerably more would be needed to soothe the bitter pain that Assumption represented to most of the southern states.
>
> It was observed, I forget by which of them, [those were Jefferson's words] that as the pill would be a bitter one to the Southern states, something should be done to soothe them; that the removal of the seat of government to the Potomac was a just measure, and would probably be a popular one with them, and would be a proper one to follow the Assumption. . . . But the removal to the Potomac could not be carried unless Pennsylvania could be engaged in it [for Pennsylvania had ample voting power to block it].

Hamilton was silent for little more than a minute before making a counterproposal: he was personally prepared to arrange for the Potomac area to become the nation's permanent capital after a ten-year period, as temporary capital status was promised to Philadelphia. At that point, Madison let only another short moment for thought pass before he slowly nodded his head in agreement and said he now acquiesced in the following proposition: that the question of assumption should again be brought before the House. And Madison added that though he himself would not vote for it, in view of the strong unfavorable stand he was known to have taken before, he would not be strenuous in his opposition, and he would undertake to arrange for sufficient favorable votes to allow the bill to pass.

The fact that this opening discussion was brief means that it was little more than a summary statement of how Hamilton and Madison now saw the matter. There was no argument, nor even any cross-talk, for that might have derailed the sense of agreement. They were not here to debate, but to confirm the fact that their basic disagreement would not prevent them from going forward on something too important to ignore.

This conversation, of course, was only a shadow of the compromise. The real substance was already understood, but still needed to be discussed. And Jefferson reported on that part of the talk in the following way: "This arrangement with Pennsylvania Mr. Hamilton took on himself, and chiefly through the agency of Robert Morris, he would obtain the vote of that state, agreeing to an intermediate residence at Philadelphia. This meant that a separate dinner with Pennsylvanians would be held the following week, arranging for Philadelphia to be the temporary capital for ten years, then yielding the permanent status to the Potomac site."

After those virtually pro forma remarks had been rather solemnly exchanged, they asked one another—in different and almost carefree voices—for reassurances of what they might do if the congressmen they asked to change their votes should refuse, or if the Pennsylvania group was uncooperative about accepting only the temporary capital plan. Madison said he expected that at least one of the people he planned to talk with would be quite stiff and pretend to be undecided. But he felt sure that he had points to make that would bring the person or people to agree rather promptly. Hamilton seemed quite candid in admitting that certain Pennsylvania people might be hard to bring around. But he spoke of having an alternate plan that would surely settle the matter, though he did not choose to explain what it was, and the other two did not press him.

They continued to talk in normal tones after that. The thing was done, after all. Both Madison and Hamilton had virtually promised that they could carry out their parts of the agreement. They were gentlemen who meant to keep their word. So now, without spelling out the deal any further, they could talk a little faster, a bit more lightly, as they sipped a fine French brandy that had crossed the ocean to join Secretary Jefferson.

Madison was even ready to name names now. He said he would probably start by speaking to Mr. Alexander White and Mr. Richard Bland Lee, congressmen whose districts lay along the Potomac, to urge them to consider how far the interests of their particular districts might be a sufficient inducement to them to yield to assumption. (This was an oblique way of saying that the congressmen would be warned that their districts might suffer future disadvantages if they failed to go along with their floor leader's request—or that they and their constituents could benefit if they cooperated.) When Madison acted on this plan in coming days, it is said that Lee came into the deal without hesitation. Mr. White had some qualms, but finally agreed. (In a separate note on this subject, Jefferson—probably quoting Madison, who had to do the convincing—described White's "qualms" more colorfully, saying that he "showed an almost convulsive sense of revulsion.")

It is typical of important conversations that the participants have slightly differing versions of exactly what words were used. So it is that one version states portentuously, "To save the Union, Madison would secure votes needed to assure the assumption of state debts. In exchange, Hamilton must help arrange for a permanent location of the government on the Potomac after ten years in Philadelphia."

And there are numerous other variations. A book by Jefferson's great-granddaughter Sarah Randolph insists that her ancestor "was too modest and downplayed what he achieved. He drove a very hard bargain, and in addition to a capital on the Potomac, he got a revision of Virginia's debt balance that saved the state over thirteen million dollars." In fact, it was Madison who won that reduction of cost for Virginia. But he and Jefferson never counted pennies between them.

The three men clearly lingered at the table, talking in short sentences about the goal they had reached and the smaller steps that must be taken in coming days, and wondering what the reactions of various states would be. Very likely, one of them mentioned that the Europeans should be promptly informed of the new arrangement, which would certainly please them mightily. If so, that would have been Hamilton, and Jefferson would have been more likely to advise, prudently, letting the Europeans find out for themselves, not leading them to believe that Americans arranged their policies with Europe in mind. It was a masterstroke, hiding the very point that had been his greatest concern. At that point, Hamilton's eyes must have opened widely, as he clearly recognized the wisdom of Jefferson's words and was probably annoyed with himself for having to be corrected.

Some states would certainly learn, or at least imagine, that Virginia had won a reduction of cost, and they would make demands for similar savings, which might force Hamilton to rearrange all his figures to balance the books. At the mention of anything he was counted on to do, Hamilton nodded dismissively, as if he had it under control.

Jefferson and Madison had noticed at that dinner table what a smile of triumph the man had. He seemed to be trying to suppress his glowing expression, but not really succeeding. Even with the anger he knew he would arouse from his fellow New Yorkers for having given away all hope of continuing to be a capital city, Hamilton looked like a man who was seeing himself at the helm of a great United States. The glowing future he had foreseen was, it seemed, like a living picture before his eyes.

There was hardly any mention of President Washington, of how to go about getting his approval, and whether he would be pleased or how this news would be conveyed to him. Hamilton seemed reluctant to be specific, but said just a few words about looking into it. As much as Jefferson and Madison hated this proprietary treatment of the president, they knew Hamilton would tell Washington in his own way and somehow convince him to join in agreement.

As he saw the others off to their waiting carriages, Jefferson knew that he had accomplished exactly what he had set out to do. But had he not also accomplished just what Hamilton had set out to do? Any satisfaction he felt had to be grim. A letter he wrote to James Monroe around this time showed how much he detested the necessity for such a compromise.

Senator Henry Cabot Lodge later said, "There is no single state paper in the history of the U.S., with the exception of the Emancipation Proclamation which was of such immense importance and produced such wide and far-reaching results as Hamilton's Report on Public Credit." But Gilbert Chinard, a Jefferson biographer, seeing it from his subject's point of view, wrote, "All the rest of his life was to be spent in trying to recover the ground he lost on that day." And even in the long run, although acknowledging that it had to be done to prevent the loss of the ability to borrow from Europe and probably even the breakup of the states, he was not happy with his own accomplishment.

"It was unjust," Jefferson said about this agreement years later, "in itself oppressive to the states, and was acquiesced in merely from a fear of disunion, while our government was still in its most instant state." He sounded almost as if the deal had been made at the point of a gun. But it was his gun.

13
The Philadelphia Story

THE RESULTING ACTION WAS FAST. There were none of the dragging delays that usually characterize government at work. While Hamilton talked with Robert Morris to make arrangements with the Pennsylvania legislators who would be vital to the compromise plan, the superpunctual James Madison had lost no time in sitting across from each of the congressmen whom he judged to be most suscepti-ble to changing their votes for the Assumption Bill that they had previously turned down.

Jefferson later recorded that one of the men, Richard Bland Lee, had no problem with changing his vote, while another, Alexander White, had responded quite distressingly. Jefferson wrote it differ-ently in two places, once going as far as saying the poor man had "a revulsion of stomach almost convulsive." This detail may have been a special embellishment by Jefferson, just to enliven the account, for there seemed to be no reason for a cold-blooded operation. Madison had been able to sweeten his request by pointing out that voting yes now was entirely different for the voters in each man's district. Now this favorable vote was buying something tangible—and it is not hard to imagine that Madison said something like: "In return for assuring me that you are voting for Assumption now, you receive the promise that the national capital will be in a new city adjacent to your district, Sir. And I need not tell you what that will do for the property values and the many opportunities open to those who live in this district. Tell me, Sir, would you have it any other way? Do you think you will meet with angry faces or broad smiles when you tell this news to your constituents?"

It is hard to see any reason why Madison should have received anything but pleasant smiles from his congressional followers, and they certainly agreed to vote as he wished. Hamilton's mission was another matter. He had to bear the brunt of very angry New Yorkers who thought much less of the assumption victory than they did of the defeat in losing any chance for even a short-term hold on the national capital for New York City. These people undoubtedly thought Hamilton had hardly tried to do anything for their city as long as he had his victory on the assumption issue—which was quite true. And then, more precisely, he had to turn away from the New York aspect and make sure the Pennsylvanians fully accepted the choice of the Potomac site. His victory would go for naught if the Pennsylvanian group suddenly tried to blur the agreement about the nation's capital with ambivalent words about the future.

Hamilton had known he would be arousing the fury of some New York followers by leaving his own city out of consideration for any part in the capital scheme. But he refused to grieve over that, and as the next dinner approached, he was seen, by the many persons who made Hamilton-watching a daily occupation, to be highly elated. He understood better than anyone else that his victory on the assumption of debt greatly outweighed the loss suffered on the capital's location. The financial greatness that he had pictured for America in those wartime days when he was only an artillery captain was about to be born, he was sure.

It had been agreed at Jefferson's dinner that in the following week, Jefferson and Hamilton would try to arrange a dinner with a group of Pennsylvania lawmakers to clear up some remaining obstacles to the compromise. Madison had excused himself from this follow-up dinner because he wanted the time free to make careful plans for carrying out his part of the deal. And as a side project, he was studying ways to maximize the considerable reduction he was trying to win for Virginia in the amount of contribution the state would have to make to the assumption program, based on the heavy debt-reduction program it had already engaged in. But Madison had suggested that Henry Knox be included in the new dinner because his knack for making others join in a good time often led to agreement on serious matters.

At this next dinner, it would be Hamilton's specific job to help persuade the Pennsylvania delegation that the ten-year temporary capital deal was the best their state could hope for. And this he felt sure of accomplishing. With wine and jollity in control of the event, he expected solid agreement that Philadelphia would serve as the nation's temporary capital for the next ten years, during which time a permanent capital would be constructed in the Potomac area.

Despite the fact that he had a mission to accomplish, Hamilton seemed totally convinced that he would prevail with the Pennsylvania group, and this proved to be exactly the case.

Hamilton had good reason not to be worried, for most of the Pennsylvanians had already made it known they were quite content with the compromise plan. He knew that there would be a variety of feelings at this festive table, with a few of the men agreeing to the deal because they were secretly convinced that once the capital got to such a major city as theirs, it would never move again. They, of course, proved to be entirely wrong. Congress took the choice of the Potomac area quite seriously. Once it had arranged for the construction of a new city near the Potomac, it never swayed from the plan, although about eight years after the initial decision attempts to alter the arrangement were made by groups that found great fault with Washington, D.C.

But on this night, Hamilton would not be troubled by the suspicion that some of those present still thought Philadelphia would exert an unbreakable hold ten years later. Their empty dream would have the merit of smoothing the way for a solid deal now.

It is noteworthy that Jefferson, too, was sufficiently sure this deal would endure that he wrote to Paris on July 1, ordering the remainder of his belongings to be shipped to Philadelphia.

But why were many Philadelphians so confident that the capital would never be moved away once they got this promise of possessing it for ten full years? The city's belief in its own superior qualities was justified, for all the things that New York and other cities were struggling to become, Philadelphia already was. Not only was it the largest city in America, it was the busiest and the richest. Its population was variously estimated at sixty thousand to eighty thousand, depending on what surrounding neighborhoods were counted in. Its exports were substantially larger than New York's, and it imported so many foreign goods that the collector of customs had one of the highest salaries in the nation, more than heads of federal departments or governors of states. This was fitting because the customs he collected made up a substantial chunk of the federal government's income. The city was proud to have a public library that was massive for its time, and it was one of the first things the many foreign visitors were told about, to show that mental superiority came first.

Philadelphia's shopping facilities were unmatched anywhere else in the nation. Because the stores were situated on wide and beautiful streets, simply strolling past these windows was a popular diversion. Numerous British companies had established branch shops along those streets, and there were enough serious shoppers to make them highly profitable. Thomas Jefferson, accompanied by one of the city's elegant ladies, had been known to buy frightfully costly gloves at three successive shops in a single morning.

Almost four years earlier, James Madison had insisted on holding the Constitutional Convention in Philadelphia because some lesser meetings in other cities to discuss the nation's future had drawn pitifully small attendance. One meeting in Annapolis, Maryland, had been such a total failure that it spurred Madison and Hamilton to call for the much larger effort of 1787. What would become known as the Constitutional Convention attributed some of its force to the rebound effect from that failure in Annapolis. Madison had hoped that his canny choice of Philadelphia would promote a considerable attendance if only because this city was a place for tourist pleasures. And the result had proved him right.

The move of the capital from New York to Philadelphia would occur in summertime, which was notoriously hot in the new destination, as all those who had attended the Constitutional Convention could attest. But most of the major players would go to their scattered homes until fall while the physical move was made—Jefferson and Madison to their own Virginia areas, Hamilton to upstate New York, and the Washingtons to Mount Vernon, of course. Then, in the fall, the president and his lady would move into Robert Morris's grand mansion in Philadelphia, while Jefferson would rent a house on Market Street, which, needless to say, he immediately and very expensively remade to accept the eighty packing cases' worth of purchases from Europe that were just arriving.

As opposed to the undoubted attractions of Philadelphia, the plan to go ahead with the Potomac site presented a mass of new questions. The place was increasingly being referred to as simply "Georgetown," even though the new capital city would be made up of land from both Maryland and Virginia. But the small and rather exclusive bit of Virginia land named for King George II in 1751 can truly be called the parent city of the national capital. In the years when Washington, D.C., was still being put together and when its muddy swamps were a sore trial to the government officials and their wives, well-bred old Georgetown, which had existed for almost 150 years, was a refuge they cherished.

This fondness for Georgetown was not at all to President Washington's liking, for he wanted to see the new capital blossom as quickly as possible. He sent a severe note to one of the District of Columbia's new commissioners, implying that he would be displeased with anyone who retreated to "an abode in Georgetown if a house is to be had in the City." And by "the City" he meant the new district, which did not yet have its full name.

Much later, in 1871, Georgetown's charter as a city was revoked, and it was incorporated into the District of Columbia. The streets were joined with letters and numbers that continued those of Washington. And its old streets proved to be such natural companions of the newer District of Columbia streets that it remains just that way today. Even one of the routes for reaching the campus of Georgetown University still involves traveling over cobbled streets and old streetcar tracks that once linked it to the original city.

Georgetown is also still a living record of the republic's architecture since its founding. Federal, Classic Revival, Victorian, and Modern homes—all are there. Most important of all are the structures built during the first fifty years of the nation's existence. Here, part of Braddock's forces passed on their way to the 1755 defeat. From Georgetown, men and supplies went to fight in the cause of the colonies. So it did not seem strange that George Washington went to Georgetown as commander in chief to oversee the planning

An early artist's impression of George Washington as a young surveyor, pausing to think while at work in Lake Drummond's Dismal Swamp.

of the new capital. Regrettably, Georgetown residents would also have a clear view of the fires that would be set by the British in 1814.

Today, Georgetown streets are among the most elegant, pricey, and desirable parts of the nation's capital. But not everybody was a winner in this move to elegance. Apart from the mansions, many of which were staffed by black slaves who lived far better lives than southern slaves, Georgetown also had a notable free black community, living in small but respectable houses. Some seven hundred free blacks were reasonably well settled, some working at paid jobs, some even running their own businesses. These free blacks attended their own churches and educated their children in small, privately run schools. But when the transformation to join Georgetown to Washington, D.C., occurred in the nineteenth century, Georgetown's black population suffered mightily. Bit by bit, the small houses gave way to large, costly ones, or to modish new apartment buildings and high-priced shops. The term *Georgetown* came to signify costly real estate and fashionable living. But there were years of painful read-justment for the original black residents. As landlords made them vacate houses they had occupied for decades, many had to leave that part of the city entirely and flee to nearby Maryland counties.

George Washington's personal trips to see the construction that was being started in Georgetown had a strange twist, with a racial importance that he himself could hardly judge. First he came from Mount Vernon with three men who had been appointed as the new city's commissioners (and note that they would later have the job of giving the city its name). Washington checked into Suter's Tavern

George Washington, near the time of his inauguration as America's first president. This painting by Gilbert Stuart is unusual because it is one of the few times when the right side of Washington's face was featured, making him seem less familiar.

on October 15, 1790. He then returned on March 28, 1791, and saw Major Pierre Charles L'Enfant's plan for the city, as well as Major Andrew Ellicott's survey. Washington recorded the latter visit in his diary:

> A few miles out of town, I was met by the principal citizens of the place and escorted in by them; and dined at Suter's Tavern (where I also lodged) at a public dinner given by the Mayor and corporation—previous to which I examined the surveys of Mr. Ellicott, which had been sent on to lay out the district of ten miles square for the Federal seat: and also the works of Majr L'Enfant, who had been engaged to examine and make a draught of the grounds in the vicinity of Georgetown and Carrollsburg on the Eastern branch, making arrangements for examining the ground myself tomorrow with the commissioners.

As a former professional surveyor, Washington was thoroughly enjoying the opportunity to study the work that was going to produce a city that he must have expected to bear his name, though that decision had not yet been made. But he did not enjoy one embarrassing incident.

A newspaperman's sudden question forced him to turn away and hide one secret that would have stirred serious political disturbances if it had been linked to the president. Washington avoided mentioning that Major Ellicott, when he accepted the job, had pointedly asked if he could choose his own staff. Washington quickly agreed, and later learned that Ellicott's choice for an assistant surveyor was a black tobacco farmer named Benjamin Banneker, one of the most brilliant men ever born in America.

Washington was not a racist, and he was against slavery, but he could not let this position be known without creating a political firestorm. In the same way, it would have caused great agitation if it were known that he approved of a black person having such a high responsibility in the construction of the new capital city. Southern slave owners would have imagined that this was the beginning of a drive to prove that black people were capable of undertaking important mental tasks, making their consignment to slavery seem even more outrageous. So when a journalist queried the president, "Sir, I understand that a black gentleman has a leading role in the planning for this new city. Is that correct?" Washington simply turned on his heel and walked away without a word.

The Georgetown Weekly Ledger, without linking this to Washington's name, referred to "an Ethiopian, whose abilities as a surveyor and astronomer clearly prove that Mr. Jefferson's conclusion that this race of men were void of mental endowments was without foundation."

Major Ellicott had named Banneker because the Ellicott family—who had never owned a slave and who judged everyone according to his abilities—knew the man well and considered him a brilliant astronomer. On the survey team for the national capital, Banneker had perhaps the most technical job of all. Among other things, he had to deploy the astronomical clock that would make certain each new morning's survey work was positioned to match where the work had left off on the previous evening.

Shortly after this work for the new capital, Banneker had the nearly unbelievable success of publishing his own almanac containing his astronomical computations, compositions, and other writings. Only a few people in the entire country, mostly men of advanced education, had the ability to create almanacs, which required skill in astronomy, mathematics, and good writing. Many families selected a favorite almanac as their only reading matter.

Banneker was almost entirely self-taught. Yet his almanac was so accurate—even meeting the needs of farmers and sailors at sea—and so readable that it became a favorite and enough of a moneymaker to enable him to quit his farming for the first time in a long life. But there was more.

Most astonishing of all, Benjamin Banneker, sometime before 1790, was the first person in history to introduce the theory that the stars were suns, much like our sun, and that they had planets circling around them. This theory was based on a mental calculation he had made that was pure genius. It proved to be correct, of course, and science finally confirmed this fact, calling the planets that encircle their star "the extra-solar planets." Banneker had said it 150 years before science confirmed that discovery. But, shamefully, science has never mentioned his name.

A part of Banneker's historic pronouncement reads as follows:

This sun, with all its attendant planets, is but a very little part of the grand machine of the universe; each star, though in appearance no bigger than the diamond that glitters upon a lady's ring, is really a vast globe, like the sun in size and glory; no less spacious, no less luminous, than the radiant source of the day: So that every star is not barely a world, but the center of a magnificent system; has a retinue of worlds, irradiated by its beams, and revolving round its attractive influence, all of which are lost to our sight in unmeasurable wilds of ether.

In the whole of science, no great accomplishment has ever fallen on such deaf ears as this statement, which Banneker made on several occasions. It was not simply a fortunate guess. It was a carefully reasoned finding, based on the following original thinking: whenever nature creates a structure or a pattern, it discards any failure but always repeats its successes. How can it be, then, that such a beautiful and balanced plan as the solar system was tried only once and not repeated? It cannot be.

There must be many other examples. Then, looking at the stars one night, he thought, "Those are all the other examples. It must be that most of the stars are suns, encircled by planets which we cannot see because they are too far away and the light of their suns is too great."

No book of astronomy's history should be considered complete without recognition of Banneker's unique contribution.

14
Doubts Settled, Doubts Revived

MORE THAN A FEW DISPUTES about the great compromise began appearing and increasing over the years—claims that such an event never happened, suggestions that Madison played no part in bringing about any vote changes, and outright charges that Jefferson's own account was totally false.

One of the most publicized arguments surfaced in 1970, when Jacob E. Cooke, a Lafayette College historian, wrote that the famous dinner, if it occurred at all, had nothing to do with the eventual compromise. He claimed, in fact, that the real compromise was a financial one, dealing with the amount of state debt and the rate of interest that funded debt would pay. Cooke, writing in the *William and Mary Quarterly*, argued that the two-part dinner bargain was never consummated.

Cooke's argument ran on for many pages of hotly contested thoughts about the many House and Senate votes that occurred and exactly which congressmen would have had to change their votes to bring about the final result. But his claim that the Jefferson dinner was not really the immediate cause of the great decision was seriously erroneous. An answering article in the same journal, in October 1971, by Kenneth R. Bowling, a University of Wisconsin professor, showed a point-by-point succession of actions whereby Thomas Jefferson and James Madison secured the votes necessary to pass the

Assumption Bill, and together with Alexander Hamilton arranged for the passage of the bill that led to a national capital on the Potomac River. Recent personal conversations with Professor Bowling (who is now engaged in a special project at George Washington University) and study of his documents have removed all doubt that the dinner did, indeed, produce the compromise and set the stage for the conclusive votes during the following month.

As we discussed earlier, Jefferson had told friends that "No funding bill could be adopted unless some plan of compromise could be agreed upon." He had written with great precision, "What is needed is something to displease and something to soothe every part of the Union but New York." Professor Cooke's theory that this clear prescription for the ultimate solution had then been ignored or bypassed and that the famous dinner meeting discussed only the financial side of the equation is more than hard to believe. There would have been no logical reason for it.

Not only was there a compromise, but it was the epitome of a classic compromise—a case study of what elevates a compromise from routine to memorable. Jefferson's dinner meeting certainly saw both subjects of the compromise laid out clearly. The nature of the bargain forced each side to work from the other's point of view. By this account, each side then concentrated on achieving the other side's goal: Madison arranged for the votes to assure Hamilton's main objective, while Hamilton took steps to give his adversaries, Jefferson and Madison, the national capital they wanted.

It might be asked why this kind of simple but perfect compromise could not have been worked out by any of the other groups that had been searching so diligently for a solution. It is chiefly because none of those others had a Madison on their team. While Jefferson was the organizer, Madison was a key person, for he alone, as the leader of the House, had a good chance of manipulating the vote as required. Not for the first time, and far from the last, the combination of Jefferson and Madison worked its magic.

The general understanding among the three diners about the assumption of debt and the location of a capital city had left them with work to be done in coming days. And we have seen that they attacked this assignment at once. But they must also have considered the possibility that they might not succeed in forcing enough congressmen to vote as they were asked to do. In that case, it would appear, they might have to turn to Pennsylvania for more than simply unblocking any objections it had to the Potomac capital site, which was basic, but also to find a "movable" congressman or two who would help to pass the Assumption Bill.

For these reasons, Hamilton very promptly set up a dinner where he and Jefferson were to meet with a Pennsylvania group on June 28. And this dinner, though less elegant than Mr. Jefferson's, was equally successful. While Madison was not needed at that second dinner, his idea of including Secretary of War Henry Knox had the favorable result that Madison had foreseen.

There was a somewhat bizarre second reason for thinking of Pennsylvania as a party to this subject: at the time when Virginia had voted to cede a ten-mile-square area of its land for use as a federal district, the state confusingly stipulated that Maryland, Virginia, and Pennsylvania were to participate in sharing the resulting benefits. The only place where the three could have taken part in such a way was the little town of Hancock, Pennsylvania, which was close to the state boundary and gave easy access into the heart of Pennsylvania. But that was not thought to be a sufficient reason for Virginia's odd stipulation. Even though the spot would have given access by water to the Tidewater cities and Western settlements, it seemed unrealistic as a potential capital city. It would appear that Virginia had just been laying down a general thought about a three-state plan, without intending to point at any specific city. Now, to everyone's relief, the great Dinner-Table Compromise could put this strange choice out of contention, but only with the agreement of Pennsylvania.

In any case, the second dinner was chiefly intended to enable the Pennsylvanians to achieve at least a minor goal by seeing Philadelphia named as the temporary capital for ten years, while the permanent capital on the Potomac was being built.

Senator Maclay wrote about this second dinner as if he had been present, which, as he was a Pennsylvania senator, is easily possible. He found Jefferson "stiff and formal" on that occasion, with a lofty gravity. And the jovial Knox, drinking to excess, said Maclay, was dignified enough to be an important member of the group, while adding a lighthearted note.

Most important was Maclay's report that Hamilton was in such high spirits that he had a "boyish, giddy manner." The all-conquering power of the assumption victory gave him all his old confidence and more.

This confidence was justified. The deal sealing the compromise was completed when two key votes took place during the month of July 1790: on July 10, the House voted in favor of the Residence Act, naming Philadelphia as the temporary capital for a period of ten years, after which the permanent capital would be a ten-square-mile site on the Potomac River, made up of small plots of land from Maryland and Virginia.

And on July 26, the House passed the Assumption Bill by a margin of 34 to 28. As arranged at Jefferson's dinner, Madison appeared to stand his ground by voting against the bill, but the additional votes he had arranged from congressmen who had previously been in opposition were more than enough to seal the victory.

But the two final yeas of Lee and White did not tell the whole story. The precise alignment of votes that made success possible was complex, and last-minute excitement must have been great because changes kept occurring up to the time of the final votes that would ensure success.

One man named Daniel Huger had been thought to be too ill to vote, but then his name appeared among the yeas. Two men named Nicholas Gilman and Samuel Livermore switched to the negative side. But meanwhile, in addition to the much-discussed White and Lee of Virginia, two Marylanders named Daniel Carroll and George Gale switched to the affirmative as a result of Madison's work after the dinner bargain.

And each of these last four, as Professor Bowling has pointed out, "represented one of the four districts along that portion of the Potomac River which the Residence Bill selected for the Federal City." These were representatives who were successfully approached by Madison and who helped to assure Congressional passage of the Assumption Bill.

The European bankers who would welcome this historic action

did not have to know how the agreement was achieved. But they understood that federal power had triumphantly taken over the role that had previously been distributed among the individual states. As lenders, they much preferred this firmer structure on which their money rested. They would never know the pain that Thomas Jefferson had suffered in arranging this blow to states' rights, but they would feel that their money was safe in Alexander Hamilton's America. It is interesting to note that this knowledge about the new country across the ocean was of major importance to them for more than financial reasons.

Those in Europe who were thoughtful enough to wonder about the radically changing new world that seemed to be emerging (and most of the bankers surely answered this description) were also caught up in wondering where the explosive growth of science was leading. And they linked the two—science and America—as twin evidences of the New World that they would have to understand and deal with.

Until the eighteenth century, science had been regarded as a unified body of knowledge that was bound to keep pace with man's moves to improve himself. But the approach of the nineteenth century was bringing whole new concepts of evolutionary change. The danger of having to adapt to a world that left the rigid Newtonian pattern behind was terrifying to thoughtful people. It had begun to seem that each branch of science—chemistry, mathematics, geology, medicine, botany—had to have its own expanding research. There was too much to know about too many things.

During the Enlightenment, Europeans had seen the universe as inflexibly and absolutely rational. Now the new century's penchant for change brought new inventions at a rate never imagined before. And it was natural for many of them to see America as one more of these—a superinvention that offered great possibilities for profit, but that also had to be watched to see what new universal pattern it might suddenly display.

Hamilton's assumption scheme was a major part of this. And now it had turned out that Thomas Jefferson had apparently signed on as one of its promoters. Not for the first time—nor for the last—Europe was misreading America.

To realize how great a sacrifice Jefferson was making in this painful move, it helps to be reminded how bad the Assumption Bill appeared in his own mind: independently of the debts of Congress, he once said, the states during the war had contracted separate and heavy debts, and the more old debt Hamilton could rake up, the more money it would create for his "mercenaries," meaning scoundrels who only backed Hamilton as a way of grabbing all the money they could get. They pretended that this money, whether it had originally been wisely or foolishly spent, had come out of the general treasury for use in fighting the war, and therefore presumably was to be repaid from the general purse. And then Jefferson imagined Hamilton saying to himself, "Though nobody knows what these debts were, no matter, we will guess." So the claims made by the several states became a scramble, with some getting more than others, but the main object was obtained, Jefferson thought: "For the phalanx of the Treasury was reinforced by additional recruits." Or, in modern terms, the numbers of speculators who were enriched by the Treasury kept growing. This was wrong, of course, but it is mind-boggling to think that Jefferson actually believed it.

Despite the extensive evidence that Hamilton worked extremely hard to measure and quantify all his financial conclusions, Jefferson honestly pictured him creating a sort of financial hash that eventually lined the pockets of men who were already wealthy (his mercenaries) and guaranteed that there would be growing sums to keep enlarging his loyal following.

It is startling to reflect that Jefferson, who was so clearly a word person and not at all a number person, took on the unlikely chore of analyzing what Hamilton was trying to do on financial affairs, a puzzle that would have seemed impenetrable even to some mathematicians. The result was that he found the appearance of massive wrongs that did not really exist. Hamilton's computations were the soul of precision, as the future would prove. But it took another financial wizard to discover this—strangely enough, in President Jefferson's term of office.

Jefferson may have been correct in fearing that Hamilton's methods were going to win him unbeatable political favor, but he was dead wrong in thinking that Hamilton was trying to create a "financial hash." It was the last thing in the world Hamilton would have done, partly because his neat mind would have hated the idea, and even more because any numbers-oriented person knows that a financial hash turns into total disaster. The huge amounts of undisciplined money that Jefferson pictured would have lost value disastrously, perhaps impoverishing many of the people Hamilton was supposedly relying on for his future greatness.

But Jefferson really had faith in the untruth he had invented. In 1796, he was still writing to Madison: "I do not at all wonder at the condition in which the finances of the United States are found. Hamilton's object from the beginning was to throw them into forms which should be utterly undecipherable." There appears to be no truth in this, but it probably seemed so to Jefferson—the impression of a man who had no ability for assessing numerical statements.

Jefferson never stopped repeating the claim that he had been duped by Hamilton when he agreed to help with the assumption scheme. Scholars have wondered why he chose to give this impression. What Jeffersonian plan could have made him insist that Hamilton had outsmarted him?

Skeptics who want to challenge Jefferson's account may simply be imagining that the secretary of state wished to be sure of getting maximum credit for having arranged the great compromise. But that simplistic view has a flaw, first because Jefferson thought boasting harmed one's image, so he was much more inclined to downplay his accomplishments, and second because he kept insisting for the rest of his life that this had been a misfortune, rather than an accomplishment. He repeatedly claimed that Hamilton had taken advantage of his unpreparedness. It is not convincing to think Jefferson wanted to get credit for something he had decided to portray as an unfortunate blunder.

So the secondary question is, why did he decide to characterize it as a mistake when he knew that it was done to avoid what he himself had called "the ultimate calamity"? He surely had not decided that it had been a mistake to protect America's credit in Europe. The compromise had accomplished its great purpose. It had helped to heal a sick situation when no other cure was in sight. Why, then, the later use of the word *mistake*?

The likeliest explanation is that Jefferson wished to put the blame squarely on Hamilton for the great sacrifice he had been forced to make. It was probably a way of showing what an impossibly divisive force Hamilton had been, deadly enough to compel others to go against their deepest principles. It was almost as though Jefferson were still arguing with the specter of General Washington, trying to make him see Hamilton's wrongs.

And apart from trying to show the evil effect of Hamilton's plans, another grim generality played a part. Even though Jefferson was often prone to speak or write somewhat deceptively, he may deserve to be credited with full sincerity in this case. Because he saw Hamilton's creation of a great financial power leading to a more urbanized, more industrialized America even during his lifetime, rather than toward the farm-based economy he favored, Jefferson genuinely considered Hamilton a destructive influence. In addition to perceiving a threat of monarchy or dictatorship, he also saw Hamilton as a destroyer. While so many others thought the great American dollar and all the accomplishments it led to were a reason for pride, the aging Jefferson was more firmly than ever opposed to that route. To him, increased federal power over the states meant failure. He was more than willing to blame it on Hamilton.

He was saying, in effect, "I do not want 'credit' for the growth of the federal government and all the other expansiveness that has come with it. There is only blame to be assigned for what is happening to America. Let Hamilton take that blame. History will prove that by forcing me to agree to a plan that made this kind of America possible, Hamilton was becoming responsible for an America that was never sanctioned by the Constitution and that will be destined to lose its way."

It is one of America's great miracles that while these two powerful men accused each other of violating the Constitution, and they both had potentially valid points, the Constitution survived all their mistreatment of it.

Before the end of 1790, as if that year had not been overflowing enough with innovative and controversial programs, Hamilton roared ahead toward his call to charter a central bank. Innocent as that now sounds, it would be a declaration of war to those who wanted the nation to remain a group of states and not a giant that treated the states as underlings.

The term *central bank*, which now seems perfectly normal, sounded like yet another way to pander to speculators while fleecing the innocent. To Jefferson, the term *bankers* doubtless conjured an instant picture of the lenders who had him in their clutches for most of his life. That the cure for this problem was to stop borrowing and start living within one's means sounded to him more like a prison sentence than a way of life.

Unlike the earlier subject of assumption, which the treasury secretary admittedly saw as a way to enormous power, Hamilton thought of a bank straightforwardly as simply an institution that could expand the money supply and extend credit principally to business—therefore a normal help to the process of government. But in this innocent view, Hamilton had more enemies than friends. Adams, for example, who had not personally suffered from debt, and therefore had not endured many interest payments, is said to have considered every bank in America as "an enormous tax upon the people for the profit of individuals." That Jefferson agreed with this is obvious, for he was paying huge amounts of interest to bankers. While he managed to talk civilly to these men when circumstances forced him to, he called the banking business "a succession of felonious larcenies."

That the president must be told to stand fast against this new outrage of Hamilton's was obvious to Jefferson. But what about his recent fear of harming America's credit standing with foreign bankers? Must he bear this in mind every time Hamilton proposed a new idea? To keep living in fear of that would provide Hamilton with carte blanche for any wild new scheme he might originate. No, he decided. The foreign bankers had ample evidence from the recently enacted measures that the United States was not about to break apart. Even the fact that the country had a national capital was a sign of new strength and permanence. Hamilton could not be allowed to keep winning his way just to impress the foreign bankers. This new bank idea of his must be fought.

For one thing, there was surely nothing in the Constitution that specifically said the government had a right to create a national bank. Hamilton would use the old argument that there is an implied right to do things that are necessary in order to accomplish some of the stated objectives. But even though that had permitted him to define the Constitution his own way on the assumption question, the argument against a national bank seemed much stronger. It was with confidence that Jefferson and Madison prepared to enter the fray against the bank.

A bill to charter the Bank of the United States for twenty years met no initial opposition at all. It went through the Senate in January 1791. But as the House studied the bank bill, it became clear that a new clash between Hamilton and Madison was forming. And it was seen to be serious. The flat disjuncture between the agricultural way of life that Jefferson and Madison prized and the money-changing ways of the business community was an invitation to real hatred. People who were debtors by nature simply could not abide the ways of the banker. If a bank took just 1 percent interest on a loan, that 1 percent was seen as robbery. Phrases like "the prostitution of money for illicit gain" and "considering a bank to be like a house of ill fame" portrayed a feeling so deep that logic could not begin to soften it.

15
Hamilton the Unstoppable?

IT HAD BEGUN TO SEEM that Hamilton's dream was the wave of the future, while Jefferson's vision of small independent farms as the basic structure of America was destined to lose. The move to Philadelphia had, of course, made no difference in the wide gap that separated these two men.

That "the Secretary of the Treasury determines the movements of government" was becoming a common opinion among politicians. His various state papers were considered masterful. His work in setting up all the new governmental structures needed to run the nation smoothly was greatly admired.

And he had developed increasing confidence as he saw that the more he attempted, the more power and acceptance he gathered— gaining ground on his detractors.

One apparent victory for Hamilton was a surprise. In December 1790, a touchy measure to put an excise tax on whiskey and other spirits—a subject that had always encountered great resistance— won full approval from James Madison. Madison even primly suggested that this would have the added benefit of increasing "sobriety and thereby preventing disease and untimely deaths."

The combative senator William Maclay, however, was a more accurate judge when he made this precise observation in his laudable diary about the results he expected from Hamilton's tax on spirits:

"War and bloodshed are the most likely consequence of all this." Just as Maclay had said, reports of trouble soon cropped up in Pennsylvania. The tax collectors, who had been instructed by Hamilton to visit distilleries "at least twice a day," stirred considerable unrest. The small local distillers felt discriminated against and armed themselves to fight back, because they were struggling to make a living with simple equipment that the inspectors could easily see and tax, while the local folk suspected that major distilleries were less transparent and easily protected from taxation. They stepped up their resistance. Still, Hamilton would not relent.

Even with such unrest to distract him, the treasury secretary did not delay in moving ahead with the new bank plan that was already expected to encounter great opposition among the president's insiders. Just before the year 1790 ended, Hamilton—flying in the teeth of known opposition from Jefferson, Madison, and John Adams—formally made the dreaded proposal that the United States should have a central bank. This, he explained, was the only way to achieve a unified currency, expand the supply of money, and manage government funds and foreign exchange. As his reason for proposing this now, he cited the European experiences that he had studied, especially the Bank of England and Bank of Amsterdam. And he quoted liberally from Adam Smith. Among other ways in which Hamilton was exceptional, he managed to use many references to foreign authorities so smoothly that he was never criticized for a practice that aroused anger when other Americans did it.

Clearly, a new struggle between Hamilton and Madison was about to break out. Every day was bringing it closer, and no one had a formula for avoiding it. Although the bank bill passed through the Senate easily in January 1791, the House began to consider it questioningly and questions turned to accusations. Bearing in mind how much Jefferson and Madison considered the farmers their prime clients—and that farmers tended to be deeply distrustful of banks—widespread opposition was a foregone conclusion. Some of the southern remarks about banks were barely printable, but Patrick Henry probably stirred more negative feelings by primly calling it "the subserviency of southern to northern interests." The way that so many questions came to be regarded as North-South issues is noteworthy. More than half a century before the fact, the physical outlines of the Civil War were discernable.

The legal battle in the House centered on the constitutional issue. The document clearly had not foreseen a national bank. But Hamilton relied on the well-known Article 1, Section 8 as giving Congress the right to pass legislation deemed "necessary and proper" to exercise its listed powers. Suddenly Madison, the Father of the Constitution, seemed to reveal a fact that had not been disclosed before: that he had become a strict constructionist of that document. If specific authorization could not be found in the Constitution itself, no amount of other sources or logic would make it acceptable. He would not relent even when his own words from the past were pointed out to him—"that wherever a general power to do a thing is given, every particular power for doing it is included." Now, he still held this to be generally true, but the bank idea, he insisted, was going much too far. The Constitution had no place for it.

When the vote was taken, a stunning result shook the political system. The House went against its own floor leader and on February 8 gave Hamilton a 39 to 20 victory. It created the worst division the nation had known. In going forward with this plan and winning, Hamilton had revealed the terrible split between North and South. Almost all northern congressmen had stood with Hamilton; almost all southerners had voted against him.

This upheaval in the basic workings of the legislative system frightened Madison more than anything that had happened since the adoption of the Constitution. Among other things, it led to more deeply entrenched political parties, with partisans putting their party ahead of any other consideration. Such emphasis on partisanship is often regarded as shallow thinking; but in many cases, even intelligent persons quickly realized that their standing in a community, or even their livelihoods, depended on adhering to party lines. This realization has often been pointed to as a basic turning point in the American system of government. Instead of a decision relying on a majority of individual opinions, a group position would determine the course of action.

Madison appealed to George Washington to realize the seriousness of the North-South split. He specifically besought Washington to respond to the bank bill with a veto—the first ever. That the Father of the Constitution should ask the president to veto a measure that had won by a two-to-one margin was like a challenge to the basic system of government that he himself had devised.

Jefferson pointed out that the vote showed the danger in Hamilton's practice of submitting his studious reports and then soon drafting bills based on them. He gave the president a statement saying that Hamilton was perverting the necessary-and-proper clause. He also repeated the argument he had made on an earlier constitutional dispute—which was now seeming a bit tired—that a measure had to be more than just convenient to fit the necessary-and-proper standard; it had to be truly indispensable in the sense that whatever was necessary and proper could not possibly be done without this approach. "To go as far as Hamilton had," he said, "was going beyond an important boundary."

Washington, deeply troubled, received mainly negative recommendations from his cabinet members, but soon found himself confronted by Hamilton's forty-page document that brilliantly set forth the horrors of a government that tried to operate "without the right to employ all the means requisite . . . to the attainment of the ends" of its power. As he had done before, he compared it to being "a people governed without government." Jefferson, Hamilton pointed out, also wanted to deprive the federal government of the power to create any corporations, and he explained why this form of organization would be essential to American business in the future. And there he had injected another fighting word into the picture, for corporations were widely distrusted. Like banks, they were suspected of moving money about mysteriously, in ways that baffled honest people.

Hamilton was now outdoing Madison—still acknowledged as the creator of the basic form of government—in shaping the extent of the document's meaning. In this sense, the Constitution we actually live under has characteristics that are more like Hamilton's vision than Madison's. The incorporation of Hamilton's ideas has come to seem quite normal because it has been done consistently. But a swing in the other direction would probably seem equally normal if Madison's preferred way had won. At the time, the pressures on President Washington were beastly, for he saw that there were points on both sides.

Jefferson's worst fears were coming to pass, it seemed. He had wanted to see America's governments "remaining virtuous for many centuries, as long as the people were chiefly agricultural," for he believed that "When they get piled upon one another in large cities, as in Europe, they will become corrupt as in Europe."

Surprisingly, although he was from the opposite party, John Adams felt very much the same way about banks. "I continue to abhor and shall die abhorring . . . every bank by which interest is to be paid or profit of any kind made by the deponent." Both Adams and Jefferson thought it was a sign of depravity that Hamilton had no such feeling.

The difference between these men was that Hamilton had set himself to study everything he could find on the long-lasting financial system of Europe. He knew that distressing excesses could happen, creating frightful public fury. But he had researched each such happening and felt there were always identifiable errors that could be avoided. Compared with the present day, Hamilton's views were very conservative, for he had a great respect for gold and silver, expressing astonishment at how firmly they could underpin the operations of a central bank, which would then distribute reliable capital that would have the total confidence of the nation because it was known to be based on something so rare and valuable.

Also staunchly conservative was his plan to issue paper banknotes that holders could freely exchange for gold or silver coins. Knowing that this paper money, unlike the disastrous and often worthless paper that the states had issued, was backed by metal, citizens would seldom come to demand gold or silver. If they did so and the government showed any hesitation about exchanging, the people would know the government had ceased to be honest and solvent.

The split between Madison and Hamilton was opened wider than ever by the bank issue. Madison, in his new role as a strict constructionist, repeatedly insisted that "it was not possible to discover in the Constitution the power to incorporate a bank." In a sense, he was turning himself inside out just to fight Hamilton, for he had held no such strict views when he was creating the Constitution.

An admirer of Hamilton's, Elias Boudinot, who had been the president of the old congress under the Articles of Confederation, read aloud in the new Congress a passage from the Federalist Paper

No. 44. The authorship of those papers was not generally known, but Hamilton assured Boudinot that Madison had written No. 44. It should have been the most embarrassing slap that Madison had ever suffered, for he had said: "No axiom is more clearly established in law or in reason that wherever the end is required, the means are authorized; where a general power to do a thing is given, every particular power for doing it is included." Madison did not deny having written that statement, but he had no reply beyond a grim insistence that Hamilton was carrying the principle too far.

It was the intensification of a move in Hamilton's favor that had begun with the assumption victory handed to him by Jefferson. Not since the days when he was being accused of cowardice for fleeing from a British raiding party had Jefferson felt so sadly defeated in politics.

He was so disturbed by his failure that there were moments when his judgment seemed affected. When the Virginia governor Henry Lee asked him for an opinion about opening a local bank in Virginia that might act in concert with Hamilton's national bank, Jefferson sent him a ludicrous response, pretending that recognizing the U.S. Congress in such a case would be like recognizing a foreign legislature in an act against the state itself. The state court reviewing such an attempt could find the offenders guilty of high treason. And, said the secretary of state, the officers of such a bank should suffer death accordingly.

Unless that was an unlikely attempt at levity, Jefferson's steady temperament had been dramatically altered.

Madison, too, was shaken by the House's overwhelming passage of the bank bill. And the jolt was much worse than the assumption affair because they had not arranged to make themselves part of the winning vote this time. There had been no dinner-table compromise. They had fought Hamilton all the way and lost all the northern congressmen, with only the southerners voting on Madison's side. This split, as Chief Justice John Marshall later wrote, "led to the complete organization of those distinct and visible parties which have . . . shaken the United States to their center." The fact that such respected persons abhorred the existence of parties puts this basic part of our system of government in an unpleasant light.

The president's dilemma in being asked to cast the first veto in history made him launch a round of requests for comments from his cabinet. But he received relatively feeble responses. Attorney General Randolph wrote him a flimsy opinion, calling the bank unconstitutional. Jefferson wrote a much stronger negative opinion, facing up to the necessary-and-proper clause, but restating the position taken earlier—that this applied only if an action was not merely convenient, but absolutely indispensable. (He did, however, omit the death penalty this time.)

With ten days to sign or veto the bill, President Washington asked Hamilton to give him an opinion on the various negative advices he had received. With his usual thoroughness, Hamilton consulted a leading Philadelphia lawyer at great length, then gave Washington a forty-page discourse boiling down to the argument of implied powers—the right to invoke all means necessary to carry out powers granted by the Constitution. The most powerful form of evidence was in the form of words taken from minutes of the Constitutional Convention itself. Hamilton was able to produce proof of the words he had used at that time, confirming the fact that his liberal interpretation of the necessary-and-proper clause on that occasion had been exactly as he stated it today. Hamilton's show of consistency was powerfully convincing.

Washington studied this paper and decided against sending it to Jefferson. It is not a surprise to find that he signed the bank bill on the day after he received Hamilton's opinion. The historian Clinton Rossiter went so far as to say, "Hamilton's works and words have been more consequential than those of any other American in shaping the Constitution under which we live."

A few months later, Jefferson and Madison were struck by harsh new evidence of Hamilton's strength as an all-conquering opponent. In May 1791 the two friends went on what they called a "harmless botanizing tour" north of New York City and up to Lake George. They were supposedly studying vegetation in the area, and they did have an interest in plant life. But historians have felt that they had a strong political reason for the trip and that they actually encountered a cause for great concern. They found evidence of a Hamiltonian juggernaut in western New England. The overwhelming support

166 DINNER AT MR. JEFFERSON'S

for him may have been decisive in confirming their belief that Hamilton had the potential for achieving a dominant position. And the two friends knew they had handed him an overwhelming victory with their compromise on assumption, after which President Washington had bestowed another great gift in allowing him to have the central bank.

Jefferson had a great wish to retire at the end of 1792. Basically, there was no clear reason to stay, because Washington was not inclined to heed his advice on questionable matters, nor was Jefferson's secretly held hope of a future presidential candidacy gaining any strength from the role he was being asked to play. If anything, his identity was being weakened by being associated with an administration that stood for policies that he deplored. And perhaps the most powerful reason for leaving was that the need to be in such close association with Hamilton was too distasteful to be borne.

But when he told this to the president, Washington said what amounted to, "No, I will not accept your resignation." What he actually said was that he himself wished to retire, but was staying on for the good of the nation—partly because Jefferson had told him he must do it. And he added that Jefferson himself would surely want to do no less. Jefferson agreed, though sadly, to stay on for another year.

The president and vice president were, of course, reelected. And Hamilton went ahead with his intensified campaign of attacking the secretary of state in newspaper articles written under false names.

Jefferson insisted that he would do nothing of that sort in response. A letter he wrote to Edmund Randolph at that time denied that he was engaging in the pamphlet wars, even though he did allow and even encourage a facile newspaperman to do that job for him:

> I have preserved through life a resolution never to write in a public paper without subscribing my name, and to engage openly an adversary who does not let himself be seen, is staking all against nothing. The indecency too of newspaper squabbling between two public ministers, besides my own sense of it, has drawn something like an injunction from another quarter.

This last reference related to the president's request that he refrain from reacting to attacks from Hamilton.

But Jefferson's next move was potentially stronger than a newspaper article. He drafted resolutions for the Republican congressman William B. Giles to introduce in the House on February 27, 1793. The motions called for Hamilton's conduct in office to be heavily censured, charging that he had misappropriated public money, made illegal transfers of funds, borrowed from the Bank of the United States, and refused to cooperate when Congress asked him to supply financial records. Giles stopped short of including a resolution of Jefferson's calling for Hamilton's removal. But in any case, the effect was not great, for the Federalists mounted a strong majority to defeat the resolutions.

Jefferson nonetheless went on discussing with Madison, Giles, and other leading Republicans various proposals that might be made, such as dividing the Treasury or abolishing the national bank. At one point, Jefferson's Republican colleagues thought of trying to destroy Hamilton's whole fiscal structure by trying to pass laws that would have divided the Treasury, attacking the bank and the excise tax, and made it illegal for members of Congress to hold government securities. It was to be a way of "seeing both Houses of Congress cleansed of all persons interested in the bank or public stocks," Jefferson said. But the Republicans were in the minority, so there was no effective action. This has to be considered a fortunate thing, considering the effect attacks on the bank might have had on the attitude of those European lenders who had so recently been one of America's prime considerations.

Moreover, the debate was sidelined by the realization that Britain and France were seriously at war, and that both those governments were pressing America to become their partisan. The Americans "owed it to the French" for having helped them to gain their independence. They "owed it to the British" for being far and away their greatest trading partner.

This context provided the occasion for Edmond Charles Genet, arriving in April 1793, as France's new envoy, to show himself as more an agitator than a diplomat. Among a number of atrocious acts, he secretly hired four American merchant vessels to attack British merchant ships and force them into Charleston. Jefferson, tending to be pro-French, had been trying to cooperate with Genet, but he was badly embarrassed by the man's conduct.

When the usually indecisive Attorney General Randolph aston-ishingly made a real decision that tended to go against the French position, Genet was wild enough to send furious criticisms of the administration to American newspapers and to insist on his right to send French privateers out from American ports. With George Washington out of touch at Mount Vernon, Jefferson was forced to make a fateful decision. Despite his firm friendship for France, he had to take Hamilton's strong anti-French view in deciding that the French-American Treaty of 1778 did not support Genet's conduct. Jefferson essentially declared American neutrality. The president supported this decision and asked that Genet be recalled.

Jefferson's mental distress was so great that he firmly decided to retire. He not only felt like a physical captive, but he was now a mental captive, being denied the right to follow his own policies. No single person had put him into this position; it had simply resulted from a set of ugly circumstances. His anger extended to Genet and even to France itself for actions that had left him no way to follow his original inclinations. The behavior of France had forced him into a series of decisions that appeared to favor Britain and, worse yet, made him seem to be swinging toward Hamilton's policies. He had never felt such an oppressive feeling of failure before.

It would appear that Jefferson had fallen into a state bordering on severe depression that made it hard for him to work effectively. His state of mind is revealed by a terrible lament he wrote to James Madison, probably in June 1793. It said, in part:

> The motion of my blood no longer keeps time with the tumult of the world. It leads me to seek for happiness in the lap and love of my family, in the society of my neighbors, and my books, in the wholesome occupation of my farm and my affairs, in an interest or affection in every bud that opens, in every breath that blows around me. . . . What must be the calculation that balances these against the circumstances of my present existence [as secre-tary of state] worn down with labors from morning to night and day to day, committed singly against a host who are systematically undermining the public liberty and prosperity . . . even the rare hours of relaxation sacrificed to the society of persons . . . of whose hatred I am conscious, even in those moments of conviviality when the heart wishes most to open itself to the effusions of

friendship and confidence . . . giving everything I love in exchange for everything I hate, and all this without a single gratification in possession or prospect, in present enjoyment or future wish.

He was trapped in a job that required him to accept and even act in accordance with the contrary views of others. A clearer statement of utter desolation had seldom been expressed. He could not have known what is so often the case at moments of despair—that a great change in his favor was forming, just months away.

At first, the Bank of the United States looked like another Hamilton success. But that was only for the first few hours on the day the bank opened, July 4, 1791. Then the American public—based on rumors that the bank's shares were going to pay 12 percent dividends—went wild with a buying spree for bank stock and they did not stop for over a month.

The $25 shares soared to more than $300. Hamilton's attempts to set up arrangments that would give southerners equal rights to get in on the buying of shares failed to work out. His worst fears about the South's being denied equal opportunities were about to be realized.

Even people of undoubted intelligence kept buying, praising Hamilton's brilliance, and enjoying the flight of the stock. Hamilton was frightened, quickly recognizing the danger. Like Jefferson, he, too, was trapped in a job that did not allow him to say what he wanted: he was afraid to issue warning words, because the treasury secretary would then be accused of giving guidance to speculators. A few sober observers suggested that this frenzy could not go on forever, but the speculators thought they knew better.

Jefferson was wise enough not to say "I told you so." He contented himself with remarks about the incurable effects of the gaming spirit, about how a tailor who makes thousands in one morning, even if he loses them the next day, can never again be content with the slow and deliberate earnings of his needle.

The bubble kept expanding until, inevitably, it burst in August. The share price fell by two-thirds to the $100 level, then began to move a little more reasonably. Hamilton had managed to find ways of limiting the movements, inventing methods in the midst of the frenzy. But because most people bought after the prices had soared, there had been more losers than winners, and for those who had bought at around $300 the losses were substantial. They were no longer Hamilton's admirers.

Although he managed to contain the financial damage that the nation was suffering from the bursting bubble, the impression that Hamilton's plans could easily go awry was growing. For the most part, Hamilton continued to give the illusion of being in full charge; yet there was an undercurrent in the nation that had begun to question Hamilton's ultimate wisdom and effect on American life. Jefferson, who so often seemed closer to the pulse of the people, strongly argued that the Bank of the United States had "taken possession of a boundless field of power, no longer susceptible of any definition." No one knew what that meant, but it seemed to describe the country's widespread frustration perfectly. It was a muted triumph for Thomas Jefferson—quiet but enduring. And it would not be the last.

16
Before the Fall

As JEFFERSON ONCE SAID, "As politicians, it was impossible for two men to be of more opposite principles." Even after the Dinner-Table Compromise and the illusion of warmth that it had ushered in, the basic enmity between Jeffersonian and Hamiltonian principles was always before both men's eyes.

The two men who had implored George Washington to allow himself to be reelected for a second presidential term made that term of office as beastly as possible for the tired and utterly frustrated old hero. Both behaved in ways that were beyond belief. But in the end, one of them lowered himself to such an extent that he completely rewrote the future.

Both Jefferson and Hamilton would talk about their hatred for factions and dislike of parties. But every move they made had a massive impact in the opposite direction—making party allegiance inevitable and factionalism an ingrown way of life. And at every turn, they and their followers were denying their involvement.

Probably the worst aspect of partisanship—and one that has proved to be sadly enduring—is the utter falseness on both sides. While one side thought mainly about the farmers and the other catered to businessmen and investors, both of them would welcome any voter they could get. Jefferson was not only willing but anxious to accumulate voters who were city dwellers, and Hamilton was just as pleased whenever he could win southerners or farming persons to his side.

171

This obvious hunger for mere numbers continued and has per-sisted because it is what democratic factionalism is all about. It takes numbers to win, and all numbers have the same weight on election day. So, in a sense, all these supremely gifted men had a certain amount of sincerity about dedicating themselves to their adored United States of America, for they truly considered it a glorious new kind of nation, but all the while they tried to ignore the ugly cancer of factionalism that moved democracy's essential engine.

This faced them at every turn virtually every day. Each bit of news from Europe cheered some and saddened others. But the deci-sion to pray for the success of England or France was not a reasoned, intelligent assessment of how that equation would affect America's future. It was the sheer excitement of political combat. And not infrequently, it also involved a petty reason based on some personal memory.

Jefferson, for example, recalled how icily he had been received by British officials when he visited London in 1786. "That nation hates us," he said at the time, and it was his firm opinion forever after, probably based on the memory of half a dozen personal meet-ings. Somewhat more understandable is the fact that many intelli-gent Americans had anti-British thoughts based on experiences in the Revolutionary War. One who had been badly treated or nearly starved as a war prisoner could hardly be expected to ignore that memory in later life. But a cool reception on a short visit—should it really be allowed to paint the picture black?

Hamilton appeared to take a very reasonable view of Britain based on its role as America's principal trading partner. But he had never gone abroad, so one cannot know whether a chilly reception in London would have affected his opinion.

All such personal reactions are normal, and their effects could be absorbed into a country's foreign policy decisions with minimal effort. But they become a malady when membership in a party tells a voter—or worse yet a leader—that everything this party decides to sponsor is to be defended. American insistence on allowing each individual to think, speak, and vote as he or she wishes certainly works to diminish this sickness, but it helps only if individuals are truly free to ignore their party repeatedly, while the exact reverse is what the party stresses to its members. Anyone who consistently opposes even a few of his party's positions risks being quickly treated as an outcast.

What makes this highly relevant to our subject is made clear when we find that Jefferson, after moving to Philadelphia as secretary of state, actually allowed this particular mind-set to prevent him from showing anything like normal civility to George Hammond, who became Britain's envoy in 1791. Hammond reported to his superiors that, "It is his fault that we are at a distance. He prefers writing to conversing." The result was that Hammond nimbly established contact with the treasury secretary. And Hamilton went so far as to makes excuses for Jefferson's manner and to tell Hammond that Jefferson's views were "far from containing a faithful exposition of the sentiments of this government." In other words, "Pay no attention to the secretary of state." Hamilton's remark was, of course, improper but occasioned by the prior impropriety of Jefferson.

If Jefferson had a serious goal of pushing Hamilton out of office, he was all too often maladroit and far short of his usual perceptiveness. He should have noticed almost immediately that Washington did not agree with a single one of the faults that Jefferson ascribed to Hamilton. Jefferson had easy access to the president, of course, which facilitated his attempts to make his points, but how could he not have noticed that he was up against an immovable object in this case? The anti-Hamilton remarks and outright attacks that he launched at Washington served only to irritate and eventually repel the president.

Jefferson seemed not to realize that almost all his complaints sounded to Washington as if he himself were under attack. They were points which, if true, the president should have recognized on his own. Washington was by no means so far over the hill that he failed to see this. So the result was a rapidly building dislike of Jefferson. There was not the slightest sign that the president would consider getting rid of Hamilton. The only reason he did not get rid of Jefferson instead was that he knew no potential substitute who was of equal caliber and therefore acceptable as secretary of state.

The interoffice warfare was greatly enhanced as the two competing national newspapers—almost openly sponsored by the two warring leaders—gained readers and became greater factors in forming political opinions. As routine as the partisan reports in John Fenno's *Gazette of the United States* and Philip Freneau's *National Gazette* appeared, their warmed-over and often erroneous positions occasionally drew blood. Hamilton, who had started the newspaper war, may have been the principal sufferer in the end, because he was a more colorful victim. The potential damage that such attacks can inflict was highlighted by Freneau's charge that Hamilton was known to drink toasts to monarchy at dinner parties. Even more memorable was Freneau's report that when one dinner guest referred to "the American people," Hamilton had slammed his fist on a table and cried out, "Your people, sir—your people is a great beast!" This phrase was endlessly repeated by Jeffersonians, as if this behavior were a nightly performance of Hamilton's.

Throughout the year 1792, this war of words continued, even while the Washington presidency attempted to function and the two highest cabinet officers undoubtedly devoted more thought to this subject than to the real affairs of the nation. The newspaper war kept overheating almost to the point where it became more humorous than serious.

As the pace of attack and response quickened, Washington, while in Mount Vernon, gathered together twenty-one grievances that he pretended to have received from George Mason. This ruse was to avoid saying that they were all from Jefferson, which showed how fearful he was of offending Hamilton. The litany of complaints was that the excise tax was oppressive, the public debt too high, speculation had drained capital and corrupted Congress, and so on. Washington undoubtedly shared with Hamilton the author's assumption (which he considered ridiculous) that these initiatives were "to prepare the way for a change from the present republican form of government to that of a monarch, with the British Constitution as a model."

Hamilton should have seen that it would have been wise to make no counterattack, since he was obviously impregnable as long as he had Washington's trust. But this was the one kind of wisdom he totally lacked. Before replying, Hamilton published a critique of Jefferson in the *Gazette of the United States*. He accused Jefferson of disloyalty for decrying the government and its measures. At the same time, Hamilton sent a fourteen-thousand-word letter to Washington, defending his work at the Treasury department. He talked of his economic feats while in office, how he had brought the interest rate down from 6 percent to 4 percent (this being opposite to rewarding his followers, as Jefferson expected) and brought money into the country to finance both commerce and agriculture.

Washington's reply was a plea to Hamilton for mutual tolerance between him and Jefferson. Washington even talked of fear that the union might dissolve. One wonders, did it strike Washington or either of the two combatants as strange or weird or utterly mad that anyone could be saying this? How could anyone be seriously thinking a nation that had been twenty years in the making, that had defeated the world's greatest empire, and that was being hailed as the great hope of all mankind, might pass out of existence because two men were having a feud and its greatest hero had to watch his words so carefully when he remonstrated with them?

Far from agreeing with Washington, Hamilton's bitterness escalated. He said he could not be as forbearing as Washington asked. In a September 9 letter, Hamilton praised Washington's attempts at reconciliation, but insisted he was the injured party. He flatly and insolently told Washington that he would not accede to his request "for the present."

It was as though the attacks had driven Hamilton almost to insanity. He couldn't seem to contain himself. Letters spewed forth from him. Hamilton sent letters saying that Jefferson had now shown himself in reality as the worst sort of tyrant, as Caesar rejecting the trappings, but tenaciously gripping the substance of imperial domination.

Jefferson did not heed Washington's plea for tolerance either. The chief difference in the behavior of the two antagonists was that Hamilton wrote his own accusations, while Jefferson let others do it for him. James Monroe, for example, prepared a number of letters with specific anti-Hamilton charges, and they were carefully reviewed by Jefferson before being published, so he could not really deny responsibility.

Some of the published attacks on both sides were simply false to the point of charging the other man with acts unrelated to his true behavior. A major article in Jefferson's *National Gazette* charged that Hamilton had a step-by-step program for "changing a limited republican government into an unlimited hereditary one." There had never been a shred of evidence to support this claim. Hamilton's *Gazette of the United States* said Jefferson had hired Freneau "to vilify those to whom the voice of the people has committed the administration of our public affairs." Here Hamilton was on somewhat stronger ground, but he had nothing that could be called proof. Nonetheless, Hamilton asked, stingingly, "Is it possible that Mr. Jefferson, the head of a principal department of the government, can be the patron of a paper, the evident object of which is to decry the government and its measures?"

Sometimes the in-house debate took the form of an argument about the relative merits of England and France, using these two warring nations as proxies for the men who were supposed to be helping President Washington. That Hamilton was pro-British went without saying, and his disgust with the bloody French Revolution seemed to him a point of pride.

But Jefferson kept trying to hold out as a champion of what was happening in France, as if any revolution that displaced the royals and the rich was bound to be a step in the direction of republican government.

Madison was fully involved in this, on Jefferson's side, of course, though he often gave the impression of being a bystander. Owing to his position in the House, he was able to create problems for Hamilton. At one point, for example, he tried to curb the Treasury's power to raise money for a Western expedition that the army planned. If he had succeeded, Hamilton might have felt forced to resign, which was probably Madison's goal. The attempt failed, but it signaled that the game was getting tougher, and some of Madison's attacks gave Hamilton a basis for strong countermeasures. He came out more straightforwardly with responses to the accusation that he aimed to replace democracy with monarchy, making the strongest statement yet to counter the charges that had been leveled against him: "I am affectionately attached to the republican theory," he insisted. "I desire above all things to see the equality of political rights, exclusive of all hereditary distinction, firmly established by a practical demonstration of its being consistent with the order and happiness of society."

This statement is the strongest Hamilton ever made on the subject, and nothing pointing in a contrary direction has ever been substantiated.

In his letters to Washington, Hamilton frequently claimed that he was deeply hurt by the false charges that were made against him, and he was particularly angered by Jefferson's pretense that he had a monopoly on patriotism and virtue.

Throughout the summer of 1792, this game of accusations and denials went on—over and around the stunned head of the president. Washington's inability to control it led Jefferson to make remarks about the great man's condition, seeing him as one who had become close-minded from too much flattery. There was nothing the president could have done, short of dismissing both of the warring men and starting over with new aides. And this Washington felt helpless to do. He had no candidates in mind. His way of finding candidates would have been to ask Hamilton. It seems that even the greatest careers in human history must have a nadir. And for the magnificent Washington, this was the lowest point.

On October 1, 1792, Jefferson met with George Washington at Mount Vernon before breakfast and tried to convince him again that Hamilton headed a monarchist plot. Washington, probably extremely worried that he was somehow about to be stripped of Hamilton's services, which were a vital crutch to him, lost all patience with Jefferson and his fixation about the existence of a plot. He said he supported Hamilton's funding plan because the assumption plan worked. As for transforming the government into a monarchy, Washington said he "didn't believe there were ten men in the country whose opinions were worth any attention at all who entertained such a thought." And as for Jefferson's charge that some legislators owned government debt, he said it "did not bother him in the least because some self-interest was natural in any government."

But no words of Washington's served to appease Jefferson, who would talk and talk, then stop, clearly unconvinced and dissatisfied, but silenced for a short while. Hamilton kept on, almost mindlessly, writing thousands of words of self-vindication to Washington and shorter attacks on Jefferson in his newspaper. The president told both men again, pleadingly, that he feared the nation could dissolve. For such a threat to have been expressed and emphasized to both of them without bringing about the slightest change of attitude on their part is one of the sorriest facts in the history of this period.

That either man could find time for other interests or pursuits during such a war seems hard to believe. Both of the combatants were affected by the feud, but in different ways. They were both grim, unwilling to budge, seeming to forget the respect they owed to George Washington. Jefferson, while he was noticeably distressed by the terrible conditions he had to work in, seemed like a changed man. The grace and elegance that usually marked him were replaced by a hardness that was probably a defense mechanism. These contentious conversations came to seem almost ugly, with none of the smoothness that had always been part of him. He may have been absorbed by the thought that his own presidential possibilities were being eroded by Washington's stubborn adherence to Hamilton's appeal, which was hard for Jefferson to understand.

On the other hand, Hamilton seemed, at times, to be exhilarated by the struggle. His production of anti-Jefferson written matter was even more voluminous than his usually prolific output. But while this, in addition to his regular work, should have left him no time for anything else, he did also find time for interests that he would have done well to avoid.

For unbelievably, when he was so much under attack and had enemies clearly wanting to undo him, Hamilton was allowing a shabby, long-running love affair to intrude grossly in his life and even lowered himself by paying the woman's husband hush money in an attempt to prevent exposure.

17

From Brilliance to Disaster

JEFFERSON'S FEAR THAT HIS Dinner-Table Compromise might lead to more and more power for a dangerous man seemed like a grim premonition. Hamilton appeared destined to have his way with his adopted nation. But that was not how this intriguing play was destined to end.

Hamilton, the extremist, the one who tended to go much too far, would stumble into a series of erratic blunders that cast an eerie new light on his dramatic history. As astonishing as his rise had been from an orphaned childhood on a Caribbean island to the pinnacle of American power, his mistakes grew to be just as startling.

In late 1791, while he was planning a massive new document to be called *Report on Manufactures*, (which will be discussed later in this chapter), Hamilton began falling into a series of misjudgments and outright wrongdoings that tarnished his reputation, threatened his family life, and put a permanent question mark over his place in American history.

The scandal that suddenly enveloped Hamilton could not have failed to provide amusement and pleasure to Jefferson and Madison. With their strong dislike for Hamilton, it would have been false to pretend that they sympathized with his largely self-inflicted woes. They might have been expected to capitalize on his sudden bad publicity. But, in fact, they did almost nothing to take advantage of his blunders or to enlarge the damage. This was probably not any courtesy or forbearance on their part. Quite simply, they would not have known how to increase the damage. Hamilton's mistakes were too stunning to be aggrandized or diminished by any outsider's comments. And Hamilton was making his situation steadily worse entirely on his own.

The many anti-Hamiltonians who had hoped that he would somehow overreach had watched him extend his victory in the assumption fight by going on to create the national bank. In seeing him win on successive major issues, they at least recognized that these victories had prevented the American crisis that could have ruined the country's credit in Europe. But their fear that Hamilton was poised to have long years of success, making him powerful enough to threaten American democracy, was destined to decline and fall without being seriously tested.

The longest-running threat to Hamilton's reputation was the catastrophic fall of his old friend William Duer. The former playboy, who had been so careless as Hamilton's assistant secretary of the Treasury, failed to heed any of his superior's warnings about his personal speculation and rising indebtedness.

Hamilton could not be called blameless in this matter, for Duer had been a poor choice for the job to begin with. Further, Hamilton had warned the terrified risk-taker not to plunge into deeper speculation. When word of his actions spread, it reflected badly on the secretary since it seemed he had given investment advice to his embattled aide. Although it was well meant, this guidance was technically improper from a man in his position.

Hamilton had finally dismissed the failed official, who engaged in an even wilder bout of speculation that plunged him into massive debt and finally thrust him into debtor's prison. He feared for his life for weeks as infuriated investors who had lost heavily clamored outside the jail for the right to come in and attack the prisoner. Hamilton's hard-earned and well-deserved image as a careful official who sought no personal profits suffered from the fact that the reckless Duer was known to have been his friend. In the end, Hamilton behaved correctly by writing Duer consoling letters, but refusing to make any financial moves that might have helped the prisoner. Nonethless, the impression that Hamilton's system of financial governance somehow could cause such excessive speculation and massive losses harmed his image.

Duer would spend seven years in prison before dying, still hoping for some form of help from Hamilton that never came. The treasury secretary was not being cold-blooded; there was simply nothing he could have done to help the unfortunate man. Jefferson tried to convince Washington that the Duer affair was proof of how Hamilton had "dealt out Treasury securities among his friends." It was a false charge, and the president refused to be taken in. Like most of Jefferson's attempts to turn Washington against Hamilton, this one backfired. Washington only grew more tired of Jefferson.

Meanwhile, by 1792, Hamilton had become deeply involved in an ill-fated plan to stimulate manufacturing industries in America. He set up a Society for Establishing Useful Manufactures, or SEUM, which aimed at increasing the nation's development of new engineering and industrial ideas. And it seemed very imaginative because American investors were to be invited to buy shares as a way of investing and hopefully participating in the profitable results.

But apart from success or failure, this venture did not seem to embody the high-minded approach previously seen in Hamilton's projects. A member of his staff, Tench Coxe, had originated the plan by pointing out the great success that England was achieving with new engineering ideas, and he suggested that American observers be sent over to learn to do such things in America.

In plain talk, these observers could be called industrial spies, and the fact that this appealed to Hamilton seemed to be a step backward, away from the high level of performance he had set. Why steal another nation's ideas, especially those of the nation that Hamilton respected most? Why not plan, instead, to encourage more inventiveness here in America? Instead, Hamilton approved the spying plan, prepared a typically careful study called *Report on Manufactures*, and began to lure foremen and other key employees away from British textile mills, some of them bringing British manufacturing secrets and equipment with them. So in addition to spying, Hamilton was stealing men and materials from another country. Then American investors who bought shares in this government-run project would be innocently joining in a somewhat shady operation.

The plan was not entirely without merit. It actually anticipated good policies, such as careful inspection of products before shipment and improved quality, that would advance the reputation of American-made exports. Hamilton had shown some of his characteristic care in gathering new information from a wide variety of American manufacturers, studying the quality of their products, the quantities produced, methods of shipment, and profitability. And because Hamilton foresaw the wisdom of making the nation self-sufficient in military weapons, his *Report on Manufactures* introduced the practical idea of arms factories owned by the government.

The new document did not result in any new legislation as his previous reports had. It was seen by Congress and then set aside because it was considered too great a contribution to federal power. Such power, of course, was just what Hamilton had wanted to promote, and it was almost certainly Madison who arranged the rebuff. But Hamilton did not fight the decision in this case, for he probably recognized that this report was harder to defend than his earlier papers. It covered such a wide array of companies that it inevitably gave a sense of being too generalized and unfocused. And, of course, the fact that Jefferson and the Republicans would interpret any promotion of manufacturing as an attack on the preeminence of agriculture was a drawback from the start. So Hamilton accepted the setback without waging a fight and apparently without any great sense of loss.

Nevertheless, Hamilton actively pursued the companion idea of a profit-making SEUM, and stock in the government-backed venture was offered to the public. Hamilton's plan was appalling to Jefferson and the Republicans, for they had long insisted that America's excess of land and relatively deficient supply of labor were naturally intended to promote farming and to discourage manufacturing. They were poised to make a strong case against Hamilton's latest scheme. But the counterattack never became necessary. Because the offer of shares to the public had come just before a new financial decline in 1792 and also because Duer had been one of its directors (and refused to resign), the hoped-for enthusiasm and readiness to invest did not materialize. There were fewer shareholders than expected and most of them soon backed out with losses. The whole venture stumbled to an early death. The public's impression of Hamilton's projects continued to decline.

It should be noted, however, that even this doomed project contained the seeds of greatness. The *Report on Manufactures* has been called the first great revolt from Adam Smith's *Wealth of Nations*, for it argued in favor of moderate protective duties to give national manufacturing interests an advantage over foreign competitors. But again—although the ideas of the report would later become a respected way of managing a nation's trade policies—it was the opposite of Jefferson's emphasis on promoting agricultural production rather than manufacturing.

While these rather manageable setbacks might have been overcome, it became known that Hamilton had been involved since the summer of 1791 in a sexual affair that would have been enough to send any normal person to bedlam. He had begun a liaison with a very attractive twenty-four-year-old woman named Maria Reynolds. It would go on for many months, sometimes seeming about to end, then gathering new force and stretching over a year, through times when his wife, Eliza, was pregnant, whether she and the children were at home or away, and when Hamilton was deeply involved in official business that should have left no moments for such an adventure. Even after the affair had ended, the echoes and reproaches went on for most of Hamilton's life.

It is surprising that accusations of misconduct had not struck Hamilton sooner, considering the bitterness of the encounters that had marred the presidential office. He was clearly and visibly flirtatious, and being an attractive man, he found it easy to draw the attention of young women. Hamilton's island upbringing and admittedly colorful beginning had been much discussed ever since his entry into American society, so it would not have been surprising if the damaging charge of indecent behavior had surfaced. Instead, people had dwelled on his early misfortunes, on pity for the lowly beginning that he could not be blamed for because it had resulted from the misdeeds of his parents. And even that stain had been largely overcome by his own charm and look of refinement.

Hamilton's sunny disposition was so winning that people were not inclined to couple the racy island stories with the genial man they saw at social affairs. Neither did they attach serious meaning to the tales about a recurring flirtation between him and Angelica Church, Eliza's married sister. Alexander and Angelica were clearly attracted to each other, and they carried on a lively flirtation, including suggestive remarks, at every meeting and in every letter. But that, as far as anyone knew, was always in Eliza's presence, and she showed every sign of being delighted that two such favorites of hers liked each other so much. When the seriously scandalous Reynolds affair nearly overwhelmed Hamilton later, his flirtatious ways with Angelica and several other ladies of his set were naturally recalled; but these were mainly noted as evidence of how much less serious those accusations had been than the atrocious misbehavior that was now coming out.

It happened that Thomas Jefferson had a troublesome record of the same kind. There were much-told tales about Jefferson's purported indiscretions in his youth—especially when it was said that he promised to look after a very good friend's wife while the man was away, and then supposedly made a strong attempt to seduce her. Gossips had harped on this so often that the husband, who had seemed only mildly disturbed at first, later began to talk of demanding satisfaction.

The feather-light attitudes of earlier days are partially explained by the fact that young and personable men and women often made harmlessly flirtatious talk a regular part of their contributions to social gatherings at that time. This innocuous flirtation was another part of America's heritage from English social manners, when dinners often began in the late afternoon and then might go on to include a vocal or piano recital as well as dancing. Those who were not performing were nonetheless expected to add clever or humorous conversation to the gathering. And a touch of coquettish talk, especially among people who knew each other well, was welcomed. So in the case of both these Anglo-American men, the earlier gossip mainly served as a contrast with the seriousness that later made Maria Reynolds and Sally Hemings into historical figures.

After Hamilton's triumph in the field of finance, Jefferson and Madison could not have been sure how far the man's talent might carry him. Now they saw—doubtless with relief—that he, as a person, had taken a new downward path that was destined to end the dazzling and perhaps even monarchical future they had once feared.

Hamilton's risk-taking habit was suddenly recognized. It was now recalled that he had a dangerous tendency to shout out a sudden challenge to any man who seemed to question his honor. Several duels had been narrowly avoided only when friends worked out intricate explanations of just what the exchange of words had meant, proving that no one's honor had been impugned. The knowledge of Hamilton's tendency to pitch into threatening situations made it believable that he might also go impetuously into a sudden lustful relationship without considering the danger. Or perhaps the danger was part of the attraction.

Hamilton's disastrous affair had begun when Maria, a clever and desirable woman, simply came to his door and asked him for help. The beginning was so mindless that it seems impossible for a person of any intelligence to have fallen for it, knowing as he did that he had many enemies who might wish to trick him into an ugly situation. Yet he did exactly that, and some have guessed that he was simply showing the bad heritage he had from a loose-living mother and a ne'er-do-well father. But before adopting such a theory, one must first wonder how this same shabby heritage had given him all his brilliance and hard-working perfectionism. If there is any science of deciphering how human nature is transmitted, it certainly has not helped to read the origin of Alexander Hamilton.

In any case, Hamilton must have been smitten by Maria at first sight, for he told this begging woman at the door that he would come to her home and bring her some money. He did, on the very same evening, and he was not at all surprised to find that she was quite willing, if not eager, to turn this into a night of love. But neither Maria nor Hamilton was willing to let it be a one-night affair. It soon developed into a regular relationship, with Maria writing him lengthy expressions of her deep love, interspersed with plaintive reports of her husband's mistreatment. As if a playwright had written it, this woman just happened to have a flair for colorful expressions, coupled with a lively way of misspelling them and a talent for portraying herself as living at the edge of a precipice. It all added to the theatrical effects that embellished the affair.

At one point, Maria's husband came directly into the picture, and he was not only demanding money in return for the loss of his wife's affection, but also asking Hamilton for a job in the Treasury, since he had been speculating on the financial markets and considered himself well qualified to help run them. Hamilton gave him no job but did give him money on several occasions, thereby exposing himself to enormous danger from a scoundrel who could prove that the secretary was not only philandering but also willing to discuss bribing his way out of his disreputable behavior.

The start-and-stop liaison went on through most of 1792, and then echoes went into 1793. In the end, Reynolds's threats were publicly known and became a more important point than the affair itself, for the public found it easier to believe that Secretary Hamilton was involved in financial wrongdoing than in a foolish affair. The need to counteract this serious suspicion later led to the bizarre situation that caused Hamilton to reassure Congress and later the public that there was no cause for concern, as he had been unfaithful only to his wife and not to the sanctity of the Treasury Department. Most everyone agreed that he really needed to level with the nation on this point, but no one was expecting him to carry the affair so far.

It was unfortunate for Hamilton that Senator James Monroe came to have a part in this affair, and undoubtedly passed his information on to his friends, Jefferson and Madison. For Monroe, who later became a very successful two-term president, and who proclaimed the incredibly durable Monroe Doctrine, felt as genuinely Republican as Jefferson himself, and he had lately taken part in writing anti-Hamilton articles on Jefferson's behalf. So he could not be called an appropriate judge of Hamilton's personal problems. But an accident of congressional assignments put him into that position.

At one critical point in the Maria Reynolds affair, several congressmen visited Hamilton to hear his explanation that her husband's charges of wrongful speculation in government securities were baseless but that the romance with his wife was true. James Monroe was one of the group. It was the time when Hamilton went into such excessive details about his relationship with Maria that the visiting congressmen became embarrassed, and one of them even told Hamilton that he need not tell all of the details. Monroe was allowed to keep a set of papers that made some of the facts clear, and he later admitted that he had left the papers with a friend, who was probably Thomas Jefferson. (In that case, Monroe broke a pledge of confidentiality.) Hamilton's most recent biographer, Ron Chernow, wrote that from that time forward, Hamilton "was shadowed by the awareness that determined enemies had access to defamatory material about his private life. This sword of Damocles, perpetually dangling above his head, may provide one explanation of why he never made a serious bid to succeed Washington as president."

In a bizarre coincidence, when Maria Reynolds decided in 1793 to file for divorce from her husband, the lawyer she chose for her case was Aaron Burr.

Four years later still, in 1797, the old accusations and exaggerations were still reverberating, especially in various forms of yellow journalism, so that Hamilton was maddened to the point of reverting to an old habit—writing at great length to tell his own story. But this was not like the times when he wrote forty or fifty pages on a technical subject to an admiring President Washington. He wrote and published a pamphlet of almost a hundred pages, describing the whole Reynolds affair in greatest detail. As always, he thought his fine words were making a winning impression. In fact, they simply completed the demolition of his reputation.

These almost unbelievable facts of Hamilton's personal behavior are highly relevant to his relationship to Jefferson and Madison, for they tend to show that although the early suspicion of Hamilton may have been baseless, there did prove to be a variety of reasons to regard this man with ever-growing distrust. An adversary who is both dangerous and inconsistent is harder to deal with than one whose threat is at least predictable. And, they must have thought, if he was capable of such duplicity and bad judgment, was there any reason to believe him when he assured the world that he was dedicated to a republican form of government? Such a statement has value only when it comes from a person of at least normal integrity.

Indeed, even the ugly remarks about Hamilton by John Adams, who called him a "bastard boy," and by his wife, Abigail, who wrote that she had "read his heart in his wicked eyes," are shown to have been at least understandable, if not necessarily justifiable.

Adams had long loathed Hamilton, insisting that he was "as debauched as old Franklin, although always pretending to morality." Much as if he was jealous of Hamilton's looks and racy relationships with women, Adams would believe anything unfavorable about the man, throwing words like "fornications" and "adulteries" about before there was the slightest evidence to support them. He even theorized that Hamilton's unusual eloquence was the result of a drug habit, that Hamilton "never wrote or spoke at the bar without a bit of opium in his mouth." Many of these remarks had been looked at askance by serious men and even tended to lower their opinion of the usually reliable Adams. But now Hamilton had given life and substance to almost anything that might be said about him.

It could be imagined that the excitement sometimes aroused by a desirable sex partner can be totally separate from a person's other inclinations and does not prove any overall lack of sound principles. But while this might be true of Hamilton's first impulse to take advantage of the opportunity extended to him by Maria, it does not at all explain the prolonged misbehavior, the outright stupidity of his dealings with her husband, and then the needless revelations in detail of every aspect of the affair. It might have sufficed for him to make a clear statement that he had been guilty of a personal indiscretion but had engaged in no speculation or any dealings that were related to his responsibilities as treasury secretary. But something had impelled him to explain, explain, and explain with the same lengthy completeness that he used in writing his great financial reports.

At every turn, there were resumptions of the relationship with Maria, even after it seemed that he had broken away, and there was off-and-on bargaining with the husband. Hamilton seemed driven to keep the adventure alive, rather than let it end. His determination would appear to signal some kind of secret delight in daring to do the dangerous thing, as if normal risks were insufficiently rewarding. And it raises the possibility that even his overwork and overperformance in all his duties may have been a form of adventure that was as captivating as sex itself.

Far from degrading Hamilton's remarkable contributions to the Revolutionary War, the ratification of the Constitution, and the early period of Washington's presidency, Hamilton's indiscretions should emphasize the innumerable aspects of human life that often have offsetting wonders and sorrows. Who can say whether the risks that are taken by persons who create our great bridges and buildings, artworks, inventions, and inspirations that have made a jungle into a world, are controlled versions of the risk-taking impulses that could make a Hamilton into a fool?

One other surprising fact in the bizarre picture is that George Washington, the steadiest of men, continued to show complete confidence in Alexander Hamilton after the publicity of the Reynolds affair and to place him near the top among America's generals, second only to Washington himself. The country was still enmeshed in the grim internal war known as the Whiskey Rebellion. The mountain people, especially in western Pennsylvania, who refused to pay taxes on their alcoholic products were determined enough to have turned tax evasion into a dangerous military challenge. They insisted that they were being unfairly taxed in a way that hit them much harder than the large distilleries of the East.

In the rebellion, there was an uprising in which several deaths occurred. George Washington wanted to be firm, but Hamilton tried to make it into a real war. He wanted to be ordered to attack. In the end, while the aging president came out of military retirement to head the armed force, he was not well enough for the physical part of the job. It was really the agile Hamilton who took charge of the action. Thus, his old ambition to become a leading general was realized when Washington named him inspector general, that is, his own first subordinate in command of the armed force that would fight the challenging rebellion.

At this point, General Henry Knox, one of the greatest wartime heroes who has already been shown to be Washington's closest friend, would explode. When he found out that Hamilton outranked every other general except Washington himself, Knox pointed out that the president had, in effect, demoted him below Hamilton. "Is that what you meant to do?" Knox demanded indignantly. And Washington told Knox yes, that was just how he meant it to be. Knox, who was accustomed to being called "immortal" for his great Revolutionary War feat of transporting the famous fifty-nine cannons from Fort Ticonderoga to Boston, did not need to keep hearing that he had become a legend—but he was more concerned with his place in the military than his place in history, and he found it almost impossible to swallow the announcement that he had dropped below the status of "Colonel Hamilton," as he often referred to him. Washington's admiration and gratitude to Knox continued to be everlasting. But knowing Washington's feelings did not change the fact that Knox had to see himself outranked by the indispensable Hamilton.

Perhaps the most surprising aspect of Hamilton's appointment was that it came after the man had made himself seem so unreliable in his affair with Maria Reynolds. There is no entirely logical way to explain Washington's unshaken confidence in Hamilton. It is possible that the president's own situation and great dependence on his aide made him ready to swallow any indignity rather than learn to do without the assistance of the man he needed so much. But Washington's judgment was entirely intact. He was still saying things we can revere today, like the currently relevant thought, "The willingness with which future Americans will serve their country in time of peril will be directly proportional to how they perceive that the injured soldiers of today were appreciated by their nation." Rather than abject need, was Washington not likelier to be recognizing his own remembered weaknesses?

The president's breadth of understanding can be sensed from a startling 1795 letter he wrote to his stepdaughter: "Beware of an involuntary passion. In the composition of the human frame there is a great deal of inflammable matter, however dormant it may lie for a time . . . and when the torch is put to it, that which is within you must burst into a blaze."

Searching beyond ordinary logic might also lead to the possibility that the general was remembering a girl named Sally Fairfax, whose spell had once caused him to write about "a thousand tender passages" and "the happiest moments of my life which I have enjoyed in your company." When Sally's furnishings were sold at auction as she and her husband left to live in England, Washington unaccountably bought her bolster and pillows. Perhaps he could not have explained what impelled him to make this mysterious purchase. Did he think, "How then could I condemn Hamilton's irrational moments?" All one can know is that when virtually everyone was ready to deride Hamilton's strange behavior, the most well-organized and tightly disciplined man in America was refusing to alter the inspector general's status in the slightest way.

A less romantic, but meaningful, reason could be given for the president's remarkable steadiness in supporting Hamilton. Washington, like all the Founding Fathers, was the heir of a great liberal British tradition. He was opposed to monarchy but was as dedicated as his ancestors had been to certain standards of behavior among gentlemen, and especially among fellow members of government.

He remembered that Edmund Burke had stood before Parliament, spoken words of support for the Americans who had broken with their king, and lived on without punishment. Other governments would not have tolerated Burke's outspokenness. But even if every man in that chamber had disagreed with Burke, all of them together would not think of stifling him for having an attitude they deplored. And in his respect for the tradition that made this possible, the president was firmly an Englishman. Washington would not have been Washington if he had not cherished a British right to define himself and to act accordingly. He might well have seen Hamilton's recent behavior as a mistake, yet never imagined the possibility of turning against him for actions that he did not choose to judge.

18

The Disappearing Cabinet

IT SEEMED AS THOUGH JEFFERSON had been talking about resignation almost from the begining of his service as secretary of state. Finally, early in George Washington's second term as president, Jefferson did firmly resign. Even then, after Washington had often expressed exasperation over Jefferson's battles with Hamilton and his insistence that Jefferson was misjudging the whole subject, the president still convinced him to stay on beyond the original departure date Jefferson gave him.

When Jefferson finally left the president at the end of 1793, a long, patient wait began for him. Several years later, we find him saying that retirement did not produce all the golden results he had foreseen.

By then, Washington had suffered irritations and furies such as he had never known in his entire career. He was a prematurely aging man, unwell with physical and dental problems that made him permanently uncomfortable. Knowing that he had the respect of the entire world was not enough to make up for the disrespect that he felt in the attitudes of Jefferson and Madison. The possibility that they were right in believing the whole principle of democratic government was at stake in the clash between them and Hamilton never seemed to occur to Washington. But it was not only Washington who had a closed mind in this respect. He, at least, carefully studied what results Hamilton's advice was producing, and what Jefferson's complaints added up to. It is a striking fact that neither Jefferson nor even the scholarly Madison ever seems to have seriously considered the possibility that their adversary might have been right. They felt justified in opposing Hamilton because if he were a secret monarchist and were left to follow his own path, he might have seized power before anyone could have stopped him. But by that standard, almost any active opponent could be denied the right to lead, which would make democracy into government by the mediocre. One wonders whether this kind of flat rejection is an oddity of the political mind, or whether a partly closed mind is a necessary part of generating leadership in any field.

At least a sampling of the true retirement that Jefferson had been longing for did come in the two years that followed his resignation. He wrote a friendly letter to President Washington, saying, in part:

I return to farming with an ardor which I scarcely knew in my youth, and which has got the better entirely of my love of study. Instead of writing ten or twelve letters a day, which I have been in the habit of doing . . . I put off answering my letters now, farmer-like, till a rainy day, and then find them sometimes postponed by other occupations.

At one early point, Jefferson was momentarily startled by a new assignment that Washington tempted him with, asking him to go to Spain to attempt to conclude a very important treaty that would be of great value to the farmers along the Mississippi. It had been dangling for much too long, and the farmers had grown impatient enough to talk about seceding from the union. Jefferson would have been the ideal man to complete the job, but he refused and went on clinging to his freedom. Visitors to Monticello commented on his easy manner and obvious interest in every aspect of farm life, including the excellent nourishment and clothing of his slaves.

Although he pretended to be entirely divorced from politics, he was moved to send angry letters to Madison in August 1794 about the president's attacks on the so-called Democratic Societies that were actively opposing his government's show of force against the Whiskey Rebellion. Mostly in Pennsylvania, the whiskey protesters were actively terrorizing neighbors whenever they complied with the law and paid the government's hated tax. The official whiskey inspector was being besieged by hundreds of rebels, and finally had called for militia help to fight them off. The call for reinforcements was gratifying to Hamilton, who, as the inspector general, was longing for a way to use the small army he had assembled and equipped with the same perfectionism that he had once applied to creating the Treasury Department. It should be noted, however, that Washington was still more commanding on military matters than he was in the presidential office, for he overruled many of the harsh methods that Hamilton wished to use against the protesters.

But on the related subject of the Democratic Societies, Jefferson was sure that Hamilton was behind what he considered Washington's excessive reaction. These societies that held meetings and criticized government policies drew the president's wrath enough to be verbally attacked in his annual message to Congress. Jefferson denounced Washington's targeting of the societies as "an attack on the freedom of discussion, the freedom of writing, printing, and publishing." He even managed to couple the president's "inexcusable aggression" with a blast at the Society of the Cincinnati, the military club (of which Washington was president) composed of former officers in the Revolutionary army who, Jefferson said, were "periodically meeting behind closed doors and corresponding secretly," as if closing doors were shocking behavior. It was a case of both Hamilton and Jefferson going much too far, one in his assessment of the unquestionable crimes that were being committed by the Whiskey Rebels, and the other in his reaction to the excessive response that was being advocated.

The situation was not without peril. Letters to newspapers kept warning that some of the rebels meant to destroy the constitutional government, and there were indications that some of the militia officers who were supposed to prevent disorder were actually encouraging the rebels. Washington delayed sending troops as long as he could, but at last, in September 1794, he ordered a move into western Pennsylvania.

Hamilton's brilliant ability to organize had equipped a larger army than Washington had commanded in the Revolutionary War. He spoke of finding dangerous elements everywhere he turned, while the president was notably as reliable as ever in showing just the right amount of firmness. Hamilton groaned at the times when Washington granted clemency to persons whom he had condemned. But the net effect was astonishing success. There were few deaths. And there was a surge of public approval for the wisdom that had been shown— basically meaning a new demonstration of Washington's impeccable judgment.

Hamilton voluntarily brought his government career to a close in February 1795 in order to return to the practice of law, hoping at last to build substantial wealth for his family's future. He would still be inspector general of the army, but no longer head of the Treasury or a member of Washington's cabinet. But as important as his new venture was, it seemed like a paltry thing compared to the work he had done in the Treasury Department. Although the change had been his own decision, he was now gripped by a strong feeling that his best days were behind him, and that the forces that wanted to crush him were likely to have their way. He was disheartened and beset by depression. For the first time in his life, he found that his law clients were leaving him and seeking other counsel, for they noticed that his other interests were often commanding his attention. They wanted a full-time lawyer, not an inspector general.

Meanwhile, Hamilton grew noticeably closer to George Washington after he retired from government, and the two shared a warmer friendship than they ever had before. Busy as he was with trying to maintain a law practice, Hamilton had nevertheless told Washington to call on him whenever and however he might need him. And Washington needily took full advantage of this. He had no one left on his staff with the brains and ability of either a Hamilton or a Jefferson.

It is inexpressably sad to think of Washington still at work near the end of his presidency with both Jefferson and Hamilton gone. Painful as their joint presence had become, it is a rude affront to our own schoolday memory of the first president to see him without his first chosen heads of departments, the lofty superiority of the presidential office sadly reduced. This office had once accorded with the earliest things each of us learned about Washington, his life, and his founding role. Now, picturing him alone with a few very ordinary and indecisive men—being forced to call others out of retirement when there was serious thinking to be done—one can't help wishing it had ended more appropriately.

And soon after Hamilton's resignation, Washington was in genuine need of the most delicate and farseeing help imaginable, for he had in his desk drawer—and was fearful of letting anyone see—a document that was bound to be hated, one that could create an unwanted war, posing the knottiest problem America had faced since it had won independence. How the president handled it would lead to either war or peace.

This problem resulted from America's long-standing troubles in trying to get along with Great Britain and to be treated as an equal. In some ways, the British treated Americans as if they were still colonials. They had strict rules against U.S. ships visiting certain destinations, limiting places where Americans could legally sell their goods. And they often seized American ships and mistreated the sailors as "escaped Englishmen," thus denying that the colonies had ever stopped being British. America's top negotiator, John Jay, had been in England for months, trying to work out a treaty that aimed to settle the near-war situation that existed between the United States and its old parent country.

Most people in America knew that something of this kind was going on, and they had confidence that the highly reputed Jay would come home with a treaty that would equalize the two nations and put an end to the abuses that American shipping regularly suffered.

Washington's shock when the treaty reached him made him call for Hamilton at once. The president immediately saw what a public commotion it would cause, for this nation had won hardly any points to offset its complaints. Jay had been forced to agree to a treaty whose only merit was that it did not call for outright war. The British had properly concluded that the United States was in no condition to fight a war, so they had given almost no concessions except for agreeing that there should be no war. Jay had correctly understood that he had no real choice: If he refused the treaty, he would condemn his country to face terrible wartime losses. If he accepted it, it would give President Washington a chance to avoid war, but Jay and the president would face the fury of disappointed Americans.

Washington quickly asked Hamilton to study the treaty and tell him the pros and cons as he saw them. Hamilton, as always, returned an in-depth study. The analysis showed what a superior mind this man had. He had faced the hard facts squarely and reduced them to two specific points that he felt should be protested and at least one alteration made. But basically (with his old splendid judgment hard at work) he understood that keeping the nation out of a war it was in no condition to fight was an accomplishment that should not be forsaken.

Hamilton also pointed out how the British had at least modified one way of treating American trade, permitting the United States to sell in places that were off-limits to others, and showed that this could lead to some very profitable trading for American shippers. In sum, he believed in approving the treaty with either one or two alterations, despite the senseless public fury it would arouse.

Washington, full of gratitude, begged him to take over the task of defending the treaty to Congress and the public, and of course Hamilton could not say no, although it brought on a series of public clashes that threatened him personally.

At last, in mid-1795, Congress debated the Jay treaty behind closed doors. There were many who found ten or twelve points that "must be changed" before approving the treaty. But by a narrow margin, the Senate went along with Hamilton's recommendation that only Article 12, putting far too many restrictions on American trade with the British West Indies, must be changed before signing the treaty. Surely, neither country would consider that one point a reason for war. But the basic facts became known, and the public was outraged.

At one moment in the long struggle to reach a conclusion on this potentially explosive subject, furious Americans demonstrated outside Hamilton's home all night long. They heckled him and almost forced him into street fights, perceiving him as a champion of the hated treaty. The idea that a man of Hamilton's standing was being challenged to fight like a common ruffian created a momentary shock. But the agitation died quickly after the painful decision was made. Meanwhile, Hamilton received another letter from Washington that was almost effusive in its gratitude for all he had done.

Hamilton's strong personal dislike of Jefferson was greater than ever. And as he left George Washington on one of his postretirement visits, he is believed to have told Washington a secret suspicion about his rival. It was a clever thought, but less than a half-truth.

Jefferson, Hamilton told Washington, had been carefully planning his way toward the presidency, and one of his trump cards was to be as different from the current president as possible. That was why he had been reluctant to accept the offer to become secretary of state and why he had talked so long about resigning. His contentious discussions with Washington had been part of his path to the presidency, said Hamilton. As he saw it, even Jefferson's constant wish to quit Washington's service stemmed from a desire to avoid carrying out duties for the president that would have weakened his political appeal to factions in his own party, and to make himself seem to be the perfect candidate who could bring peace and stability to the presidency.

And by this account, it is said that Washington later told Hamilton he had always remembered those remarks and had concluded that Hamilton was completely right about Jefferson's motives because "you foretold what has happened with the spirit of prophecy." Ron Chernow's splendid biography of Hamilton gives credence to this story, which was written by Hamilton's son, John C. Hamilton. Chernow writes, "The story's likely veracity is bolstered by the fact that Jefferson exchanged no letters with Washington during the last three and a half years of the general's life." (But it should be pointed out that Jefferson wrote at least one friendly letter to Washington after leaving his service—the one that is reproduced on page 194. It had been written on April 25, 1794, throwing doubt on the story, which may explain why John Hamilton left it out of the biography he wrote of his father's life.)

In fact, Jefferson did not set out to be different from Washington. He had reluctantly agreed to join the government because he hoped to find that Washington shared most of his views. Their ample correspondence over the years had given this impression, but the subjects had never been political, so he could not be sure. As Jefferson grew more suspicious of Hamilton's objectives, he began trying *to make Washington different from Hamilton*, which would have enabled Jefferson to serve Washington and still maintain his conservative views and heavy emphasis on states' rights. When that failed, resignation was the only way he could continue to advocate personal policies that he deemed consistent with democratic government.

It is probable that Jefferson's thoughts about eventually winning the presidency had been with him since his return from France. But there was a curious lack of urgency, as if he had a timepiece running that had set the proper moment some years away. At first he was probably hesitant to become Washington's secretary of state because he was unsure of how that would relate to this larger ambition. And soon after arriving in New York, he must have realized that he had hitched his wagon to a star with ideas that were hopelessly different from his own. After innumerable attempts to overcome this gap, he had apparently decided, though reluctantly, that his ultimate goals required him to separate from Washington, since the latter was clearly wedded to Hamilton's Federalist view, one that Jefferson could never pretend to support. He may even have felt that Washington had no fixed political view, but was neutral enough to blend easily into Hamilton's firm opinions, which amounted to the same thing. If so, Jefferson would never have uttered this thought—except for whispering it to Madison—for only a candidate for the madhouse would have called George Washington a pushover.

Jefferson was wrong to have badgered Washington in hopes of turning him against Hamilton's views. He had acted out of desperation, which was not like him, hoping that any slight success in that direction might change the picture. But since Washington would not be budged from leaning toward Hamilton's federalism, he had to be considered an obstacle to Jefferson's hopes—not just of gaining the presidency, but of subduing the Federalist Party that he regarded as a danger to democracy and to the vision of America that he had always wanted to promote.

One could not be a Federalist's employee and a Republican leader at the same time, so moving away from Washington became a must, though it was vitally important to avoid any appearance of a real break with the president. Being an apparent enemy of George Washington would have been a disastrous political position, and in actuality, it was the farthest thing from Jefferson's mind.

There was no surprise when Washington decided that he must retire after two terms as president. His first move was to ask his former aide to draft a final speech for him, which resulted in Hamilton's usual yeoman job of preparing two complete drafts. But Hamilton also suggested that they might edit the whole thing jointly. And they did, sitting together and working as partners, almost line by line, so that the final version had the smooth perfectionism of the old Hamilton and the perfect taste and restraint of a Washington.

Because Hamilton had been disloyal to John Adams by working against his election in 1796, the new president now excluded him from everything. So Hamilton went from unlimited access to President Washington to no access at all to President Adams. Only because Adams had found it useful to retain some lower-level employees who had links to Hamilton was the former treasury secretary able to say that he knew someone in the president's office.

Hamilton had only a decade to live before his premature end in the duel with Aaron Burr. But the years after Washington's presidency closed found him depressed, knowing that his tremendous influence in government had evaporated for good.

On any occasion when he made a political appearance, Hamilton's performance was still superb, making people long to see him back in office. Some of his courtroom appearances brought forth the ringing vocal abilities that still riveted audiences. In one case, in 1803, his defense of Harry Croswell, an editor charged with seditious libel against President Jefferson, moved every eye in a large courtroom to tears, and the attorney who opposed him called him "the greatest man this country has produced."

But the apparent enthusiasm that Hamilton could project was a pretense. Hardly anything could happen to him now that was a match for what he had left behind. Even this was not the low point in Hamilton's assessment of his own standing, Robert Warshow wrote in his book *The Declaration of Independence*. "When Jefferson became president in 1801, the Federalist sway was over. Hamilton found himself a private citizen in a world he could not tolerate. He could hardly hope for a renewal of power in his lifetime. A pronounced personal depression became evident, mingled with bitterness towards the men and circumstances that had contributed to his dismissal from a strong participation in public affairs."

Hamilton wrote, in an 1807 letter to a friend: "I often dare to think our nation began self-government without the education for it. Like negroes freed after having grown up to man's estate, we are incapable of learning and practicing the great art of taking care of ourselves." This remark was not intended to be racist, for he abhorred slavery. But the thought was strangely applicable to his own life. In saying it, did he ever apply it to his own great failings— being involved with William Duer, being madly involved with Maria Reynolds, overestimating how long his ties to George Washington could prevail against all foes, underestimating the power of Jefferson and Madison to block his plans in the end? He had such an incredible collection of knowledge and skills, but did he realize that he had gone through most of his great career setting up pitfalls for his own future? Where other, and lesser, politicians would at least have arranged political alliances that safeguarded their future, he had concentrated so hard on astonishing achievement that he set up no fallback position for troubled times. Like the unprepared slave, he had been incapable of "learning and practicing the great art of taking care of" himself.

For entirely different reasons, Thomas Jefferson would soon also find himself left out of the presidential circle, though he was not at all discomforted by it.

"Farmer Jefferson's" idyllic life at Monticello had been threatened when the presidential campaign of 1796 showed him, with no effort and not a single move on his part, to be a leading candidate. The magic of his name, creating new support with every wild falsehood about him spread by his enemies, astonished the political world. Jefferson did not expect anything to come of this, and did not seem to feel that it was time for a real push to win, even though his friend Madison had a much more active attitude toward the coming vote.

In fact, the election had turned out to be a close one, but even before the results were known, Jefferson sent John Adams a congratulatory letter. "I knew it impossible that you should lose a vote north of the Delaware," it said, "and even if that of Pennsylvania should be against you in the mass, yet that you would get enough south of that to place your succession out of danger. I have never one single moment expected a different issue; and though I know I shall not be believed, yet it is not the less true that I have never wished it."

This letter had been, in effect, both a concession and a graceful suggestion of how closely the two of them should work together, with Adams as the clear leader. In the end, the Federalist John Adams became president, by winning 71 electoral votes to 68 for the Republican Jefferson. The latter, therefore, was to be vice president.

Even though Jefferson had not felt like leaving Monticello, he was not greatly disturbed, because he thought it was properly Adams's turn to be president, and the two of them had always gotten on well. As he put it, with perfect grace, he was Adams's "junior in life, his junior in Congress, his junior in the diplomatic line, and his junior lately in the civil government." He fully expected and planned to be supportive of Adams, making the fact that they belonged to opposite parties as trifling as possible. But when they dined together two days after the inauguration, his words about close cooperation seemed to confuse his old friend. It became obvious that Adams was embarrassed by the fact that his Federalist government quite naturally had an accumulation of Hamiltonians in his cabinet, making it awkward for the new president and vice president to work together.

So Jefferson was basically free again—a vice president who did not have to be physically present or to simulate impartiality. He could not pretend to be happy about it, for he had not believed that party differences should prevent loyal Americans from working together. He had planned to make at least a few perfunctory visits to Philadelphia, the temporary capital. But now he found a gap that he was not even expected to bridge.

It soon developed that Jefferson had nothing but scorn for some of the new legislation he was glad to stay away from, and especially for the deplorable Alien and Sedition Acts—decreeing "un-American" actions against immigrants and persons who circulated "defamatory materials." Adams had signed these laws against his better judgement because there had been a flurry of such shrill criticism of government that even his intelligent wife, Abigail, had urged him to take this defensive step. But Vice President Jefferson was so horrified by the clearly unconstitutional laws that he spent four solid months at Monticello to avoid having to preside over the Senate when such bills were being considered.

But being sidelined in this way at a time when the political issues had grown so much more intense was not the joy Jefferson hoped for. Four years after he had finally carried out his desire to leave the position of secretary of state, he said that "From 1793 to 1797, I remained closely at home, saw none but those who came there, and at length became very sensible of the ill effect it had on my own mind." He did not rush right back into political life openly at that time, but he was giving a great deal of thought to it, exchanging ideas on strategy with James Madison, who had resigned from Congress because of ill health, but was actively applying his own rare mind to his friend's future.

And, of course, Jefferson's greatest years were yet to come.

First, however, four years of a John Adams presidency loomed— a strange term of office, headed by a man who could be crudely bombastic in talking about fine men and scoundrels alike, who could even deride the recently deceased Benjamin Franklin, a man who seemed simple at times but addicted to pomp and ceremony at others, who was quick to take offense, yet who had a very clear intelligence that often rose to exceed the commonplace thoughts around him.

John Adams, for all his comical looks and ways, had a mind that could be precise and tough on serious subjects. Contrary to what the foolish stands Adams had taken on the matter of presidential titles and protocol would suggest, important issues brought out his great ability to see through distracting details, to focus on key facts, and to stay on course regardless of the excitement or opposition around him.

As Adams moved into the presidency in 1797, he appeared to have inherited a crisis of his own. Both France and England were demanding that the Americans declare themselves to be on their side in the war building between them, and the presidential office, mainly staffed by mediocrities, found itself almost as divided as it had been in the previous administration.

The choice between favoring England or France as they prepared for yet another military confrontation was critically important. Once again, France obviously expected America to be pro-French because she had helped America to win its liberty. England expected to be favored because of its historical ties to America and current close trading partnership. But unlike the earlier years when each of these great powers had worked to win America's favor, now they were headed by truculent leaders who behaved abominably. Americans were demanding safety for their ships, but receiving harsh warnings instead.

Despite these facts, Adams had a stubborn belief that an honorable peace with France could be arranged without infuriating Britain. But every circumstance seemed to work against him. The American people had turned warlike over the treatment of their ships—France had captured three hundred—and the nation was showing a great demand for war. To make things infinitely worse, when Adams risked the anger of Congress and the public to send a three-man delegation to Paris, the destined meeting with Foreign Minister Talleyrand never took place. Talleyrand would not start until he got his $250,000 *douceur*, or "sweetener," and a $10 million loan to the French Republic to compensate for insulting remarks that France accused Adams of having made. This set off the famous XYZ Affair, named for three agents who presented the foreign minister's demands to the startled Americans.

Although the rebuff seemed to be calling the American people to rise to war against these insulting French, Adams was pleasantly surprised to find that the first fury was followed by a wave of patriotic feeling that approved of his stand against rushing into war. It was a rare moment, because the much-maligned public opinion was not being "a great beast," as Hamilton might have expected, but seemed to find its footing and to fall into line with a leader's moderate approach. The history of a nation is sometimes written in such brief paragraphs that are barely audible amid the churning sounds of the ages.

A startling development came when, as the rebuffed American deputation in France sailed for home, it was learned that one member, Elbridge Gerry, had elected to stay behind in Paris. There was general consternation. Was Paris that magical? What could the respected Boston stalwart be thinking? But when the others landed back in America, John Marshall, a member of the delegation, reported that Gerry had stayed behind because Talleyrand had told him that France did not want war with the United States, but would attack if Gerry left. Judging by Talleyrand's actions, the French foreign minister preferred to avoid war but knew that someone a notch higher in the government would order an attack unless the presence of Gerry—who was known to the French as a leading figure—made it appear that negotiations with America were still under way. It had the mark of a typical Talleyrand ruse for getting his own way even if he was outranked or outnumbered. Without paying his "sweetener," America had the benefit of his talent.

Everyone, including Adams's wife, had thought war must be at hand. But when John Marshall, just off the ship, told Adams the welcome news of Gerry's continuing effort, it was clear that a way to avoid war still existed, and Adams's courage in averting it against all opposition is one of the noteworthy presidential feats in our history.

Sadly, Adams would never make history forget his signing of the outrageous Alien and Sedition Acts. They were passed by a Federalist-controlled Congress that was seeking political advantage by muzzling the clamor of dissenting voices and also by ridding the country of alleged enemy aliens with little or no reason. Adams was somewhat ashamed of having let those measures become law. And he later blamed Hamilton (after his death) for having made the mistake by convincing Congress that they were "necessary war measures." But his administration is better reflected by his superb judgment in outlasting the warmongers and almost single-handedly avoiding a needless war.

In some ways, Adams, giving harsh names to people he disliked, saving his worst epithets for his fellow Federalist Hamilton, and denouncing the "turbulence of all factions," seemed almost out of control. Yet, under all this bombast, there was a singular undercurrent of judgment about him. For example, he immediately saw the evil of the killings that the French Revolution produced. At a time when even Jefferson fell into the foolish mistake of blaming Marie Antoinette for the murderous events and then spoke of salutary results for a reborn society, Adams alone refused to see any merit in the French Revolution.

While any number of prominent Americans saw the French Revolution as a breath of fresh air, leading to a great new day, John Adams, as reported in David McCullough's biography, was "ahead of anyone in the government in foreseeing that the French Revolution would lead to chaos, horror, and ultimate tyranny." The will of the majority, if out of hand, could lead to horrible ravages, he believed.

It would soon be learned, he said, that the brutality of a crowd is even worse than that of any individual, and those were the wisest words on the subject.

This call for crowd control, by the way, was a smart precautionary note for an American to sound. Wild behavior has been known to jump from country to country. If American crowds started sounding too enthused about revolutionary killings, there was the danger that demonstrators in New York City or Philadelphia might be tempted to try the Parisian methods. Nothing of the kind occurred, but Adams's timely warning was well taken.

Jefferson, who was Adams's inactive vice president, took an opposite position, called the president's building of new ships a waste of money, and pretended to see no difference between Adams and those who wanted war. But that was because he was already looking beyond Adams, looking to a run for the presidency. His attitude did not have a great effect, but for one short moment he appeared to be giving credence to Hamilton's theory about his tendency to take up a position against whoever was the incumbent president.

19
One Heart and One Mind

IT HAD BEEN A DECADE SINCE the Dinner-Table Compromise had forced Jefferson to hand Alexander Hamilton the assumption victory that might have made him the most powerful man in America for a full lifetime. The theory we have heard that Jefferson spent the rest of his life trying to recover the ground he lost on that day is an exaggeration. But it is certain that whatever was lost at that dinner had been regained.

In the last few years of the eighteenth century, Jefferson had seemed almost uninterested while friends, led by James Madison and James Monroe, had urged him to make a determined run for the presidency. Every time his name was mentioned publicly, masses of people responded. It was clear that he was a charismatic figure, even with no effort on his part. But by November 1799, at long last, we find words on paper to show that he was indeed ready to seek the presidency. He wrote Madison a statement of strategy for the coming election of 1800. It was on a short slip of paper that stated:

Our objects, according to my ideas, should be these:

1. Peace, even with Great Britain.

2. A sincere cultivation of the Union.

3. The disbanding of the army on principles of economy and safety.

4. Protestations against violations of the true principles of our constitution, merely to save them, and prevent precedent and acqui-
escense from being pleaded against them; but nothing to be said or
done which shall look or lead to force, and give any pretext for
keeping up the army. If we find the monarchical party really split
into pure Monocrats and Anglo-monocrats, we should leave to
them alone to manage all those points of difference which they
may choose to take between themselves, only arbitrating between
them by our votes but doing nothing which may hoop them
together.

This was the platform on which the Republicans in 1800,
directly and pointedly, asked for votes for Thomas Jefferson for president. It forbids toying with the Constitution, and proposes letting
the "Monarchical Party" (by which he meant the Federalists) split, if
possible, as it did. It led to a turbulent campaign because there were
four active candidates—all closely matched on the Electoral College
count, although Jefferson had a large lead in popular votes.

The personal attacks on Jefferson became furious. He was
charged with treason, with plans to form a dictatorship, with destroying all property rights, freeing the slaves, and being personally
immoral. He was said to have fathered countless negro children, to
have robbed widows and stolen funds entrusted to him by friends. It
was heartening that this form of publicity appeared to create more
favorable sentiment for him, giving him the large popular vote lead.

Nonethless, the electoral vote count was agonizingly close, with
a widely distrusted Aaron Burr somehow reaching a 73 to 73 tie with
Jefferson, despite being involved with a variety of secession plans
to separate New England from the rest of the nation. The odd situation left the incumbent John Adams with only 65 votes, so he was
considered out of the running, as was General Charles Cotesworth
Pinckney with 64 votes.

The tie had to be settled by Congress, but there, too, the dead-
lock continued, which put Hamilton in the strange position of
endorsing Jefferson in a backhanded fashion. He had written repeatedly to the Delaware congressman James A. Bayard, who had been
casting his single vote for Burr on every ballot. Any change by
Bayard could make Jefferson president. Hamilton's strongest letter

ended by saying that Jefferson was not as bad as Burr. "I admit that Jefferson's policies are tinctured with fanaticism, that he is too much in earnest in his democracy, that he has been a mischievous enemy to the principal measures of our past administration, and that he is a contemptible hypocrite, but it is not true as is alleged that he is an enemy to the power of the Executive." It was strange repayment for the dinner of a decade ago, almost indigestible, but it appears to have played a part in changing Bayard's mind. On the thirty-sixth round, Bayard submitted a blank ballot, giving Jefferson the advantage. As there were other vote changes in that last round, Jefferson suddenly won by an eleven-vote margin. So it is not possible to say that Hamilton's intervention was decisive, but it is pleasant to recall that Hamilton, so late in his spectacular life, ended the political career of the man who would cause his early death and also played a key role in elevating Jefferson to the presidency.

At the inauguration of March 4, 1801, all Jefferson had to do was appear in plain clothes, walking alone from Conrad's boarding house to the Capitol, to make watchers gasp at the thought of what a new day this was. Suddenly, the shopworn elegance of the first two presidencies seemed quaint. Jefferson was his own man, the first modern president. Because of doing it his way, he seemed more truly in charge.

Senator Maclay, who had snickered at the pretentious semiroyal arrangements surrounding the first two presidents, would have put down his cunning pen in respectful silence.

After taking the oath in the crowded Senate chamber, speaking in his soft voice, Jefferson was at last in a position to express the precious thought he had always believed in, but that only a president could say with meaning:

> Let us then, fellow-citizens, unite with one heart and one mind. Let us restore to social intercourse that harmony and affection without which liberty and even life itself are but dreary things. . . . We have called by different names brethren of the same principle. We are all republicans—we are all federalists!

Some have considered that last thought a pleasant sentence empty of any real meaning, but this presumption is untrue. By far the major part of the population could easily have been said to approve the republican system, the state-by-state governments, but also to recognize that more and more major projects could best be created by the nationwide effort of Federalism. They did want states, and they did want a union. They were indeed all Republicans, all Federalists, if only their leaders would let them be—and so are Americans still, it seems. For the tendency of states' rights to dwindle has usually been at least partially balanced by a comeback in the power of individual states. And we are seeing a particularly striking example of this return of state power in the twenty-first century, when states have taken the lead in steps to control global warming and in several other contentious issues. Jefferson was simply saying that, like a great family, Americans can have different approaches to many problems and still work to make most decisions take one another's points of view into account.

Less simplistic is the fact that we go through phases when this effort to find common ground is relatively easy to accomplish and longer phases when it is devilishly hard. And if we are right in imagining that Jefferson had a sort of clock running in his mind that guided him toward choosing his presidential moment, we have to say that it was one great timepiece. For Jefferson took office at the most favorable moment imaginable.

Those troublesome Alien and Sedition Acts did not have to be repealed; the sedition law was set to expire after three years—and its expiration was happily allowed. The "alien" immigration law was relaxed by the Congress after Jefferson asked in an annual message, "Shall oppressed humanity find no asylum on this globe?" Those words still resonate for us today.

The first two presidents, although highly respected, had allowed the people who surrounded them to give a self-important, quasi-monarchical tone to even the simplest occasions. All Jefferson had to do when he entertained was just appear, somewhat underdressed, and tell dinner guests to sit wherever they liked, and though not all approved, they knew they were in modern America.

Jefferson needed a new treasury secretary, and there was Albert Gallatin, a congressman of such brilliance that many said he would certainly have become president if he were a native-born American. He was Swiss, highly accomplished, and ready to attack the new post with almost as much energy as Hamilton, except that in his case, he was reducing the size of the department and lowering costs. His cuts, in turn, enabled Jefferson to please even more people by killing the unpopular excise tax.

Gallatin was also honest enough that when Jefferson asked him to review Hamilton's "financial mess" and report what he found, he announced, "I found the most perfect system ever formed. Any change made in it would injure it. . . . Hamilton made no blunders." He also reported that the Bank of the United States "had been wisely and skillfully managed." And he added, "I think Mr. Jefferson was disappointed."

Jefferson was politician enough, partisan enough, to fill as many offices as possible with Republicans, but he made a conscious effort to retain enough Federalists to prevent unnecessary political resentment. His own cabinet—beyond the inevitable Madison and Gallatin—was made up of highly qualified men from a variety of states—all Republicans, but none famous standouts who would reopen old wounds.

There were politico-religious questions, especially in New England, that had favored the Federalists. But Jefferson cleverly worded a statement calculated to help dissenters who wanted to change religions to be less concerned with parties. "I shall see with sincere satisfaction," wrote Jefferson, "the progress of those sentiments which tend to restore to man all his natural rights." That meant the right to choose, to change, or to avoid any religion.

Glorying in the wonderful power of the presidency, Jefferson quickly released from jail all persons who had been sentenced for violating the Sedition Act. He abolished the old whiskey tax. And he began cutting back the navy, although dealing effectively with the Barbary pirates.

Another laudable move he made was to quickly remember persons who had meant a great deal to the nation at the time of the revolution, but whom the Federalists had turned against because they had become old and inconvenient. He wrote to the forgotten Samuel Adams, the Boston firebrand who had so much to do with the early attempts to make Americans into patriots. Now Jefferson's letter told him that his name would live forever.

Tom Paine was another one—the author whose great works, such as *Common Sense* and *The Rights of Man*, had raised the revolutionary spirit to heights that brought numberless volunteers into the military. He had gone to France after the war and stirred up trouble there with his constant flow of contentious ideas. Most knowledgeable people agreed that American independence would never have been won without him. But many of the nation's greats would now cross the street if they saw him approaching. Paine had been wanting to come home, but he was getting no help from anyone. Jefferson quickly wrote him an admiring letter and sent a warship to France to bring Paine home.

A momentary disappointment came when James Hemings— who, as a free man, had become the well-paid chef of a new employer—decided not to accept Jefferson's offer to make him the White House chef. But a Frenchman named Honoré Julien took the job and was soon living up to the new president's exacting standards. Describing a meal there in 1802, Benjamin Latrobe, a famed British-born architect, said, "The dinner was excellent, cooked rather in the French style, with larded venison. And the knick-knacs after withdrawing the cloths, profuse and numberless."

But not everything facing Jefferson was that simple. There were questions that, in Jefferson's opinion, concerned the life or death of the nation. Topping them all was the riddle of what Napoleon Bonaparte was going to do with Louisiana—occupy and try to turn it into a thriving, growing, even fighting French colony in the West, perhaps? Jefferson had been pondering that question even before the presidential race began, thinking that whoever became president would face a great potential threat to the Atlantic immunity Americans had enjoyed.

This kind of thinking was what he liked most to do with "the greatest man in the world," as he called James Madison, and he was not jesting when he said it.

The time had come for the incomparable team of Jefferson and Madison to move even closer together as president and secretary of state. Sending that message to Madison was one of Jefferson's first moves as president, and it marked a new phase in the greatest political partnership in American history.

Even though Madison had already had an incomparable year in

1787, when he became the Father of the Constitution, and then a brilliant period as floor leader of the first Congress, he now came into the moment when, oddly enough, being in the second position made his role even more memorable.

Madison's principal advantage over almost everyone was his deep knowledge of antiquity. Knowing what had happened in similar situations centuries ago seemed almost always to guide him toward a better feel for what was likely to happen in the modern world. At every point in his life, Madison's long studies and research into the distant past put him far ahead of almost anyone he worked with or against.

In studying materials even older than ancient Rome and Greece, for example, he was searching not for what made some of the ancient cities endure, but what had brought them down. He saw that they were all long gone, so he had no reason to consult them about longevity. But was there a single factor that appeared to be the cause of every state's eventual disappearance? The answer seemed to be corruption of the upper class. And that was why he thought the best chance of permanence, or at least very long durability, was to keep government in the hands of the widest possible base—literally all the people, with no class or property distinctions. (Here he was in disagreement with Jefferson, who believed that some property ownership should be required to qualify as a voter.) And when doubters asked, "But could that possibly work in a very large country? If we should grow to cover the entire continent, for instance?" Madison's answer was that it would be even better, for it is always when a relatively small group takes control that it begins to become corrupt. The larger the country and the voting base, the safer it is from the corrupting tendency of centralized power.

Madison was suffering badly from chronic intestinal ailments when Jefferson's presidential victory in 1801 brought the immediate call for him to become secretary of state. He gladly accepted, but had to work from home for several months. It was well worth the wait, for he was the president's indispensable partner through two memorable terms that totally changed the map of the United States. And it could not have been done without their joint effort.

Madison and Jefferson were an ideal team during Jefferson's

presidency, and especially in the struggle to outwit Napoleon and turn Louisiana from a major threat into America's bonanza.

During those eight years as secretary of state, Madison would always carefully refer to Jefferson as the leading figure, writing letters as though every word was what "The President wishes." But in fact they were doing it all together. And in private moments, there were times when Madison led the discussions.

They also played a repeated game of good cop–bad cop to achieve certain results, notably to convince the French envoy, Louis-André Pichon, that America had tens of thousands of troops ready to repulse the French if they dared to send forces to Louisiana. Often, Madison would receive the very bright, youngish envoy in his office, then Jefferson would have him to dinner the same week. They would seem to have slightly different attitudes in order to lend real-ism to their stories—Madison a bit harsh, Jefferson all charm. But the story was always the same on one point, the troop buildup. There were actually fewer than a thousand men in uniform scattered around the country, and hardly any equipped for battle. But these two spinmeisters talked of ten thousand and more, building up month by month.

Napoleon, having heard warnings from his man in America and foreseeing a great defeat if he tried to take possession of Louisiana, especially after he suffered a huge loss of troops to yellow fever in the Caribbean, decided to accept a modest payment and give up the territory.

"The whole place is nothing to me without New Orleans," he told a minister. "Sell it all." Until almost the last moment, the American negotiators in Paris—Robert Livingston and James Monroe—had no notion that the prize included over one-third of the entire continent, rather than just the New Orleans area. But the result proved to be world-changing. The size of the United States was doubled for a bit less than $16 million.

And when the deal had been agreed upon and only congressional approval was pending, it had been Madison who saved the president from a monumental mistake that could have ruined it all. Jefferson had agonized over the fact that he was making a huge territorial purchase that the Constitution gave him no power to do. As

Alexander Hamilton later gleefully pointed out, Jefferson was making a thundering misuse of the "implied power" that he had so firmly opposed when assumption or banking was the subject. The truth was that Jefferson's several days of deep introspection on this very point had led him to decide that he must first ask for an amendment to the Constitution in order to legalize the purchase.

He was saved from doing this only by James Madison's sudden flash of anger, when he warned Jefferson in words to this effect: "You will be throwing away this opportunity of the ages. Bonaparte is not a man who will wait months or years for his money." Jefferson, chastened, had to agree. Hamilton must have realized that it was no ordinary case of turning away from one's principle. It was a clear one-time situation that presented no danger to the Constitution because it could never be repeated. To have thrown away the opportunity would have been totally irresponsible, as Hamilton very well knew.

Madison's role at every turn in the Jefferson presidency was as overwhelming as it was securely hidden. His willingness to apparently remain in Jefferson's shadow was just one part of their great equation. But the otherworldly perfection of the Jefferson-Madison partnership was best described by John Quincy Adams, who called it "a phenomenon, like the invisible and mysterious movements of the magnet in the physical world."

Before the Louisiana Purchase was made, most New Englanders and many other easterners tended to oppose any moves toward the West. Because Britain, France, and Spain all owned land west of the Mississippi, many Americans thought we would be creating a potential war situation if we moved into those areas, and they wanted no part of it.

But from the moment the deal with Napoleon was announced, there was a surge of national joy. The most determined New Englanders who had originally opposed westward expansion were calling the Mississippi "our river." Jefferson was lionized, and both houses of Congress—all parties included—joined in giving a dinner in his honor.

James Madison's brilliance when he was Jefferson's secretary of state makes it appear that his skill as a team player was greater than his ability to head the nation. When Madison had two presidential terms of his own, they would be blemished by a war (of 1812) that he was forced into politically by great orators in Congress who espoused the idea and fanned the people to virtually demand war. He saw the ragtag American military effort collapse, allowing the British to occupy his capital and set fire to parts of it. But even when he was forced to escape and exist in nearby woods for a short time, he survived the experience more gallantly than the military men around him, defying his fragile looks and constant physical complaints.

Although Madison endured some withering written attacks on his presidential decisions, he had the good fortune to be associated in the public's mind with the brilliant Battle of New Orleans, in which Andrew Jackson scored the most decisive numbers in military history—2,700 British casualties to 13 American ones—producing the real end of the American Revolution. Only then did Great Britain stop planning ways to get "its colonies" back. So Madison left office as a relatively successful president, and survived into his eighties.

Hamilton left his wife, Eliza, with very little money and six children to educate. With the help of Gouverneur Morris, who urged others to join him in raising a secret fund for her, Eliza gave them all fine educations, and she lived to be ninety-seven, still loyally talking of her Alexander's greatness. She also was still being invited to White House dinners, adored by people who had not even been born when she became a widow. Whoever was the current first lady always gave Mrs. Hamilton her chair. Eliza also had a memorable presidential visit, when ex-president James Monroe came to her door. Because she held him responsible for spreading what she insisted were falsehoods about her husband (in the Maria Reynolds affair), she would not ask him to sit down, rebuffed his suggestion that they should let the lapse of time heal all the wounds, and stood her ground until he bowed and walked out.

As for Jefferson, whatever he may have thought as age depressed him, he continued to express absolute faith in the people. Much as he had written to David Humphreys, a former military aide, in 1789, "Whenever our affairs go absolutely wrong, the good sense of the people will . . . set them to rights," he was still insisting to another aide, William Short, in 1820, "Public opinion is the lord of the universe." And near the end, in 1826, he was even more combative in writing to yet another friend, Nathaniel Macon, "Manfully maintain our good old principle of cherishing and fortifying the rights and authorities of the people in opposition to those who fear them, who wish to take all power from them and to transfer all to Washington."

Jefferson held firmly to his spendthrift ways, making it no surprise that he would actually have ended life as a bankrupt, except that lenders did not take action against him because of his great name. Although he had been a meticulous manager of the nation's money, it was almost a part of his charm that he seemed to consider it beneath him to put restrictions on his way of life. His property and slaves all had to be sold after his death, leaving almost nothing to his heirs. In the last years of his life, he even had to change the wine orders he sent to France, buying slightly lower grades. That, presumably, was his idea of thrift.

20

The Jefferson Factor

WHAT WAS IT THAT MADE JEFFERSON gather so much support without seeming to work as hard for it as most other leaders had to do?

Why is his name, even today, a magnet that draws our attention?

Say "Madison" softly in a crowded room, and only a few heads will move.

Say "Jefferson" and nearly everyone turns to ask, "What about Jefferson?"

Why? They were the closest of partners. Many of one man's ideas really originated with the other. What makes one of them so alive today?

Hardly anyone has ever been regarded as somebody special for so long a time as Jefferson has been. The idea that one can be long dead and still be special is rather intriguing. His renown began when he was a boy, asking for books well beyond what others his age were studying, showing eager excitement as he attacked each new one. It continued when he went to the College of William and Mary at age seventeen and soon joined two of his most intellectual professors at dinners, holding his own in discussions of Europe's Enlightenment that few Virginians had even heard of. And his sense of enterprise made him special when he had just come of age and worked to clear the nearby Rivanna River, making it a practical waterway. It continued when, at age twenty-five, he shocked the smug House of Burgesses with startling proposals on property inheritance—and some were actually adopted.

He was special when he kept buying an outrageous number of new books being published overseas and then spent hours soaking up the wisdom. Many such people are demeaningly called bookworms. Not Jefferson. His reading seemed adventurous. And he converted much of it to new activities that affected others.

Just to converse with him was golden. The marquis de Chastellux, accustomed to talking with great men, came by chance to Monticello and went away saying, "Several days talking of art, literature, and natural history in his company disappeared like minutes."

Jefferson became a center of activity in Paris when he went to replace the great Benjamin Franklin as America's representative in France. That the young United States was able to send first Franklin and then Thomas Jefferson as its envoys to Paris filled the advanced world with wonder. It made the French think all of America must be filled with exceptional people. These two men seemed to validate their nation. When the French translation of the Declaration of Independence reached France in August 1776, it electrified Paris. A nation who had never had a written charter was stunned to know that the Declaration had come from a young nation surrounded by forests and natives.

And when Jefferson came back from five dazzling years there, Washington had already thought of him in choosing America's first secretary of state.

How could a man who appealed so strongly to French intellectuals of that day come home after five years and still be remembered excitedly by Kentucky backwoodsmen who thought him their greatest protector?

Jefferson had, perhaps, an inner warmth that is not common to most political leaders. For even as much as he had grown to hate Hamilton, something impelled him, in a private letter to Madison, to admit in this unusually warm tone: "Hamilton is really a colossus to the anti-republican party. . . . We have only middling performances to oppose to him. . . . In truth, when he comes forward, there is nobody but yourself who can meet him." (Here, he complimented two persons in one line.)

Without being a full-time professional philosopher, for he had too much else on his mind, Jefferson had a love of pure thought that became almost tangible when one talked with him. His mind was a birthplace of ideas. And although he talked softly, seldom seeming to insist on any point, a listener usually had the feeling that he had heard something out of the ordinary. When he talked of Bacon, Newton, and Locke, one had the impression that he knew these men, that he was talking of friends. He was a lover of learning for its own sake. His friend Madison was almost unequaled in his knowledge of the past, which could also mean his respect for the value of what other ages have thought. Jefferson had no peer in his love of pure thought, his interest in the wonders that a human mind can achieve, with emphasis on the present. And he did not hesitate to add his own thoughts to those of the great thinkers he studied.

Even when he deliberately violated the law, it was done with a flair. During the clamor over the Alien and Sedition Acts, when Vice President Jefferson retreated to Monticello for months to avoid presiding over the Senate while these laws were considered, he went farther and illegally proposed a resolution for the state of Kentucky to override the bad laws. This action was, in itself, a punishable offense against the wrongful legislation. At the same time, Madison, although a congressional leader, proposed a similar resolution for Virginia. Both men were violating the Constitution that Madison had created. Under no circumstances can a state decide to reverse or ignore a federal law. Only the Supreme Court could contemplate such an act. Nobody in the world knew this as well as these two did. Their actions were principled, meant to show their sense of outrage, but technically illegal, and could have resulted in jail terms, for they could not have pleaded ignorance of the law. Fortunately, these illicit protests were lost in the turbulence of the time.

If Jefferson's subtle ambition to become president caused him to behave unkindly during some of his attempts to change George Washington's position, his behavior was less than most men have resorted to in the quest for that office. Above all, the fact that he did become president was decisive, for he went on to give the nation its majestic continentwide expanse.

If Jefferson himself were asked to explain what made him so memorable, he would surely not wish to answer. But it is amusing to note that on one occasion, he turned away such a question by using

Jefferson supervised work at Monticello every time he broke free from political
duties, as a retired secretary of state, as a virtually unemployed vice president,
and finally as a retired president. An unknown artist imagined this typical scene
in 1930.

a small writing trick that forces the reader to reach his or her own
conclusions.

Having been asked—after leaving the presidency and retiring
from politics—what services he had rendered to the nation and the
world, he wrote a strange list that leaves us shaking our heads. But
you will find a method at work here. Jefferson has intentionally created surprise, forcing us to correct some of this composition for him.
Note how he emphasizes some accomplishments that seem minor
and glosses over or skips some of his best-known contributions. He is
not in the least indicating the true weight he gave to each accomplishment. He is quite clearly using a device to catch our attention
and make us take part. Knowing that we the readers will judge the
proper weight to be given to some items that he passes over rapidly,
he makes us doubly impressed to find that we seem to know his
greatness better than he knew it himself.

The following words are his:

I have sometimes asked myself whether my country is the better for my having lived at all? I do not know that it is. I have been the instrument of doing the following things, but they would have been done by others; some perhaps a little better.

The Rivanna [a small river near his boyhood home] had never been used for navigation. Scarcely an empty canoe had ever passed down it. Soon after I came of age, I examined its obstructions, set on foot a subscription for removing them, got an act of Assembly passed and the thing effected, so as to be used completely and fully for carrying down all our produce.

The Declaration of Independence.

I proposed the demolition of the Church Establishment and the Freedom of Religion. It could only be done by degrees. [Jefferson enumerates the steps, then very properly gives credit to James Madison for getting a law passed on this subject in 1785.]

The Act putting an end to Entails. [Laws that complicate inheritances of real property.]

The Act concerning citizens and the natural right of man to expatriate himself, at will. [That is, everyone's right to change citizenship.]

The Act changing the course of Descents and giving the inheritance to all the children equally.

The Act for Apportioning Crimes and Punishments [which included Jefferson's extensive study of solitary confinement as a substitute for the death penalty].

In 1789 and 1790, I had a great number of olive plants of the best kind sent from Marseilles to Charleston, for South Carolina and Georgia. They were planted and are flourishing, and though not yet multiplied, they will be the germ of that cultivation in those states.

In 1790, I got a cask of heavy upland rice from the river Denbigh, in Africa, which I sent to Charleston in hopes it might supersede the culture of the wet rice which renders Ga. & S. Car. so pestilential through the summer. . . . It has spread in the upper parts of Ga., and is highly prized. Perhaps it may answer in Tenn. & KY.

The greatest service which can be rendered to any country is to add a useful plant to its culture; especially a bread grain; next in value to bread is oil.

Jefferson also mentioned his "Act for the General Diffusion of Knowledge," though not knowing if it would be carried into effect. This act would eventually lead to universal public education. He said it was read by the legislature with great enthusiasm, and a small effort was made in 1796 to establish public schools.

Notice that he made no mention of the Louisiana Purchase—doubling the nation's size. Nor of the Northwest Ordinance, which helped to populate the Midwest. Nor of his arranging for the Lewis and Clark Expedition that opened the continent to this nation. Nor of the Dinner-Table Compromise that saved the nation's unity and its financial standing.

Those four unmentioned accomplishments, and the ludicrously underplayed Declaration of Independence, now become the loudest sounds on the page, don't they?

But Jefferson was also teaching us something else, more significant than the writing trick: what sort of things give a real leader satisfaction, such as making a river available for practical use, changing laws that can simplify or enrich the lives of many persons, and, best of all, adding useful plants like bread grains and oils. These are things that can affect thousands and even millions of people over centuries to come.

Whatever the subject, Jefferson always seemed to find a method for getting the job done. And so we might say in ringing tones that whatever methods Jefferson used to reach the presidency, the results were well worth the cost. Without him, it is far from certain that America would have grown as it did. And bear in mind that without the Dinner-Table Compromise, America might have broken into several parts or, worse yet, might have dwindled into a decline because the inflow of European money would have stopped.

Jefferson's inaugural address included extreme statements that left people puzzled, for he seemed to speak of a day when Americans would plant their feet on every inch of this continent—at a time when most of the continent was owned by foreign powers. Yet such thoughts were on their way to becoming a reality during his presidency. In part, this was because he began laying plans for the Lewis and Clark Expedition almost at once.

If the methods for bringing about such vast events sometimes escape our understanding, we can only marvel and hope the spirit that drove them is being born in many new Americans today. More than simply the territorial aspects of a great America was the determination to give her people an endless appetite for genuine self-improvement. How much more special can anyone be?

John Adams called it "a glittering generality of Jefferson's that all men are created equal," and he seemed to be questioning it when he added that there would never be a nation whose individuals were all equal. Adams is right, of course, but Adams knew, as we know, that this glitter of Jefferson's has brightened the world. And we know, too, that this generality of human equality is based on an essential truth, for the sameness of most people far exceeds their differences.

It has been said that the men who created the American government were trying to adjust politics to human nature. Jefferson and those who shared his dream occasionally found reasons to be petty, but never strayed for long from the conviction that they were privileged participants in a "bold, sublime experiment to live together in a society founded on liberty, equality, and justice." If Jefferson deserves to be remembered because he was different from most people, it was because he believed this passionately and lived with it as an everyday reality. Could it be done? Can his "bold, sublime experiment" still succeed? It was left to a Frenchman, the vicomte Honoré Gabriel de Mirabeau, to remind us of a thought we should revive regularly: "The human race puts this great question to the United States of America, and if by chance they should answer badly, it would be necessary to ask it again."

APPENDIX A
Recipes from Monticello's Kitchen

(With special thanks to Daniel P. Jordan, president of the Thomas Jefferson Foundation, Beth L. Cheuk, coordinator, and Damon Lee Fowler, editor of *Dining at Monticello: In Good Taste and Abundance*, published in 2005 by the University of North Carolina Press.)

Dining at Monticello, a beautiful book, contains dozens of recipes that were saved by Jefferson's wife, daughter, and granddaughters. In a few cases, Thomas Jefferson himself is known to have written recipes, even though he almost never went into the kitchen. But he did keep a "garden book" with careful notations about food that was prepared for his table, and his comments tell of his great interest in vegetables—even greater than his interest in meats. He found it exciting to follow the progress of peas, lettuce, and other products of his own farm as they matured and came indoors.

Fowler points out that the African presence was an important influence in Jefferson's kitchen. He mentions products such as okra, black-eyed peas, and red peas, as well as eggplants and sesame seeds, which came by way of Africa: "In Virginia cuisine, this African influence was a caress, creating a remarkably successful and sophisticated cuisine that reflected many influences."

Fowler also stresses the compelling fact that Jefferson had a truly elevated taste in food, with an interest in what was really fine, rather than what was complicated or impressive: "One might say that he appreciated the elegance of simplicity, a quality that characterizes

the finest French cuisine, especially that of the eighteenth century."
He might have made a great show at dessert time, creating a sensation, but he knew the difference between a stunt and real elegance.

Here are a few recipes that were favored and frequently used at
Monticello, chosen because they require only materials that are
easily available today. These recipes could be combined to make up
an entire meal.

Monticello Muffins

The cooks at Monticello probably used an iron griddle, but a coated
aluminum griddle will work well. Note that the griddle should not be
greased.

Makes about 16 muffins

¼ teaspoon active dry yeast, or ½ ounce compressed fresh yeast

2 cups water, at room temperature

4 cups unbleached all-purpose flour, including
    ¼ cup whole-wheat pastry flour

1 rounded teaspoon salt

Rice or corn flour, or fine wheat cornmeal, as needed

Unsalted butter for serving

1. Dissolve yeast in water in a small bowl and let it proof for 10
   minutes. Whisk or stir together the flour and salt in large bowl.
   Make a well in the center and pour in the yeasted water, gradually stirring the flour into it. Aggressively stir the dough until it
   is cohesive and smooth. (It will be almost too stiff to stir, but
   too slack to knead by hand.) Cover with plastic wrap, or
   double-folded damp towel, and set aside to rise until almost
   doubled, about 3 hours. The dough can also be covered with
   plastic wrap and allowed to rise overnight in refrigerator.

2. Lightly dust a work surface with rice or corn flour or cornmeal.
   If dough has been refrigerated, let stand for several minutes

until warmed almost to room temperature. Beat the dough down with a wooden spoon, and sprinkle the top with a little corn flour or meal. With lightly floured hands, scoop up small handfuls of dough, shaping each one into a round, flat disk, about ½ inch thick and 2½ inches in diameter. Put them on the flour-dusted surface spaced at least 1 inch apart, and let them rest for 15 to 30 minutes.

3. Heat a griddle or wide shallow skillet over medium-low heat. With a spatula, transfer as many muffins as will fit to the griddle, with at least one inch around them. Cook slowly until the bottoms are lightly browned, about 8 to 10 minutes. Turn, lightly pressing with the spatula, and cook until uniformly browned and set, but still moist at the centers, about 8 minutes longer. Serve hot with butter.

Beef Soup Monticello

Jefferson's granddaughters subsequently copied his technique for the broth in this soup, based on the classic French practice that he explained in his "Observations on Soups." At Monticello, this soup would have been cooked in the stew holes, in either a lined copper or iron soup kettle, after the drawing of the broth was begun on an open fire. Today's Monticello experts say a heavy-bottomed soup kettle of lined copper or stainless steel is an appropriate substitute for a modern cook.

Serves 8

2 tablespoons unsalted butter

3 pounds beef shanks, boned, rinsed, and marrow removed

Salt

Whole black pepper in a pepper mill

2 large sprigs each fresh parsley and thyme, tied in a bundle with twine

1 large white onion, peeled and chopped (about 2 cups)

12 cups water

3 large carrots, peeled and diced (about 2 cups)

2 medium turnips, peeled and diced (about 1½ cups)

2 medium parsnips, peeled and diced (about 1½ cups)

1 small green cabbage, cored and thinly sliced into 1-inch strips

3 large ribs celery, peeled and diced

2 cups toasted croutons (Butter and grill-toast them in a skillet over over medium heat, turning them, until golden brown. Put them in the bottom of a warm tureen or divide them among warm bowls.)

1. Melt the butter in large heavy-bottomed soup pot over medium-low heat. Add the shank meat, season with salt and several grindings of pepper, and toss in the herb bundle. Strew the onion over the top, cover, and reduce heat to the lowest possible setting, cooking at a bare simmer until the juices are fully extracted and reduced almost to a glaze, about 2 hours.

2. Pour in the water, increase the heat to medium, and bring the broth to a simmer, skimming any scum as it rises. Add the carrots, turnips, parsnips, and cabbage, let the broth come back to a simmer, and reduce the heat to medium low. Cook at a bare simmer, again skimming any scum as it rises, until the meat and vegetables are very tender, about 2 hours, or until the broth is reduced by about one-third, adding the celery after 1½ hours.

3. Remove and discard the herbs, remove the meat, and let it cool enough to handle. Cut it into bite-size pieces, cover, and refrigerate until just before finishing the soup. Let the broth cool and skim away the fat (or chill the soup until the fat hardens, about 4 hours or overnight. Lift the fat off the top and discard it.)

4. Put the meat back in the soup, bring to a simmer over medium heat, and simmer for about 5 minutes. Remove the meat and arrange it over the croutons in a warm soup tureen. Ladle the soup over the top.

Stuffed Cabbage

This recipe is one Jefferson copied out himself. And it was a great favorite, partly because the cabbages of the Monticello gardens were beautiful to begin with. When Jefferson thought (mistakenly) that he was leaving politics in 1792, his way of telling his daughter Martha the news was to write, "The next year we will sow our cabbages to-gether." This dish was originally entitled "A Cabbage Pudding," because when cooked whole and wrapped in a cloth, it resembled the puddings of the day. The experts suggest that although the beef was originally finely chopped by hand, readers may substitute ground beef if they choose. Today's home cooks may substitute a heavy-bottomed stewing pan or Dutch oven for the tin-lined copper or iron pot that was used on the stew stove in Jefferson's time.

Serves 4 to 6

1 large green cabbage (about 2 pounds)

8 ounces very lean beef sirloin, finely chopped (or ground)

8 ounces beef suet, finely chopped

1 small white onion, peeled and minced

1 tablespoon chopped fresh parsley

1 tablespoon chopped fresh herbs, such as thyme, marjoram, summer savory, or 2 teaspoons crumbled dried herbs

¼ cup dry bread crumbs

3 large egg yolks, lightly beaten

Salt

Whole black pepper in a pepper mill

2 tablespoons unsalted butter

1. Bring a large pot of water to a boil. Remove the outer green leaves of the cabbage, saving several if they are unblemished, and wash well under cold water. Slip the cabbage and any reserved outer leaves into the pot. Return it to a boil, and cook until the outer leaves soften and can be pulled back easily, about 15 minutes.

2. Lift the cabbage out of the water and drain in a colander, leaving the water in the pot. Carefully pull back two or three rows of leaves, but leave them attached to the stem. Cut a large cross through the center, going all the way to the stem, but taking care not to puncture any of the outer leaves. Bend back the outer layers of the center and cut out the rest of it, leaving the outer leaves attached at the base.

3. Finely chop the center portion of the cabbage and toss in a large bowl with the beef, suet, and onion. Stir in the herbs, bread crumbs, and egg yolks and season liberally with salt and several grindings of pepper.

4. Spread a 14-inch-square piece of double-folded cheesecloth flat and place the cabbage in the center. Gently pull back the leaves and pack the stuffing into the center, being careful not to break the outer leaves. Fold the leaves back over the stuffing and wrap any reserved leaves around it so that the cabbage appears whole. Fold the cloth over the cabbage, wrap it with twine, and knot it securely.

5. Bring the cooking liquid back to a boil. Carefully lower the cabbage into it, return to a boil, and lower the heat to a gentle simmer. Simmer until the filling is fully cooked and the cabbage is tender, about 2 hours.

6. Lift the cabbage from the pot, draining well, and remove the cloth. Transfer it to a warm serving platter and rub it with butter. Serve whole, cutting it into individual wedges at the table.

Salad Dressing

Salads were of the greatest interest to Jefferson and his family, partly because they had such fine supplies from their own garden. And not surprisingly, Jefferson favored imported olive oil and vinegar "brought to the table in handsome cruet sets to create the classic French vinaigrette."

Serves 6

2 tablespoons wine vinegar or tarragon wine vinegar

Salt

Whole black pepper in a pepper mill

6 to 8 tablespoons extra virgin olive oil

6 cups mixed salad greens, such as seasonal lettuce, spinach, endive, radicchio, and cress

Fresh herbs, such as sweet basil, marjoram, mint, and summer savory

6 small scallions, trimmed

1. Put the vinegar, a small pinch of salt, and several generous grindings of pepper in a salad bowl and beat with a fork until the salt is dissolved.

2. Gradually beat in about 6 tablespoons of olive oil, a little at a time, in a steady thin stream, beating constantly until emulsified. Taste and adjust the salt, pepper, and oil as needed.

3. Add the greens and herbs to the dressing and toss lightly to coat. Taste and adjust the seasonings again, toss and arrange the scallions around the edges of the bowl.

Anne Cary Randolph's Elegant Peas

This granddaughter of Jefferson's, who lived at Monticello while he was president, kept a very clear account book. Among the preparations that she recorded was this way of lifting peas to a lovely level of elegance. The peas were special to begin with, for neighbors engaged in a friendly competition to see who could bring the first fine English pea to the table. There is a traditional belief that Jefferson once harvested the first pea of the late spring but kept it a secret in order to avoid spoiling the record of a neighbor who was regarded as the undisputed champion. It's an unlikely story, but it matches the classic tone of this simple dish.

Serves 4 to 6

1 pound freshly shelled green peas

2 tablespoons unsalted butter

2 teaspoons all-purpose flour

1½ cups chicken broth or water

1 small white onion, peeled and studded with
   3 whole cloves

Salt

2 teaspoons sugar

2 large egg yolks

2 tablespoons water

1. Rinse and drain the peas and put them in a medium saucepan. Add the butter and cook over medium heat, shaking the pan gently until the butter is melted. Cook, shaking the pan frequently, until the peas are bright green. Sprinkle in the flour and shake the pan or stir until it is incorporated and smooth.

2. Stir in enough broth or water to completely cover the peas and bring to a simmer. Add the onion and return to a simmer, stirring occasionally, until the peas are tender, about 20 minutes. Taste and add salt as needed.

3. Remove and discard the onion, stir in the sugar, and return to a simmer. Whisk together the egg yolks and water in a small bowl until smooth. Gradually beat a few spoonfuls of the hot broth into the egg yolks. Slowly add the yolk mixture to the peas, stirring constantly, and heat until the sauce begins to thicken, about 30 seconds. Immediately pour the peas into a warm bowl and serve at once.

Jefferson's Vanilla Ice Cream

Damon Lee Fowler has been careful to explain that Jefferson did not introduce ice cream to Americans, as he has often been credited with doing. But he was one of ice cream's greatest early promoters, and the imaginative ways he served it—whether vanilla or chocolate or even peach flavors—made his desserts unfailingly exciting.

Here is the recipe for his famous vanilla ice cream, which he often enclosed in a warm pastry, creating surprise and excitement. But anyone who takes the trouble to use an ice-cream machine can come close to duplicating Jefferson's wonderful texture and flavor, with or without a dazzling presentation.

Makes about 2½ quarts

2 quarts heavy cream

1 vanilla bean

6 large egg yolks

1 cup sugar

1. Bring the cream and vanilla bean to a simmer in a heavy-bottomed saucepan over medium-low heat, stirring frequently until fragrant, about 5 minutes. Whisk the egg yolks in a bowl until smooth and whisk in the sugar. The mixture will be quite thick.

2. Slowly beat about 1 cup of the hot cream into the egg yolks and gradually stir this egg mixture into the hot cream. Cook, stirring constantly, until lightly thickened, enough to coat the back of the spoon, about 5 minutes. Strain the custard through a double layer of cheesecloth or a fine strainer, and remove the vanilla bean. Stir until slightly cooled. Cover and refrigerate until chilled, at least 1 hour or overnight.

3. Freeze the custard in an ice-cream machine according to the manufacturer's directions until set but still a little soft. Scoop the ice cream into a 3-quart mold, or several smaller molds,

running a spatula through the ice cream and tapping the mold firmly to remove any air bubbles. Fill the molds completely. Cover and freeze until set, about 2 to 4 hours.

4. To serve the molded ice cream, dip the mold briefly in hot water, or wrap briefly in a towel that has been heated in a clothes dryer. Run a knife around the top edge to separate the ice cream slightly from the mold. Invert the mold over a serving dish and gently lift it from the ice cream.

Alexander Hamilton's Letter to New Coast Guard Officers

Treasury Department,
June 4th, 1791

Sir:

As you are speedily to enter upon the duties of your station it becomes proper briefly to point them out to you. Accordingly I send you a copy of the Act under which you have been appointed, and which are contained your powers and the objects to which you are to attend, and I shall add such observations as appears to me requisite to guide you in fulfilling the intent of that act.

It may be observed generally that it will be in a partial manner, the province of the Revenue Cutter to guard Revenue laws from all infractions, or breaches, either upon the coasts or within the bays, or upon the rivers and other waters of the United States, previous to the anchoring of vessels within the harbors for which they are respectively destined.

Hence, it will be necessary for you from time to time to ply along the coasts in the neighborhood of your station, and to traverse the different parts of the waters which it comprehends. To fix yourself constantly or even generally at one position, would in a great measure defeat the purpose of the establishment. It would confine your vigilance to a particular spot, and allow full scope to fraudulent practices, everywhere else.

The 63d section of the Act herewith transmitted, declared that the officers of the Revenue Cutters are to be deemed officers of the Customs, and enumerates certain powers with which they are to be invested. The 30th section treating of the same powers, that of demanding manifests and that of searching vessels, enters into some details concerning them. These sections require particular attention as marking the outline of authority and duty, but in the capacity of officers of the Customs you will possess some other powers, and be bound to perform some other duties which are not mentioned in those sections. You will have a right for examination, and it will be your duty to seize vessels and goods in the cases in which they are liable to seizure for breaches of the Revenue laws, when they come under your notice, but all the power you can exercise will be found in some provisions of the law and it must be a rule with you to exercise none with which you are not clearly invested. In every case of doubt you will follow the advice of the officer to whom you will be referred in a separate letter. On points of importance which admit of delay you may correspond with the Secretary of the Treasury.

The 9th, 10th, 11th, and 12th sections which relate to manifests will also require your particular attention. The clear observance of the provisions of these sections is considered as of material consequences to the Secretary of the Treasury, and ample time having been allowed for them to be generally known and compiled with, it is now indispensable that they should be strictly enforced.

You will perceive that they are only required in respect to vessels belonging wholly or in part to a citizen or citizens, inhabitant or inhabitants of the United States. It is understood that by inhabitant is intended any person residing in the United States, whether citizen or foreign. The reason of the limitation is that citizens and resident foreigners are supposed to be acquainted with the laws of the country; but that foreign citizens residing in foreign countries, have not the same knowledge, and consequently ought not to be subjected to penalties in regard to a thing which they might not know to be necessary.

But since you cannot be presumed to know beforehand what vessels are owned in whole or in part by citizens or inhabitants, it will, of course, be your duty to demand the manifests of all indiscriminately, and to report those from which you do not receive them, to the Collector of the District for which they are bound, and you will at the end of every month (pursuing the division of the year by the calendar) send me an abstract of your records.

Careful attention is likewise due to the 13th and 14th sections of the Act. It is of importance that vessels should not break bulk, or put out any part of their cargo even temporarily, previous to a regular entry and permission obtained, except in cases of real necessity, to be duly reported and proved. You will observe that besides the penalties on the masters and mates of the vessels from on board of which any goods shall have been illegally removed, the master or commander of the vessel or boat into which they may be received, and all persons aiding in the removal, are liable to a forfeiture of treble the value of the goods removed, and the vessel or boat into which they may be received is also subject to forfeiture. It is well known that one of the most extensive cases of illicit trade is that which is here intended to be guarded against—that of unlading goods before the arrival of a vessel into port, in coasters and other small vessels, which convey them clandestinely to land. Hence, the bare removal of goods from one vessel to another is made penal, though they may not have been landed. Nor will the pretext of their being intended to be replaced avail anything. The provisions of these sections admonish you to keep a careful eye upon the motions of coasting vessels, without, however, interrupting or embarrassing them unless where some strong ground of suspicion requires that they should be visited and examined.

The execution of the 15th section of the Act essentially depends on the Revenue Cutters. It is easy to see that it would be dangerous to the revenue for vessels to be permitted to go at pleasure from one part of the United States to another without announcing themselves to some proper officer. Hence, though each may proceed on her voyage from a more exterior to a more interior district to which she may be bound—yet none can go back from a more interior to more exterior Districts, or from one part of the United States to another without first reporting himself to the Collector of the District, in order that he may come under the notice and precautions of the law. Nor can this be deemed a hardship; seeing her report will not oblige her to unlade any part of her cargo, but she may afterwards proceed with it wheresoever she pleases.

I have now noticed to you the principal parts of the law which immediately relate to the execution of your duty. It will, however, be incumbent upon you to make yourself acquainted with all the revenue laws, which concern foreign commerce, or the coasting trade—a knowledge of the whole spirit and tendency of which cannot but be a useful guide to you in your particular sphere. You will observe that the law contemplates the officers of cutters in certain cases remaining on board of vessels, until they arrive at their places of destination; and with a view to this it is that so many officers have been assigned to each cutter. It is not, however, expected that this will be done in every case, and it must be left to the discretion of the commanding officer when it shall be done—when there is a vessel, the lading of which is of very great value, or which has any considerable quantity of goods on deck, or in other situations from which they can readily be removed; or where the nature of the cargo is such as to admit more easily a clandestine landing, or from the highness of the duties to afford a more than ordinary temptation, or where a vessel is bound to a very interior district up long bays or rivers, or when any suspicious circumstances appear; in these and the like cases, it will be well to let an officer accompany the vessel to her place of destination. The want of a manifest will be a circumstance in favor of so doing. It will not, however, be advisable to make known the circumstances under which it is deemed most peculiarly proper to use these precautions; as it might sometimes unnecessarily give offense. It may be always left to be understood, that it is the practice whenever the state of the cutter renders it convenient. You are empowered, amongst other things, to affix seals on packages found in certain situations. For this purpose, proper seals will be prepared and transmitted. Till they are required, any other may be made use of. The principal design of this provision is to identify the packages found in such situations.

It will be expected that a regular journal be kept in each cutter, in the same manner, as far as circumstances are applicable, as is practiced in sea voyages, and that all occurrences, relative to the execution of the laws, and to the conduct of all vessels which come under their notice, be summarily noticed therein, and that a copy of this journal to the end of each month be regularly forwarded to the Treasury.

It has also occurred that the cutters may be rendered an instrument of useful information, concerning the coast, inlets, bays and rivers of the United States, and it will be particularly acceptable if the officers improve the opportunities they have (as far as shall be consistent with the duties they are to perform) in making such observations and experiments in respect to the objects, as may be useful in the interests of navigation, reporting the result, from time to time to the Treasury.

While I recommend in the strongest terms to the respective officers, activity, vigilance and firmness, I feel no less solicitude, that their deportment may be marked with prudence, moderation and good temper. Upon these last qualities, not less that the former, must depend the success, usefulness and consequently continuance of the establishment in which they are included. They cannot be insensible that there are some prepossessions against it, that the charge with which they are intrusted [sic] is a delicate one, and that it is easy by mismanagement, to produce serious and extensive clamour, disgust and alarm.

They will always keep in mind that their countrymen are freemen, and, as such, are impatient of everything that bears the least mark of a domineering spirit. They will, therefore, refrain, with the most guarded circumspection, from whatever has the semblance of haughtiness, rudeness, or insult. If obstacles occur, they will remember that they are under the particular protection of the laws and that they can meet with nothing disagreeable in the execution of their duty which these will not severely reprehend. This reflection, and a regard to the good of the service, will prevent, at all times a spirit of irritation or resentment. They will endeavor to overcome difficulties, if any are experienced, by a cool and temperate perseverance in their duty—by address and moderation, rather than by vehemence or violence. The former style of conduct will recommend them to the particular approbation of the President of the United States, while the reverse of it—even a single instance of outrage or intemperate or improper treatment of any person with whom they have anything to do, in the course of their duty, will meet with his pointed displeasure, and will be attended with correspondent consequences.

The foregoing observations are not dictated by any doubt of the prudence of any of those to whom they are addressed. These have been selected with so careful an attention to character, as to afford the strongest assurance, that their conduct will be that of good officers and good citizens. But, in an affair so delicate and important, it has been judged most advisable to listen to the suggestions of caution rather than of confidence, and to put all concerned on their guard against those sallies to which even good and prudent men are occasionally subject. It is not doubted that the instructions will be received as it ought to be, and will have its due effect. And that all may be apprized [sic] of what is expected you will communicate this part of your orders, particularly, to all your officers, and you will inculcate upon your men a correspondent disposition.

The 5th section of the Act, requires that all officers appointed pursuant to this Act, should take a certain oath therein specified. The Act of the 1st of June, 1789, requires that you should also take the oath to support the Constitution of the United States. These oaths, each of your officers must take before some Judge of the United States, if access can conveniently be had to one. If not, before some other magistrate, duly empowered to administer oaths, and a certificate from him, of the taking of it, must be transmitted to the Comptroller of the Treasury.

I am sir, your obedient servant,

ALEXANDER HAMILTON,
Secretary of the Treasury

Notes

Chapter 1. Before the Clash

Jefferson's return from five years in France has been described by such a multiplicity of books that it might seem unnecessary to seek more facts. Yet the rich pile of sources contains conflicts that have added to the doubts, especially about precisely when Jefferson first heard the news that President Washington wanted him to be secretary of state and how he reacted. By comparing bits from Henry Randall's 1857 *Life of Thomas Jefferson*, Princeton University Press's massive *Papers of Thomas Jefferson*, Merrill Peterson's *Thomas Jefferson and the New Nation*, and two personal letters, it has been possible to verify that President Washington wanted Jefferson enough to send him three letters at different locations and that Jefferson was wary enough to voice the fear that "this job might end disagreeably."

Several books in the bibliography spell out facts about Jefferson's daughter's approaching marriage, which delayed his move to New York, and the added financial burden that his wedding gift would create.

Chapter 2. An Old Friend's Bombshell

A deceptively small book, *Thomas Jefferson*, by Stuart Gerry Brown, written for the Great American Thinkers Series, is replete with important insights, among which are remarks that the dying Benjamin Franklin made to Jefferson. One is the revelation of a secret that might have prevented the American Revolution.

Hamilton's foreign affairs activities before the real secretary of state even arrives are, in themselves, evidence of the treasury secretary's intrusiveness.

Olivier Bernier's *The World in 1800* makes it very clear that Hamilton was not only prepared to dabble in foreign policy matters, but also thought George Washington's government "lacked sufficient power to rule the United States properly."

Unusually pregnant facts that affected Jefferson's actions are touched on in Jack Larkins's useful book, *The Reshaping of Everyday Life*, published in 1988 by Harper and Row, for the very high percentage of farmers that constituted America's population and the change that was soon to take place in road travel were basic indicators of the looming future.

David McCullough's fine biography of John Adams gives us a further confirmation of the poor impression made by the first vice president when he wanted Washington to adopt exaggerated titles to exalt his presidency. And most important of all is the confirmation in several books listed in the bibliography that the president and Hamilton soon formed a relationship that would ultimately force Jefferson to leave Washington's cabinet.

For the time being, however, Jefferson's enormous spending on household arrangements, even when the cost was all out of keeping with the short stay in New York, is featured in almost every book on this period, but Fawn Brodie's *Thomas Jefferson: An Intimate Story* is especially thorough on this subject.

Chapter 3. The Mounting Anger

Concentrating on Hamilton's early years, his incredible ability to learn on his own, and the speed of his rise in America are all facilitated by the splendid insights that Chernow's biography has given us. Having these facts so clearly presented might be expected to diminish their effectiveness, but instead, they add to the astonishment that any person could accomplish so much. The comparison with Napoleon Bonaparte's ability to function with so little sleep is an obvious one, and it is not at all an exaggeration.

It is Hamilton's refined attention to detail that makes any reading of his works nearly incredible. As he created a new arm of military service that came to be the U.S. Coast Guard, we read long and meticulous instructions that make us think, "This man must be trying to make his works last forever." And then we soon begin to see that this is virtually true. The details that he preached to the early American customs inspectors seem to warrant such a conclusion. We read his detailed letter of instructions (reproduced in appendix B on page 239), and learn that it is, indeed, must reading for the Coast Guard officers of today. And what's more, the Coast Guard seems to be our most esteemed branch of the service. In this and many other ways, Hamilton still lives.

Chapter 4. The Radical Conservative

The series of books written by Dumas Malone, who was the most complete analyst of Jeffersoniana, helped to provide many of the facts that show the young Jefferson growing into the mature but excessively anxious secretary of state. By now, his awareness that it had been a mistake to join Washington's staff was vivid, but the realization that a hasty change was unthinkable gave him a feeling of imprisonment.

Being reunited with Madison is seen to have been a stabilizing factor; but the pair of friends—both in powerful positions—sensed that Hamilton's power over President Washington could allow him to vault over them in his drive for control.

And Robert Rutland's massive *Papers of James Madison* makes it possible to see how Madison was able to inject a much-needed positive note to alleviate Jefferson's seriously depressed condition.

Chapter 5. Aggressive Lobbying

The author's own book *Young Patriots* was useful in analyzing how state loyalties were still playing a major role in prompting certain states to confront neighboring ones on the right to cross with imported products. The substantial charges that were leveled in some cases hampered or prevented certain transactions entirely.

Sparks's *Life and Works of Gouverneur Morris*, volume 3, was particularly helpful in enabling us to see Hamilton in a balanced way through the eyes of this eminently stable friend.

Papers of Thomas Jefferson, issued by Princeton University Press beginning in 1950, were important in many cases, one of which was in showing Jefferson's astonishment at the number of Americans in New York City who appeared to be longing for the former royal rule. This percentage was confirmed by Lorenzo Sabine, the leader of a large group of American loyalists. Sabine claimed that his people were a majority in New York State.

Chapter 6. Thoughts of Breaking Up

The intensification of tension between Jefferson and Washington reached nearly unthinkable new force, as the secretary of state repeatedly told the president that he and Madison had thoughts of resigning because Hamilton wanted to run the government alone. This tension is covered in several of the older books listed in the bibliography, but it is emphasized even more strongly in Chernow's book on Hamilton. The almost unbelievable fact that Washington said, "You appear to feel that I am either too old or too stupid to judge these things for myself" is surely one of the saddest things we have heard about what the great Washington had to bear.

Even in Russell Blaine Nye's *Cultural Life of the New Nation*, there are several indications that few persons of that day shared the feeling of Jefferson and Madison that Americans might perfect themselves to a remarkable degree. Washington, Adams, and nearly all other leading Americans thought, "Men are men, and not angels." The degree of self-improvement that Jefferson talked about seemed mind-boggling to most others.

Chapter 7. Jefferson's Awakening

This chapter takes up the time when Jefferson and Madison went on what they called a "harmless botanizing tour" to the north. While they did look at floral beauty, they were also taking political soundings. Every source consulted shows that they were shocked to realize what great strength Hamilton appeared to have everywhere they went.

Worse yet, this grim news combined with Jefferson's sudden realization that European lenders might be on the point of concluding that the United States was about to break apart, perhaps into three or four separate nations. At any moment, they might cut off all new lending to America, and even ask for repayment of existing loans. This danger has been a rather muted note in most American histories, but we have firm evidence—especially in comments to James Monroe in 1790—that Jefferson did see the United States facing disaster if their loan sources in Europe dried up.

This frightening thought was softened for obvious reasons, but books— notably *The American Sphinx*, by Joseph Ellis, and *The Works of Thomas Jefferson*, edited by Paul Leicester Ford—and notes to his friend Monroe show that Jefferson referred to it as "the ultimate catastrophe." This fear made Jefferson decide that he must back Hamilton's plan for assumption. From that point on, Jefferson, Madison, Monroe, and a few other intimates made it their first priority to arrange a deal with Hamilton—letting him have his assumption plan, but hopefully in the form of a compromise that would force him to give up something in return.

Chapter 8. A Country without a Capital

Because the proposed compromise with Hamilton was likely to ask the latter to accept the Potomac River area as a permanent national capital, this chapter takes a look at the proposed area—its ancient Native American roots and even a clumsy poem in a George Washington University book that theorizes that Eurasians and Phoenicians teamed to become its earliest pioneers. In fact, we know that Native American tribes did inhabit the area, but their numbers were decimated before Jefferson's day.

Sheehan's *The Making of American History* shows that Jefferson arranged numerous deals that deprived the Native Americans of their land, believing that this was justified as a way to make land available to white Americans.

The Chernow biography of Hamilton helps to show Jefferson's key role in arranging the compromise solution, for he outlined it unmistakably in a note to friends just prior to the event.

Chapter 9. Doubters and Believers

Two persons featured in this chapter are General Henry Knox, one of Washington's closest friends, and the Pennsylvania senator William Maclay, who served only two years, but whose keen insights illuminate the actions of many others. These are neatly described and dramatized in the Chernow and McCullough biographies mentioned earlier, and even further clarified in *The Journal of William Maclay* (New York: F. Ungar Publishing Company, 1965).

Maclay's completely honest reporting is a clear contribution to history, despite the fact that he was admittedly biased, a conservative who has been called "the first Jeffersonian." Even though he was often tart in his comments about Hamilton, for example, the facts he relates are entirely accurate. And although he was opposed to Washington's largely Federalist views, his respect for the president leads him to report very honestly on Washington's courtesy to him.

Henry Knox presents us with another profile in courage and honesty. There was a vast difference between his jovial reports as he traveled about the country and his sudden, sharp wake-up calls to George Washington whenever he found something seriously wrong. Although there were some (Senator Maclay being one) who questioned why we needed a secretary of war when there was no war in sight, Knox, as a trusted correspondent who kept Washington precisely informed on affairs that could seriously threaten the nation, was invaluable.

Chapter 10. Nearing a Decision on the Capital

Stuart Gerry Brown's biography of Jefferson again takes up a point that few others have troubled to cover—the effort to give America a viable currency of its own. Under the old Articles of Confederation, the nation's currency was in a chaotic condition. A few states had circulated coins and nearly all had issued paper notes. But although the old Congress was authorized to coin money and regulate currency, it had no metal to coin and no credit to back up its paper. Robert Morris had proposed a system, but Jefferson considered it too complicated for general use, and he proposed an approach based on the decimal system that went on to establish itself under the Constitution. It was even respected internationally and was published in Paris.

Chapter 11. That Day on the Street

Most of the books about Jefferson that appear in the bibliography or have been otherwise cited contain parts of what is presented here—Jefferson's personal account of the meeting on the street with Hamilton. It describes Hamilton as being excessively agitated and even somewhat disheveled, and it tells of the excited conversation that led to the invitation for dinner on the following day. Some of this may be an exaggeration by Jefferson. But we know from other sources that Hamilton's followers were, indeed, sunk in gloom over the looming failure of their hopes for assumption.

Chapter 12. Dinner at Secretary Jefferson's

The food selections at the famous dinner were based, in part, on the book *Dining at Monticello* by Damon Lee Fowler, and on a personal luncheon that was given at Monticello for the author by Daniel Jordan, the president of Monticello. Several of his leading staff members were present to contribute ideas on the probable flow of events at Jefferson's dinner for Hamilton and Madison.

Fowler has said, "I am left with the impression that Jefferson actually had very simple tastes in food. He could be more excited by the first new peas of spring than by the most elaborate dish. He was, in other words, a true connoisseur."

In addition, a book called *Thomas Jefferson on Wine* by John Hailman was used in determining which wines were probably served at the crucial dinner. And a book called *Domestic Life of Thomas Jefferson by His Great-Granddaughter, Sarah Randolph* was also consulted for her comments on the dinner proceedings, although some inaccuracies in the book have been noted.

Chapter 13. The Philadelphia Story

All of the sources consulted agree that Hamilton seemed highly elated as it became clear that his chief objective was being achieved. He still faced the job of making sure that Pennsylvania would agree to accept Philadelphia's ten-year period as a temporary capital with no subplots that might endanger the Potomac area's clear right to the permanent role. But he seemed so confident that Senator Maclay wrote of his having a "boyish manner" at the subsequent dinner that was held with the Pennsylvanians.

Several virtually unknown books about Georgetown's old houses and its unusually stable black population (*Georgetown Houses* and *Black Georgetown*, both published with the help of George Washington University) give an intimate view of the rare old city that has since been totally absorbed by the nation's capital.

And in telling about a visit that President Washington made to the emerging capital city, the author recalls an incident in his own biography of Benjamin Banneker. If the president could have looked into the future, he would have known that Banneker's work on the city of Washington was trivial in comparison with his astronomical insight that many of the stars would prove to be encircled by "extrasolar planets."

Chapter 14. Doubts Settled, Doubts Revived

A rare dispute between two academic experts about the truth of the Dinner-Table Compromise dominated many pages of the *William & Mary Quarterly* in two successive issues. The author of this book chooses to disbelieve Professor Cooke's view that no real compromise took place. There was a discussion about certain financial aspects of the assumption dispute, Cooke believed, but no compromise dealing with the choice of a capital city. The author, having studied the contentions of both Cooke and Bowling, and having discussed the subject in person with Professor Bowling, is convinced that the latter is correct. The author is further inclined to credit Thomas Jefferson with more truthfulness on the subject than some other commentators have done.

The one aspect of this matter on which the author faults Jefferson is his insistence that he was duped. Jefferson's extreme agitation at the danger that America might, at any moment, find itself denied further credit by foreign lenders makes it absolutely clear that he had mastered that aspect of the subject, even if he was not clear on all parts of Hamilton's plan. It is virtually certain that Jefferson's repeated mention of an "ultimate catastrophe" was based on a clear understanding of what was at stake.

Further, it has to be noted that Jefferson did not make this deal alone. James Madison, whom he trusted implicitly, understood the issue perfectly. He had been against Hamilton's plan for political reasons and because he thought his own state, Virginia, was being unfairly treated. He was not the least bit duped, nor could Jefferson have been.

Chapter 15. Hamilton the Unstoppable?

Up to this point, Hamilton appeared to be unbeatable. While Jefferson's vision of a nation dedicated mainly to the farming life appeared to lose ground, most of Hamilton's new proposals—which were anathema to Jefferson's Republicans—won the necessary backing to move forward. Just before the year 1790 ended, Hamilton's demand for a central bank brought on another great congressional clash. And the House gave the Federalists a shocking victory—39 to 20—meaning that Madison's opposition had won only southern votes, while the rest of the nation stood firmly with Hamilton.

It was the worst division of this kind that had ever been recorded—almost like a clear call to split the country. James Smith's *The Republic of Letters: Correspondence of Jefferson and Madison* is especially useful in its coverage of this stark situation.

Because this reversal was soon followed by the dramatic problems with France's Edmund Charles Genet, the secretary of state was forced to order Genet's eviction from the country. Jefferson was plunged into despair at the thought that he was now being forced to take an anti-French stand, which reversed his normal position. In cooperation with the Virginia congressman William B. Giles, he drafted resolutions opposing many of Hamilton's moves, hoping to dislodge the latter from office. But since the treasury secretary had a clear majority in Congress, this attempt failed.

The Bank of the United States seemed, at first, to be another Hamilton triumph, as its stock quickly soared from $100 to $200 and then to $300. But that was excessive, and the tumble back to $100 created many losers. The result was a feeling that Hamilton's ideas were somehow unsafe, raising questions that had not existed before.

Chapter 16. Before the Fall

Two full years after he had joined Washington's staff and soon begun to suspect Hamilton, Jefferson was taking every opportunity to convince Washington of Hamilton's corruption, attempts to lure citizens into financial gambling, and preparations for a change to monarchical government. Here again, the Chernow biography of Hamilton is the most complete source of such charges. Jefferson even warned Washington that Hamilton's father-in-law had advocated hereditary government at a recent dinner. Madison was entirely in agreement with Jefferson's suspicions and felt it his duty to block Hamilton whenever possible. The establishment of two competing newspapers that specialized in such attacks raised the number and level of accusations. And Washington's pleas to both sides to abstain from these attacks had no effect.

Chapter 17. From Brilliance to Disaster

But a weird new factor had entered the fray. Hamilton, with everything seeming to be in his favor, had involved himself in a foolish affair with a young woman who had simply come to his door asking for money. When he promised to bring some to her home, he got the reception he hoped for and began a relationship that even caused him to bribe the woman's husband, and later to make confessions to congressional investigators. As the tale dragged on for months and brought suspicion of dishonesty in his Treasury duties (which was untrue), he wrote a long paper describing the whole affair in far too much detail. During all this, President Washington's confidence and full support never wavered. Hamilton had resigned from his government duties, but he remained inspector general of the army—the highest officer next to Washington himself.

Chapter 18. The Disappearing Cabinet

Left with a staff of sadly diminished quality, Washington called on Hamilton several times for help in handling difficult problems. One was the long-awaited Jay Treaty that had been expected to clear up problems with England. But when Jay's treaty produced no such result, Hamilton recommended that it should be accepted, if only to prevent a war for which the United States was not prepared. The public was infuriated, but Hamilton succeeded in getting the treaty passed, though at the expense of personal attacks on him. The strongest complaint came from Congressman Rufus King, as reported in *1903 State Papers and Correspondence Bearing upon the Purchase of the Territory of Louisiana*, House of Representatives Serial Set #4531, 57th Congress, 2nd Session, Doc. 431, Letter of 3/29/1801.

Also, a virtual war had arisen over attempts to collect duties from the Whiskey Rebels, who became violent in avoiding payment. General Hamilton rather enjoyed this one, as it gave him the chance to build an army larger than the one Washington had led in the Revolutionary War.

Jefferson spent most of this time at Monticello, writing about how dedicated a farmer he had become. But after two years, he became President Adams's vice president and his presence was not required. He later admitted that the rest was not as pleasant or stimulating as he had expected.

Chapter 19. One Heart and One Mind

One of Jefferson's biographers, Gilbert Chinard, in *Thomas Jefferson, Apostle of Americanism*, wrote that Jefferson had spent the rest of his life trying to regain what he had lost at the compromise dinner. Although this claim seems exaggerated, there is more than a little truth in the fact that the upsurge in Hamilton's Federalist style of government after that dinner continued to have more effect on American life than Jefferson's Republicanism, even after Hamilton himself was gone. Jefferson's personal popularity and triumphant presidency make it seem wrong to speak of "what he had lost." But his dream of a nation devoted mainly to farming was dying. It was not, however, because of the compromise dinner, but because the widespread wish for a growth-oriented national life favored the Hamiltonian approach.

By this point in the book, the cliff-hanging election that made Jefferson president was won, incredibly with a halfhearted assist from Hamilton. And the new leader had everything going his way for a time. Although few are willing to rank Jefferson with Lincoln as our greatest, he can easily be called our most successful president, simply by comparing where we were in 1800 and what size and power we had gained by 1808.

The curious fact that this statistic is largely based on the overwhelmingly great Louisiana Purchase that Jefferson considered a mischievously unconstitutional act makes no difference at all. It was Jefferson who selected Madison as his partner, and he gets the credit for having heeded that partner's advice when he told him to forget his scruples and keep Louisiana.

Chapter 20. The Jefferson Factor

By now, an accumulation of facts has told us that Jefferson was far from a perfect man. We have seen that he was a singular achiever all his life, commanding the attention of his elders even when he was not yet fully grown. We have seen him take great risks when anything threatened the freedom of the press and speech that he held so dear.

But on the negative side, it is possible that he and Madison misjudged Hamilton. And it is a certainty that he behaved badly to George Washington when that great man was begging for patience and forbearance. In the end, however, Jefferson was exactly like his friend Franklin—determined that in America people "must never inquire concerning a Stranger, *What is he?* but *What can he do?*" (as shown in Russell Blaine Nye's *The Cultural Life of the New Nation*).

Jefferson's writings show that he was not a great believer in any of the usual faiths, but his dedication to the "bold, sublime experiment" that was America was as intense as a deep religious attachment.

Bibliography

Adams, James Truslow. *The Adams Family*. Boston: Little, Brown, 1930.

Becker, Carl L. *The Declaration of Independence: A Study in the History of Political Ideas*. New York: Vintage Press, 1970.

Bernier, Olivier. *The World in 1800*. New York: John Wiley & Sons, 2000.

Boutell, Lewis Henry. *The Life of Roger Sherman*. Chicago: McClurg & Co., 1896.

Bowling, Kenneth R. *The Creation of Washington, D.C.* Fairfax, Va.: George Mason University Press, 1997.

Brodie, Fawn M. *Thomas Jefferson: An Intimate Story*. New York: W. W. Norton & Co., 1974.

Brown, David S. *Thomas Jefferson: A Biographical Companion*. Santa Barbara, Calif.: ABC-CLIO, 1998.

Brown, Stuart Gerry. *Thomas Jefferson*. New York: Washington Square Press, 1966.

Burke, Edmund. *Reflections on the Revolution in France*. Indianapolis, Ind.: Hackett Publishers, 1787.

Burstein, Paul. *The Inner Jefferson: Portrait of a Grieving Optimist*. Charlottesville: University of Virginia Press, 1995.

Butterfield, L. H., Leonard C. Faber, and Wendell D. Garrett, eds. *Diary and Autobiography of John Adams*, Cambridge, Mass.: Belknap Press, 1991.

Cerami, Charles A. *Benjamin Banneker: Surveyor, Astronomer, Publisher, Patriot*, Hoboken: John Wiley & Sons, 2002.

Chernow, Ron. *Alexander Hamilton*. New York: Penguin Press, 2004.

Chinard, Gilbert. *Thomas Jefferson: Apostle of Americanism*. Boston: Little, Brown & Co., 1929.

Curtis, William Eleroy. *The True Thomas Jefferson*. Philadelphia: J. P. Lippincott Co., 1901.

DePauw, Linda, et al., eds., *The First Federal Congress Project*. Vols. 1–14. Baltimore: Johns Hopkins University Press, 1972–1997.

Earle, Alice Moore. *Stage-Coach & Tavern Days*. New York: Haskell House Publishers, 1968.

Ellis, Joseph J. *American Sphinx*. New York: Alfred A. Knopf, 1997.

Ernst, Robert. *Rufus King: American Federalist*. Chapel Hill: University of North Carolina Press, 1968.

Flexner, James Thomas. *The Young Hamilton: A Biography*. Boston: Little, Brown & Co., 1978.

Foley, John P., ed. *The Jeffersonian Cyclopedia: A Comprehensive Collection of the Views of Thomas Jefferson*. New York: Funk & Wagnalls Co., 1900.

Ford, Paul Leicester, ed. *The Works of Thomas Jefferson*. Vols. 6 and 7, Federal Edition. New York: G. P. Putnam's Sons, 1904.

———. *The Writings of Thomas Jefferson*. 10 vols. New York: G. P. Putnam's Sons, 1894.

Fowler, Damon Lee, Ed. *Dining at Monticello: In Good Taste and Abundance*. Chapel Hill: University of North Carolina Press, 2005.

Hailman, John. *Thomas Jefferson on Wine*. Jackson: University Press of Mississippi. 2006.

Halliday, E. M. *Understanding Thomas Jefferson*. New York: HarperCollins, 2001.

Hamilton, James A. *Reminiscences of James A. Hamilton*. New York: Charles Scribner & Co., 1869.

Hendrickson, Robert A. *The Rise and Fall of Alexander Hamilton*. New York: Van Nostrand and Reinhold Co., 1981.

Hirst, Francis W. *Life & Letters of Thomas Jefferson*. New York: The Macmillan Co., 1926.

Jacobs, Major James Ripley, and Glenn Tucker. *The War of 1812*. New York: Hawthorne Books, 1969

Kennedy, Roger G. *Burr, Hamilton, and Jefferson*. New York: Oxford University Press, 2000.

Kline, Mary-Jo, ed. *Aaron Burr, Correspondence and Papers*. Princeton, N.J.: Princeton University Press, 1983.

Larkin, Jack. *The Reshaping of Everyday Life: 1790–1840*. New York: Harper & Row, 1988.

Malone, Dumas. *Jefferson and His Time*. 6 vols. Boston: Little, Brown, & Co., 1948–1981.

Mayo, Bernard. *Jefferson Himself: The Personal Narrative of a Many-Sided American*. Charlottesville: University Press of Virginia, 1942.

McCullough, David. *John Adams*. New York: Simon & Schuster, 2001.

Nye, Russell Blaine. *The Cultural Life of the New Nation, 1776–1830*. New York: Harper & Row, 1960

Peterson, Merrill D. *Thomas Jefferson and the New Nation*. New York: Oxford University Press, 1970.

Randall, Henry S. *The Life of Thomas Jefferson*. New York: Derby & Jackson, 1858.

Randolph, Sarah N. *The Domestic Life of Thomas Jefferson by His Granddaughter*. Charlottesville, Va.: Thomas Jefferson Memorial Foundation, 1978.

Rutland, Robert A. *The Papers of James Madison*. Vols. 8–10. Chicago: University of Chicago Press, 1962.

Sheehan, Donald, ed. *The Making of American History*. New York: The Dryden Press, 1954.

Smith, James Morton, ed. *Republic of Letters: The Correspondence Between Jefferson and Madison*, Vols. 1 and 2. New York: W. W. Norton & Company, 1995.

Staloff, Darren. *Hamilton, Adams, Jefferson*. New York: Hill & Wang, 1994.

Twobig, Dorothy, ed. *Papers of George Washington*. Presidential Series. Charlottesville: University Press of Virginia, 1996.

U.S. Senate Library. *Debates and Proceedings, Important State Papers*. Vol. 2. March 3, 1789, to March 3, 1791.

Various Editors. *The Papers of Thomas Jefferson*. 33 Volumes from 1760 to 1801. Princeton, N.J.: Princeton University Press, 1950.

Warshow, Robert Irving. *Alexander Hamilton: First American Businessman*. Garden City, N.Y.: Garden City Publishing Co., 1931.

Index

Note: Page numbers in *italics* refer to illustrations.